# Bach's *Church Cantatas*

# ABS GUIDES

*Series Editor*
Steven Zohn

Bach's *Art of Fugue and Musical Offering*
**Matthew Dirst**

Bach's *Well-Tempered Clavier*
**Paul Walker**

Bach's *Church Cantatas*
**Ruth Tatlow**

# Bach's *Church Cantatas*

RUTH TATLOW

Oxford University Press is a department of the University of Oxford.
It furthers the University's objective of excellence in research, scholarship,
and education by publishing worldwide. Oxford is a registered trade mark of
Oxford University Press in the UK and in certain other countries.

Published in the United States of America by Oxford University Press
198 Madison Avenue, New York, NY 10016, United States of America.

© Oxford University Press 2025

All rights reserved. No part of this publication may be reproduced, stored in a retrieval system, transmitted, used for text and data mining, or used for training artificial intelligence, in any form or by any means, without the prior permission in writing of Oxford University Press, or as expressly permitted by law, by license or under terms agreed with the appropriate reprographics rights organization. Inquiries concerning reproduction outside the scope of the above should be sent to the Rights Department, Oxford University Press, at the address above.

You must not circulate this work in any other form
and you must impose this same condition on any acquirer.

CIP data is on file at the Library of Congress

ISBN 9780197622513 (pbk.)
ISBN 9780197622506 (hbk.)

DOI: 10.1093/9780197622544.001.0001

The manufacturer's authorised representative in the EU for product safety is
Oxford University Press España S.A. of El Parque Empresarial San Fernando
de Henares, Avenida de Castilla, 2 – 28830 Madrid (www.oup.es/en or
product.safety@oup.com). OUP España S.A. also acts as importer into Spain
of products made by the manufacturer.

*To the reader*

*May this book help open your heart, ears, and mind
to the wonders of Bach's music*

# Contents

| | | |
|---|---|---|
| *Series Editor's Foreword* | | ix |
| *Acknowledgments* | | xi |
| Chapter 1 | *Glory from the Gallery* | 1 |
| Chapter 2 | *Music for a Mühlhausen Occasion:*<br>*'Gottes Zeit ist die allerbeste Zeit'* | 34 |
| Chapter 3 | *Advent Music for Weimar and Leipzig:*<br>*'Nun komm der Heyden Heyland'* | 66 |
| Chapter 4 | *Music for Winter and Summer: 'Hertz, und*<br>*Mund, und That, und Leben'* | 87 |
| Chapter 5 | *Pastoral Music for a Leipzig Springtime:*<br>*'Du Hirte Israel, höre'* | 113 |
| Chapter 6 | *Candlemas in Leipzig: 'Ich habe genung'* | 133 |
| Chapter 7 | *Glory from New Galleries: Reimagining*<br>*Bach's Church Cantatas* | 163 |
| *Glossary* | | 185 |
| *Select Bibliography* | | 187 |
| *Index* | | 195 |

Sponsored by the
**RUTH AND NOEL MONTE FUND OF
THE AMERICAN BACH SOCIETY**

*Ruth and Noel Monte were deeply devoted to Bach and his music, sensing its great impact on the human brain and culture throughout the world. To them, Bach represented a bright planet appearing in the sky only once, requiring centuries for the human mind to observe and fully comprehend. The Monte Fund has the goal of supporting and promoting this living musical treasure for present and future generations.*

# Series Editor's Foreword

Few composers of any time or place have inspired as many words as Johann Sebastian Bach. For well over two centuries, generations of writers have contributed to a now voluminous literature on the composer's life and works. Yet because a large portion of this literature approaches the music from a highly technical perspective, Bach enthusiasts who lack extensive musical training find themselves looking in from the outside, as it were. More accessible writings often avoid discussing the music itself, which is of course what draws listeners to Bach in the first place; instead, they tend to limit themselves to investigating Bach's biography, the social contexts for music-making in his time, or the theological interpretation of his sacred vocal works. Non-specialist literature that does focus on the music often perpetuates myths or engages in misguided (if well-meaning) attempts to reveal supposed compositional secrets.

The present volume, as with others in this series of guides sponsored by the American Bach Society, is by an expert in the field who aims to offer a lucid, engaging, and timely exploration of Bach's music for a broad audience. Central to this exploration is the experience of listening to Bach's music in his time and ours. Attention is also devoted to the music's genesis, history, organization, meaning, and contexts, this last category encompassing perspectives that may be musical, biographical, social, political, performance-practical, and theological. Authors assume no technical knowledge about music on the reader's part, and although musical examples make occasional appearances, they are intended to be illustrative of the discussion rather than integral to it. Finally, the brief suggestions for further reading that follow each chapter and the selective bibliography at the end of the volume emphasize literature in English.

Among the many people who have made this series possible, special thanks are due to my predecessor Daniel R. Melamed, without whose vision and advocacy it could never have materialized, and to Norman Hirschy and Rada Radojicic at Oxford University Press, whose enthusiasm and support for the project have been essential to its realization.

Steven Zohn<br>
General Editor, American Bach Society

# Acknowledgments

Writings on Bach's church cantatas now span over two and a half centuries of scholarship, and are almost exclusively by men. As a woman in what continues to be a male-dominated field, I am therefore particularly happy to have been invited to add a female voice to the cantata narratives. My thanks go to Daniel R. Melamed and Steven D. Zohn of the American Bach Society for entrusting me with the church cantatas volume in this ABS series, to Matthew Dirst for permission to adopt the glossary definitions from his volume, and to Norman Hirschy and the team at Oxford University Press for shaping my files into a beautiful book.

The research and illustrations for this monograph have been aided beyond measure by the 24/7 access to rare books and sources made possible by countless unnamed librarians and archivists working behind the scenes, and to whom I am indebted. The freely available annotated translations of Bach's cantata texts by Michael Marissen and Daniel R. Melamed on BachCantataTexts.org have also been an invaluable resource.

I would like to thank the Tobias Norlind Memorial foundation and the Royal Swedish Academy of Music for awarding stipends that enabled me to focus on this project in Leipzig and Cambridge. Special thanks are also due to Christiane Hausmann and Bernd Koska at the Bach-Archiv Leipzig, Antje Schloms of the Stadtarchiv Mühlhausen, and Daniela Stein-Lorentz at the Universitäts- und Landesbibliothek Darmstadt for their timely help with images and sources that were difficult to track down.

I am deeply grateful to the readers of the manuscript, including Andrew Frampton, Steven D. Zohn, Fredric Fehleisen, Robin A. Leaver, Francis Knights, and Joel Speerstra, whose detailed comments have made this a much better book. If kindness and joy radiate the writing, it is in large measure due to the humor and companionship of my friends at Emmanuel College and Clare Hall, Cambridge, Bach Network, and at the weekly online tea-time meetings where knowledge is generously shared, and every new research discovery enthusiastically discussed.

Above all, though, I am grateful to my family for their support as I worked on this volume, and particularly to my husband Mark for his understanding, encouragement, and love.

Danderyd, Sweden<br>24 November 2024

# 1
## Glory from the Gallery

The phrase "Glory from the Gallery" is a deliberate allusion to Bach's stated aim to serve and glorify God with his music, much of which was performed from the choir gallery or organ loft. Early in his career Johann Sebastian Bach (1685–1750) wrote that his life's aim was to create church music to the glory of God, and several title pages show that his compositions were designed to delight the hearts, minds, and emotions of his listeners. At this time well-constructed music was seen as a mirror of God's wisdom, a deep concept that motivated the composer and musician. As Bach's cousin Johann Gottfried Walther (1684–1748) explained in his composition manual, musical harmony was not the result of simply following artistic or compositional rules: it came to fruition when music was used for virtuous and God-pleasing practices. In this book I will explore how Bach applied these ideals to his music. Taking five well-loved cantatas as examples, my aim is to help Bach's church cantatas come alive in a new way, whether the reader is a novice or expert, listener, or performer.

There are many things we do not know about Bach's church cantatas. How and why have some become more popular than others? Are the more famous and popular any "better" than those less well known? Was their popularity caused by the availability of printed sheet music, or because of repeat performances by esteemed musicians, or because of a memorable theme or two, or even because of a combination of cultural and practical factors that have influenced musical taste over time? I will look at some of the most beloved cantatas that illustrate their wide variety of styles, occasions, texts, and compositional contexts. The selection is personal, and some readers will find it limited, maybe even disappointed that their favorite cantata is not mentioned. But this would be to miss the point. In the five case studies my goal is to give new ideas that will empower the reader to study and understand all of Bach cantatas more deeply. In the final chapter I will look beyond, at how these compositions might be reused and adapted for future generations.

Bach's music is often thought of as deeply serious, with a tendency toward joylessness. This is a hangover from the way his music was perceived in the nineteenth and early twentieth centuries. There is no doubt that life in Bach's time was often hard, and the harsh reality of death was an ever-present fact, but the teaching and theological reminders in the Lutheran liturgy were there to help. There were smiles as well as solemnity during the long hours spent in the sacred space of church buildings. Public worship aimed to inspire joy for Christian living and to infuse daily life with celebration. As an integral part of the liturgy, Bach's cantatas were devised to contribute to this overall aim.

Love, joy, and peace are recurring themes in Bach's church cantatas. The word "joy" (Freude) appears several times in the cantatas that I have chosen, including in those associated with death. In fact, "joy" is a prominent word in the first line of one of the most common funeral chorales, Martin Luther's paraphrase of the Song of Simeon (Luke 2:29–35) "Mit Fried und Freud ich fahr dahin" ("With peace and joy I journey yonder"). Lutheran musicians in Bach's day thought about life in the service of God as a joyful, love-inspired calling. They understood that music had a special role in that calling, both now, in this life, and after physical death, in heaven. A typical affirmation of these beliefs was formulated by the much-respected music theorist, author, and diplomat Johann Mattheson (1681–1764), in *Behauptung der Himmlischen Musik* (1747): "Given that all possible kinds of joy will, without question, be encountered in eternal life, surely it stands to reason then that fine music (indeed in all its possible styles) will be the very first?"

## Bach and Church Cantatas

The word "cantata" has had different meanings across the history of music, and there are various suggestions as to its etymology, whether from the Latin "canere" meaning "to sing," or the Italian "cantare" also meaning "to sing." The cantata had been the main form of vocal chamber music since the early 1600s in Italy, whereas in German-speaking lands the word was slow to catch on, first used around 1700, and then primarily associated with vocal church music. When Bach and his contemporaries gave titles to their church cantatas, they usually used the words "Concerto," "Kirchen Musik" (church music), "Kirchen-stück" (church piece), or just "Musik." Bach did, however, use the word "Cantata" in the heading of the full score of his Cantata (BWV) 82 for solo voice (see Chapter 6).

Bach composed what we now know as "cantatas" in various styles and for very different occasions from his early twenties until a decade before his death. All have a combination of vocal and instrumental elements, ranging from a single soloist to a full choir, and from a small five-part string ensemble to a full orchestra with trumpets and drums. Most were written for use in church, but there were also cantatas for special occasions, for example, to celebrate royal birthdays, university festivities, and for private individuals. Those composed for a church service are sometimes called "sacred" cantatas, in contrast to "secular" cantatas. This is a contradiction in terms, because as a faithful Lutheran musician Bach would have seen all his musical activities as part of his sacred Christian calling. It is important nonetheless to recognize the different purposes his cantatas served. So as to avoid the misleading "sacred-secular" division, I will differentiate the cantatas by their functions, and use the terms "church cantata" and "occasional cantata."

Authors and composers in Bach's day frequently included a dedication to God in their publications and manuscripts, using phrases such as "Soli Deo Gloria" ("to God alone be the Glory"), "Omnia ad majorem Dei gloriam" ("All for the greater glory of God"), and "Gott allein die Ehre" ("To God alone be the glory"). Two dedicational abbreviations are frequently found on Bach's cantata scores: "J. J." standing for *Jesu Juva* and meaning either "With Jesus' help" or "Help, Jesus!" and usually positioned immediately above the top staff of music in the full score; and "S.D.Gl." or "S.D.G." or "D.S.Gl.," standing for variations on *Soli Deo Gloria* meaning "to God alone be the Glory" and usually written at the very end in a convenient space after the final double bar line. Contrary to popular belief, these do not appear on every Bach cantata score. Many of Bach's Leipzig cantatas were composed in just a few days under less-than-ideal circumstances and with minimal time for their composition, copying, and rehearsal. Whenever he asked for and acknowledged Jesus' help with "J. J.," I suspect his plea was heartfelt, rather than just a habitual formula. Likewise, I suspect that the aspiration in "S.D.G." was sincere, after the massive weekly effort, that the new composition on Sunday would glorify God.

Bach's earliest surviving cantatas are thought to date from 1706 to c. 1709, a period that straddles his service in Arnstadt, Mühlhausen, and the first years in Weimar. These works have a distinctive seventeenth-century flavor and form, with short contrasting musical sections in different time signatures and texts running without a break to create longer movements. The texts typically contain Bible verses, chorales, and freely composed phrases. Another way to recognize Bach's early vocal works is that they do not have recitatives. An example is Cantata (BWV) 106, the focus of Chapter 2.

During his Weimar period, Bach composed church cantatas from around 1713 until he moved to Cöthen in 1717. In general, these established a musical model that Bach would take up again when he arrived in Leipzig in 1723. He gave many a new lease of life, revising the texts of some, adding new recitatives to others, and occasionally reusing or reworking a movement or two. Cantata (BWV) 61, discussed in Chapter 3, and Cantata (BWV) 147, discussed in Chapter 4, were both originally composed in Weimar and then revised in Leipzig. When Bach moved to Cöthen to become court Capellmeister, his compositional focus turned to instrumental music. With one exception, his Cöthen cantatas were for celebratory non-church occasions at the Calvinist court for his employer, Leopold, the Prince of Anhalt-Cöthen. Although the music of most of these occasional cantatas has been lost, it is thought that Bach also reused it, and that it survives unrecognized in new guises in some of the Leipzig cantatas.

The church cantatas that Bach composed, or rewrote, for the Leipzig churches typically have five or six movements made up of arias and recitatives for solo voices, and movements for a choir, such as the opening choruses and final hymns or chorales. His cantatas were integral to the set liturgy and order of the main morning and afternoon service at St. Thomas Church and St. Nicholas Church. The cantata was heard before the sermon, although when Bach composed a longer cantata, he would divide it into two parts, the first part to be performed before the sermon, and the second during the distribution of communion. An example of a two-part cantata is the Leipzig version of Cantata 147, discussed in Chapter 4. The Leipzig cantatas are often arranged symmetrically, with alternating aria-recitative-aria movements surrounded by the opening and closing choral movements. The arias are normally settings of contemplative free-texted poetry on the biblical theme of the week. Arias are often accompanied by a small instrumental ensemble so that the solo voice can be heard clearly, in contrast to the movements with choir, which are usually accompanied by a larger instrumental group. The recitatives are in an almost speech-like form, which allows many more words of text than in a typical aria. Most of the recitatives are accompanied minimally by a **continuo** section, usually made up of harpsichord or organ and cello or violone: these are known today (but were not in Bach's time) as *secco* (literally dry) recitatives. Sometimes a recitative is given a lyrical-style accompaniment with a small instrumental group, and these are known as accompanied recitatives. As the word "recitative" suggests, their purpose is to narrate or "recite" the storyline, which in the case of the church cantatas is often the biblical narrative. Pastor Erdmann Neumeister (1671–1756) is said to have introduced the recitative into church cantatas in 1705, adapting for church use models that were well known in Italian opera. Neumeister also set a trend for writing and publishing collections of poetic reflections on the prescribed biblical readings, or lectionary, for each Sunday of the church year. These annual collections of texts are known as cycles, and always begin with the first Sunday of the church year, Advent Sunday, and continue to the last Sunday of the Trinity season.

It seems that Bach composed up to five annual cantata cycles, although the music and texts of many are now lost. Contrary to the collections of textual cycles, Bach's annual cycles start on the First Sunday after Trinity, when he took up official duties in Leipzig, starting with Cantata (BWV) 75 on 30 May 1723. His second cantata cycle, known as the chorale cantata cycle, contains a corpus of cantatas that share an almost uniform structure. Structurally, the first movement presents the first verse of the chorale unaltered and usually has an elaborated orchestral setting. The texts of the following movements, whether recitatives, arias, or duets, are paraphrases of the middle movements of the chorale, and the final movement tends to be an unembellished four-part setting of the chorale's final verse. The chorale cantata cycle runs only from the First Sunday after Trinity 1724 to Easter 1725. Bach composed a few chorale cantatas after 1725, possibly as a way of completing the cycle. These include Cantata (BWV) 140 'Wachet auf, ruft uns die Stimme', which he composed for the rarely occurring Twenty-Seventh Sunday after Trinity. Some of Bach's earlier cantatas are also based on a chorale, for example Cantata (BWV) 61 'Nun komm der Heyden Heyland' (see Chapter 3), which quotes and paraphrases Luther's Advent hymn.

It is not known how many cantatas Bach composed. About two hundred church cantatas have survived in part or in full, in original scores, parts, and in copies, the majority of which were composed during his tenure as Thomaskantor (Cantor at St. Thomas Church) in Leipzig. Relatively few occasional cantatas have survived in original scores or parts, but this is possibly because Bach reused these materials in later compositions. There is no complete record of what he performed in Leipzig, and despite expert reconstructions and redating, there is still great uncertainty about how many of his church cantatas have been lost. Records show which biblical texts were used Sunday by Sunday, and sometimes there are details of who preached the sermon. Small text booklets containing the words of the cantatas heard in the main Leipzig services were printed every month or so. These were available for purchase so that members of the congregation could study the meaning of the words in advance. To keep up with the schedule of the booklet publication, Bach had to select the texts for his cantatas well in advance. Unfortunately, only a few of these fragile booklets have survived. Without them, information about the dating and potential performance of the cantatas must be sought elsewhere; for example, clues can be found by studying the watermarks on the paper used for the original score and parts, by studying the handwriting of the copyists, and Bach's handwriting from different periods of his life.

The main Sunday services at the churches of St. Thomas and St. Nicholas in Leipzig included a celebration of communion. The early service started at 7 A.M., the sermon began promptly at 8 A.M. and lasted an hour, and the whole event, including communion, took between three and four hours. The order of the liturgy and the content of a church service for Saxon cities and the villages were stipulated in the published *Kirchen-Ordnung* (Church Order), and the *Kirchen-Agenda* (Church Agenda). Words that did not change from Sunday to Sunday were known as the "Ordinary," and the materials that differed each Sunday or feast day were known as the "Proper." The changing materials included the opening Psalm, the collects, the prayers, the biblical readings, the sermon, and the cantata. The cantata had to be timed precisely to make sure the sermon could begin with the 8 A.M. bell.

## How Bach Composed the Cantatas

Bach's primary materials were the set biblical readings—the Gospel and the Epistle texts for the day—the prayers, and the cantata text or libretto that he had chosen, commissioned, or even maybe adapted himself.

## Studying the Libretto

It would be natural to assume that Bach started to compose each cantata in the order in which we hear it, from the first movement to the last, but this was not necessarily the case. His compositional choices were affected by the available instrumentalists and singers, the musical ideas and materials at his disposal, and his libretti. On page 240 of *Der Vollkommene Capellmeister* (1739), Johann Mattheson explained how Agostino Steffani (1654–1728) set about composing texted music:

> §28 The world-famous Steffani once said to me that before he put pen to paper he carried the text of the work around with him for a long time until he had decided how and in what order he would organize the work. And only then would he commit his musical thoughts to paper.

We do not know to what extent Bach was involved in the writing of the cantata texts. In Leipzig he seems to have collaborated closely with both Christian Friedrich Henrici (1700–1764), known as Picander, and Christiane Mariane von Ziegler (1695–1760), and there was a supply of talented students, including Christoph

Birkmann (1703–1773), who were willing to try their hand at writing. He could also consult reading materials in his library for inspiration and ideas. Once the cantata texts had been sent to the printers, Bach had some time to think about the allusions in their poetry and in the Bible readings before he worked on the composition itself.

## Mapping Out the Score

Bach was also bound by practical constraints of the service order. The cantata was placed after the Credo, and before the Gospel reading and the Lord's Prayer, before the 8 A.M. bells sounded (see Suggested Further Reading, Petzoldt/Bratz, 17). Ensuring that the cantata did not go on too long had been a long-term conundrum for Lutheran church musicians. In 1619 the composer, theorist, and organist Michael Praetorius (1571–1621) described the method he preferred to solve this practical issue: he always noted the number of *tempora* or breves (double whole notes) at the end of the continuo part:

> it is necessary to take into account how many breves can be played in a quarter of an hour at a moderate tempo, that is 80 breves in half of a quarter of an hour, 160 in a full quarter of an hour, 320 in half an hour, and 640 in a full hour. In this way one can judge more accurately how long a particular composition might last so that the sermon is not delayed and can begin at the proper time, and so that other parts of the liturgy can also be arranged accordingly. (*Syntagma Musicum*, Vol. 3 (1619), 87–88)

Over a century later a similar guiding principle was circulated to the sixteen members of the Corresponding Society of the Musical Sciences, founded in 1738 by Lorenz Christoph Mizler (1711–1788), and limited to twenty invited members. Mizler, who studied theology, as well as some music, at Leipzig University called Bach his "good friend and patron." Bach joined the society in 1747, becoming its fourteenth member. The aim of Mizler's society was to encourage leading composers and theorists to discuss musical science, which they did by letter rather than in personal meetings. Mizler included much of the discussion material in the four volumes of *Musicalische Bibliothek*. Bach's death was announced in the final volume, Vol. 4, Part 1 (1736–1754), page 108, and on the very next line, directly beneath the announcement, was the following description:

> In winter the cantata should be shorter than in the summer due to the cold, to help the congregation concentrate. From experience a cantata of 350 bars of varying time signatures will take approximately 25 minutes, which in winter is long enough, whereas in summer one can add 8–10 minutes to make a cantata of 490 [*sic*] bars. . . . The point is that a composer should commit himself more to bringing a movement into beautiful order (*schöner Ordnung*) than to keeping an eye on the clock. It is not about the number of minutes.

As a member of Mizler's society Bach would have read this updated version of the 1619 guideline by Praetorius. In fact, its positioning, immediately after the announcement of Bach's death, suggests that Bach himself might even have written it as a contribution to the society's discussions. The complete essay gives valuable insights into the practical nuts and bolts of church cantata composition.

Although the anonymous author did not specify how to "[bring] a movement into beautiful order," all members of the society would have understood what this phrase meant without further explanation, because it was documented, both philosophically and practically, in many a music treatise of the period. For example, in a passage written specifically for the German Capellmeister, Johann

Mattheson explained how to create beautiful order in compositions, and why:

> §29 Moreover if this true uniformity of order contributes so much as to make it pleasant to the human senses, it will also become more enduring, as is well known to good architects.... §30 Whoever wishes to use this method should outline his complete project on a sheet of paper, sketch it roughly, and then order it before proceeding. In my opinion this is the absolute best way to organize a work so that each part demonstrates a true proportion, uniformity, and agreement, for nothing in the world is more pleasing to the ear than this. (*Der Vollkommene Capellmeister* [1739], 240–41)

Mattheson then describes the elements of ordering, proportion, symmetry, the keys, the time signature, and the importance of putting these in good order. Composers of the time understood that equality and symmetry within and across a composition were important because they were pleasant to hear, and because they made the composition more enduring. Composers observed and learned about compositional form through transcribing music by others, carefully counting the bars to ensure the copy was accurate. Organizing the number of bars in a melody, in consecutive sections, between movements, and across the larger structure of a composition to create balance and proportion was one way in which composers could bring music into beautiful order.

Mattheson's move from a description of making beautiful order in a composition to his focus on symmetry, proportion, and the emotional effect and endurance of music rings strangely in the ears of the modern reader. Its explanation, however, is self-evident when one understands how Bach and his contemporaries understood the nature of music and its significance in creation and the universe.

## A Creational Theology of Music

Bach and his contemporaries thought about music in a very particular way, which had a direct influence on how they composed and constructed their art. Music was fully integrated into the theology of creation. It was understood to be quintessentially numerical, and a mirror of God's creation. Wisdom 11:20: "God has ordered everything according to mass, number, and weight" ("Gott hat alles mit Mass, Zahl und Gewicht geordnet") was frequently cited in music books. Order and proportion were integral to the Lutheran understanding of the world. This was because they believed that God had used the proportions of the harmonic series of music (1:1, 1:2, 2:3, 3:4, 4:5, 5:6—creating the unison, octave, fifth, fourth, major third, and minor third respectively), the foundation of *numerus musicus*, when He ordered the entire universe, from the furthest distance between the stars and planets, that could be viewed through a telescope, to the tiniest organism seen through a magnifying glass. It was an ancient belief known as Universal Harmony, which, surprisingly, had survived into the eighteenth century. Furthermore, the most perfect proportions of all were still thought to be 1:1 and 1:2 (the unison and the octave) because they were closest to the unity. And, as Lorenz Mizler commented in 1742, this explains "why philosophers always had to consider God to be the simplest of beings above all others, and hence, logically, also the absolutely most perfect" (Fux, *Gradus ad Parnassum*, trans. Mizler [Leipzig, 1742], 35–36, note 12).

The idealized perfection of the first two harmonic numbers, and their proportions 1:1 and 1:2, favored the development of symmetrical forms in every creative endeavor: 1:1 symmetry can be seen literally in the proportions of Classical and Neoclassical architecture, and in the facades of buildings designed in Leipzig in Bach's time, such as the King's House and the Bose House. Every well-ordered object in creation was a useful reminder of God's perfect creative act, and this was a visual reminder that music and its harmonic proportions lay at the heart and soul of the universe.

**Canon** and **counterpoint** particularly were understood to flow from the purity of creational harmony: canon, because it is literally the repetition of unison lines, and counterpoint, because it is made up of unison lines that always resolve any passing dissonances, and so combine to create harmony. Whenever Bach chooses a clearly contrapuntal style in his cantatas, it is important to remember the significance of his choice, for example, in Cantata (BWV) 106/2 where he uses fugal entries for the words "Es ist der alte Bund: Mensch, du musst sterben" ("It is the old covenant: Man, you must die") (Chapter 2), and the contrapuntal lines in Cantata (BWV) 104/5, 'Beglückte Herde' (Happy Flock) that cause a simultaneous mirror symmetry (Chapter 5).

It will always be impossible to know exactly how these techniques resonated in Bach's innermost being, whether he saw them as metaphorical, as images, or as literal and essential expressions of God's perfection. On page 92 of his short musical tract *Kurtzer Entwurf von der Music* (1754), Heinrich Georg Neuss (1654–1716) put it like this:

> §2 For music is primarily a bright mirror of the eternal invisible God, from whom it [music] has its origins. . . . Therefore, music takes the prize above many other works in creation, on account of both its external Harmony, and its secret power, which is hidden in its internal proportion, number, measure, and form, which is itself the clearest and most beautiful mirror of the eternal Godhead.

Beyond architecture, this profound understanding led to many different creative techniques that involve proportions, symmetry, and parallel ways of reading. Among these are emblems, with their combined images and cryptic mottos to puzzle over and meditate upon with the help of a commentary. Bach owned several books that contained emblems, including *Evangelische Schatzkammer*, a collection of sermons by August Pfeiffer published in 1686 (reprinted 1717) (see Chapter 5). In 1678 a pastor and preacher Gustav Adolph Hiltebrandt (1632–1695) published a collection of 100 emblems on different topics in his *Picture Treasury . . . for joyful contemplation and the delight of the mind/emotions*. The twentieth emblem (Figure 1.1), printed on pages 96–99, rehearses the standard, accepted views of music. Its title reads: "In Praise and Honor of Music" (Der Music Lob und Preiß). The motto around the image reads: "It [Music] brings forth the infinite and the finite" (Finitum Infinitum Producit). The Latin couplet beneath the image reads:

> A countable number produces innumerable numbers,
> Just as a song brings forth variations in wondrous modes/ways.
> (Innumeros numerus numeros numerabilis edit
> Cantio ceu miris fert variata modis.)

And the German couplet:

> Great mystery is hidden in music
> That not one in a thousand has seen.
> (An der Music groß Geheimnüß stickt
> Daß der Tausend nicht eins erblickt)

In addition to the tongue-twisting riddling of "numeros" in the first line, the Latin couplet is difficult to understand because its form, an elegiac distich, requires a particular rhythm and scansion, which causes the words to be put in an unusual order. The German couplet is similarly contorted, allowing it to be understood in several ways. These deliberate ambiguities and double meanings contribute to the positive intellectual challenge of meditating on emblematic imagery.

Figure 1.1 Gustav Adolph Hiltebrandt, *Neu-Eröffneter Anmüthiger Bilder Schatz . . . Zur Lustigen Beschawung und Gemüths-Ergötzung* (1674), 96. https:diglib.hab.de/drucke/xb-5991/start.htm?image= 00107. Herzog August Bibliothek Wolfenbüttel.

Hiltebrandt's explanation is liberally seasoned with biblical references. It begins:

> Just as God himself in Heaven is pleased by the eternal and immortal, so should we mortal humans on earth also be pleased. For God himself has a great love for devotional well-formed music, as we can see because he created angels and men to his Praise and Glory, as well as sensible and clever creatures to sing praises to him.

The message of his twentieth emblem is that music draws forth the finite in this life and leads to the infinite in the next. He claims that the finite, quantifiable numbers seen in the infinite variations of music produce infinite unquantifiable numbers, because all music is based on just six numbers, the *senarius*. This is fundamentally a repetition of the accepted theory of music from *Le istitutioni harmoniche* (1558) by Gioseffo Zarlino (1517–1590) and widely copied in theory books published over the subsequent two centuries. It is what theologians and pastors would have taught their congregation about music and its place in everyday life and in worship, and, importantly, it is the view of music that Bach would have been taught at home, in church, and at school.

In Bach's time, the numbers and proportions of music usually went by their Latin name, *numerus musicus*. These were the building blocks of every aspect of musical composition and performance, and they are integral to understanding Bach's music. The *senarius*, numbers 1, 2, 3, 4, 5, and 6, generated all musical intervals, pitches, tuning, and harmonic progressions and were taught by means of the proportional divisions of a length of string on a monochord. The *numerus musicus* also included the arithmetical division of the bar in different time signatures (C, 4/4, 3/4, 2/4, 9/8, 6/8, 3/8, etc.), the arithmetical division of rhythm (double whole notes, whole notes, half notes, quarter notes, eighth notes, sixteenth notes, thirty-second notes, etc.), the regular pulse of the bar that is counted across a piece, and, importantly for the understanding of Bach's cantatas, in the overall proportion of a movement or work, measured in breves or bars (see Praetorius and Mizler above), remembering that the most perfect manifestation of creational number was the 1:1 unison, and its formal equivalent, the symmetry.

## Meaning Embedded in Music and Structures

Artistic creations of all kinds in Bach's time were full of rich and ambiguous meanings. His was not an age of one single code with one single decipherable meaning. Creativity was not a dualistic process with its this-is-right-and-this-is-wrong notion fundamental to so much thinking in the twentieth and twenty-first centuries. Bach's time was the period of allusion, with layers and shades of meaning that encouraged contemplative understanding. Naturally this mitigates against today's musicians giving one "symbolic" interpretation to compositions. Take as an example the understanding of how the musical sounds of keys, different instruments, and rhythms affect the listener and performer emotionally. In Chapter 2 of the third section of *Das Neu-Eröffnete Orchestre* (1713), 252, Johann Mattheson tried to catalog the qualities and effect of the most common musical keys and modes, yet he had to conclude that there were no hard-and-fast rules, writing:

> § 25 If everything that could be said or thought were to be mentioned [on the subject], each key/mode (Tohn) would fill a chapter of its own; but the more one would endeavor to state something positive, the more contradictory things would be found, since the opinions in this matter are almost innumerable, which I can account for in no other way than through the differences of human complexity.

There were, however, some fundamental physical properties of music that musicians believed in and tried to put into words. Among these is how they understood the physiology of music-making. Another is how they understood the physical vibrations that made up music. In 1712 Gottfried Wilhelm Leibniz (1646–1716) expressed this phenomenon in the well-known phrase "*Musica est exercitium Arithmeticae occultum, nescientis se numerare animi*" ("Music is a secret exercise of arithmetic where the mind is unaware that it is counting"), explaining that "even if the soul does not realize it is counting, it nevertheless feels the effect of this insensible calculation, that is the pleasure in consonances [closest to 1:1 unison] or the vexation of dissonances [furthest from the unison]." Eighteenth-century physicists and music theorists believed that the pulses and sonic vibrations traveling through the ear and bodies of the listener and performer caused an unconscious emotional response, with the strongest and most efficacious reactions caused by the purest consonance of the 1:1 unison. This was part of the "science" of music. Bach and his contemporaries could incorporate such features in their compositions confident that these most perfect proportions would elicit the most powerful emotional impact.

These vibrational impulses could be used to affect or even "control" the human being, from the extremes of heroic trumpet sonorities rousing an army to battle, to music at excessive tempi triggering frantic dancing. This was partly why some theologians feared the negative impact of music, discouraging music-making for dances, taverns, and unlicensed coffeehouses, and characterizing some music-making as sinful. At the other end of the spectrum there were perfect vibrations that embodied the divine perfection of God and that were thought to be healing. These could be expressed in the form and order of a work of art, such as 1:1 symmetry, or in the unison (1:1) or octave (1:2) when two or more instruments or voices play the same melody or repeat the same pitch (as seen in BWV 106/1). Combined with words expressing attributes of the holy God, George Frideric Handel

(1685–1759) can be seen to harness this power in *Messiah*, HWV 56 (1741), when he suddenly changes from multivoice writing to voices in unison and octaves for the words: "For the Lord God omnipotent reigneth," "King of Kings and Lord of Lords," and "The Lord gave the Word." Of course, not every unison or octave composed at this time indicates an intentional representation of the Godhead, but given the prevalent philosophy and science, it should give pause for thought.

Although differently proportioned, the triad (2:3:4:5 in its simplest formation) was also considered a fitting expression of God. The triad was named after the Trinity, as it was believed to reflect the threefold nature of God himself. Some even believed that God revealed it specifically to Christians, for whom the Trinity was a fundamental tenet of faith. When combined with words expressing attributes of God, it is possible that triadic figuration too might have been significant. Cantata (BWV) 147 opens with trumpets playing a triadic motif. This figure is also heard at the end of the opening movement, in the final ***ritornello*** immediately after the words "dass er Gott und Heyland sey" ("because he is God and Savior"). I suspect Bach may have chosen the triadic trumpets deliberately to represent the qualities of Christ, "God and Savior."

The term "chiastic" or "cross-shaped" is often used today in the study of ancient texts, and the word has found its way into musicology. Musicians have often noticed cross-shaped **sequences** in melodies by Bach, and some attribute symbolic value to these observations. The term is also used to describe the organization of movements in a composition. For example, Chorus-Duet-Solo-Chorus-Solo-Duet-Chorus, as in "Christ lag in Todesbanden," Cantata (BWV) 4, or Chorus-Aria-Recitative-Aria-Recitative-Aria-Chorale, as in "Christ unser Herr zum Jordan kam," Cantata (BWV) 7. This kind of symmetrical organization is common in Bach's cantatas. Even though *chiasmus* has long been used for cross-shaped figures or motifs in the arts, I do not use the term in Bach's music. Instead, I prefer to describe such formal ordering as symmetry, associating it with the perfect ideal of the 1:1 so fundamental to the philosophy and theology of music found in publications from Bach's time.

## Poetic Forms in the Cantata Texts

The poetic texts, or *libretti*, designed to be set to church music vary widely in structure and quality according to the experience, agendas, and talents of their authors.

### The Poets

Many of the authors of the cantata texts were pastors and theologians, whose primary calling was to convey the Gospel message. To be frank, their poetic talent rarely matched their theological zeal. As privileged members of the community—university-educated, with stable salaries, and guaranteed social status—pastors were frequently called upon to provide memorial or dedicatory writings in honor of their patrons, local dignitaries, friends, and colleagues, in addition to commissioned sermons. Many of these occasional poetic writings appear in prefatory materials to printed books, in memorial poems accompanying funerary pamphlets, or reprinted as individual dedicatory pamphlets.

As seen above, creating annual cycles of poetic texts based on the readings for each Sunday and festival of the church year became fashionable. Theologians and pastors seem to have produced these as an aid to their own meditations as they prepared their sermons each week. Other non-theologian poets also wrote and published texts intended to be set to music, and there are numerous examples of such in Bach's cantatas. In Weimar, his primary librettist was the court lawyer and poet Salomo Franck (see Chapter 4), and in Leipzig he often worked with texts by Picander, who was a government official. Very few women feature among the published authors of cantata texts, the major exception being Christiane Mariana von Ziegler, nine of whose texts Bach set to music for church cantatas composed in April and May 1725.

For the five cantatas featured in this book, Pastor Erdmann Neumeister wrote the libretto of Cantata (BWV) 61, Salomo Franck wrote the early text of Cantata (BWV) 147, and Pastor Christoph Birkmann the libretto of Cantata (BWV) 82. The compiler of the texts for Cantatas (BWV) 106 and 104 are unknown. It has been suggested over the years that Bach may have written the words for some of his cantatas. Theoretically there is no reason why he could not have done so. Lack of time, though, is the strongest argument against. It is nonetheless within the bounds of possibility that members of his household, or his students provided some texts. Indeed, it has recently come to light that Birkmann was among the previously unseen helpers available to Bach as provider of cantata texts while he was still a student in Leipzig.

Poems were frequently based on a model. In 1685 Johann Christoph Männling (1658–1723) called this technique "Parody." Parody in music and poetry was common and was not thought of as plagiarism. If done well the reader or listener would never recognize the original model. One method in music was for the composer first to change the bass line of a beloved aria to create a different harmony, and then to write a new melody over the top. Bach frequently reused and reclothed his own musical material, which explains why certain melodic fragments feel familiar (see Chapter 6).

Among his description and illustration of many common poetic techniques, Männling explains on page 92 of his *Europäische Parnassus* (1685) that to create a parody one should take a well-known hymn or song text and rework it to create something new and meaningful. Männling regularly used this technique when called upon to write occasional arias. See Chapter 6 for his use of Franz Joachim Burmeister's 'Es ist genung' for a funeral aria. There are many examples of the parody technique in the church cantatas, where Bach upcycled melodies and whole movements from earlier compositions. His parodies might also involve changing the text, structure, rhyme, and meter of the original to create a cantata suitable for a new occasion—for example, Cantatas (BWV) 30.2 and 36.1 and 36.5, and the Christmas Oratorio (BWV 248), reconstructed mostly from the occasional Cantatas (BWV) 213 and 214; and at other times they involved assembling movements or sections from earlier compositions to create a new work—for example, the B Minor Mass (BWV 232) where movement 7, "Gratias agimus," is taken from Cantata (BWV) 29/2 'Wir danken dir, Gott', and movement 9 "Qui tollis peccata mundi" from Cantata (BWV) 46/1. Bach's parody technique is a rich topic, worthy of further reading (see below).

The poetic equivalent of *numerus musicus* was *numerus poeticus* (poetry numbers), which is defined and afforded a full chapter in the famous language tutor *Unterricht von der teutschen Sprache* (1682) by Daniel Georg Morhof (1639–1691). The *numerus poeticus*, like its musical counterpart, embraces the numbers in the rhythm of a text counted in syllables or feet, the scansion of lines, rhyme scheme, and form. The *numerus poeticus* had the same theological significance and meaning as *numerus musicus* (see above). Composers of texted music were aware of the *numerus poeticus* of their libretti and could either imitate it in their musical setting or, more interestingly, go against it to create a different rhythm, as Bach frequently does, including in Cantatas (BWV) 106/4, and 147/1. Many symmetrical forms were developed in poetry, with 1:1 reflecting the most perfect manifestation of creational number. Examples of these symmetrical forms can often be seen in the free-texted arias and choruses of Bach's cantatas. Whenever Bach opened books of mixed poetry looking for inspiration for his cantatas, he would have seen symmetrical poetic forms, including in the five volumes of *Picanders Ernst-Schertzhaffte und Satyrische Gedichte* (1727–1751) by his Leipzig collaborator Christian Friedrich Henrici.

## Symmetrical Forms in Free-Texted Verse

Examples of poetic forms inspired by the ideal 1:1 and 1:2 proportions include the paragram, anagram, and chronogram, the acrostic, the picture rhyme, and the head form. Appearing in dedicatory materials to collections of poetry books, although not used in cantata texts themselves, the paragram was a common symmetrical form with a parallel structure. In this technique, the poet took a Bible verse and a personalized verse, translated them into numbers with a number alphabet, and, through deft manipulation of the spelling, the totals were made identical, thus creating a numerical parallel between the two verses. The techniques could be adapted so that the parallel lines create a date, as Beer uses in the dedication of Pachelbel's *Hexachordum Apollinis* (1699). This technique was popularized by Johann Christoph Männling and made commercially successful by Johann Friedrich Riederer (1678–1734).

Bach will have seen many paragrams, including one composed by Riederer published in the prefatory materials to the double cycle of cantata texts *Das Saiten-Spiel des Hertzens* (1721) by Benjamin Schmolk (1672–1737), and one by Picander (Figures 1.2a, 1.2b, and 1.2c) included on pages 30–32 of his *Ernst-Schertzhaffte und Satyrische Gedichte* (1732), Vol. 3, which contains numerous cantata texts for which Picander claimed Bach composed the music. Number alphabet techniques were regularly used as emblematic devices to give extra allusive meaning to important words. The simplest alphabet was $A = 1$ to $Z = 24$, in which I and $J = 9$, and U and $V = 20$. Bach and others appear to have used this number technique to incorporate the name "Jesus" at key moments into the form of some of their church cantatas: Jesus is 70 ($J = 9 + E = 5 + S = 18 + U = 20 + S = 18$), and Jesu is 52 ($J = 9 + E = 5 + S = 18 + U = 20$), although these are less obvious to recognize than a printed paragram. Examples of Bach's potential use of these numbers are cited in Chapters 2 and 6.

The acrostic is another emblematic technique used to give words a parallel meaning. It is regularly seen in the texts of dedicatory

Bey der D. und T. Hochzeit, den
1. Jun. 1730.

PARAGRAMMA CABBALISTICUM TRI-
GONALE. Ex Lib. Sir. XXVI. v. 16, &sp.

| Bey | - | - | 294 | Ein | - | - | 151 |
| dem | - | - | 103 | freundlich | - | - | 653 |
| Daumischen | - | - | 663 | Weib | - | - | 294 |
| | | | | | | | und |

(31)

| und | - | - | 311 | erfreuet | - | - | 772 |
| Thomischen | - | - | 944 | ihren | - | - | 340 |
| Hochzeits- | - | - | 904 | Mann | - | - | 261 |
| Festin | - | - | 533 | und | - | - | 311 |
| wolte | - | - | 607 | wenn | - | - | 428 |
| dem | - | - | 103 | sie | - | - | 231 |
| Herrn | - | - | 448 | vernünfftig | - | - | 1075 |
| Bräutigam | - | - | 724 | mit | - | - | 313 |
| und | - | - | 311 | ihm | - | - | 159 |
| Jungfer | - | - | 563 | umgehet | - | - | 572 |
| Braut | - | - | 557 | erfrischet | - | - | 805 |
| beyden | - | - | 410 | sie | - | - | 231 |
| wahre | - | - | 436 | ihm | - | - | 159 |
| Liebe | - | - | 144 | sein | - | - | 322 |
| wahre | - | - | 436 | Hertz | - | - | 694 |
| Beständigkeit | - | - | 874 | Ein | - | - | 151 |
| wahre | - | - | 436 | Weib | - | - | 294 |
| Treu | - | - | 568 | das | - | - | 182 |
| reichlich | - | - | 408 | schweigen | - | - | 638 |
| Auskommen | - | - | 804 | kan | - | - | 147 |
| und | - | - | 311 | das | - | - | 182 |
| alles | - | - | 319 | ist | - | - | 406 |
| vergnügende | - | - | 866 | eine | - | - | 166 |
| Wohl | - | - | 438 | Gabe | - | - | 47 |
| nebst | - | - | 470 | GOttes | - | - | 699 |
| folgenden | - | - | 442 | Ein | - | - | 151 |
| aus | - | - | 382 | wohlgezogen | - | - | 984 |
| der | - | - | 178 | Weib | - | - | 294 |
| heiligen | - | - | 341 | ist | - | - | 406 |
| Schrifft | - | - | 643 | nicht | - | - | 368 |
| ein | - | - | 151 | zu | - | - | 510 |
| | | | | | | | alter |

(32)

| alter | - | - | 425 | bezahlen | - | - | 527 |
| Teutscher | - | - | 986 | Es | - | - | 186 |
| und | - | - | 311 | ist | - | - | 406 |
| naher | - | - | 296 | nichts | - | - | 539 |
| Befreundter | - | - | 686 | liebers | - | - | 468 |
| beständigst | - | - | 930 | auf | - | - | 232 |
| antwünschen | - | - | 943 | Erden | - | - | 284 |
| | | | 20699 | denn | - | - | 207 |
| | | | | ein | - | - | 151 |
| | | | | züchtig | - | - | 815 |
| | | | | Weib | - | - | 294 |
| | | | | und | - | - | 311 |
| | | | | nichts | - | - | 539 |
| | | | | köstlichers | - | - | 1013 |
| | | | | denn | - | - | 207 |
| | | | | ein | - | - | 151 |
| | | | | keusches | - | - | 679 |
| | | | | Weib | - | - | 294 |
| | | | | | | | 20699 |

Schweigt, ihr schmähenden Verächter,
Die ihr sonst nur ein Gelächter
Aus den lieben Weibern macht;
Und bereut, ihr grossen Sünder,
Daß ihr sie vor keine Kinder
Wohlgerathner Menschen acht.
Weiber sind auch Menschen-Köpffe,
Und ein edeles Geschöpffe,
Das man in der gantzen Welt
Wie das Brodt so nöthig hält.

Über-

Figure 1.2a, 1.2b, 1.2c  Paragram using the trigonal alphabet devised by Henrici and printed in *Picanders Ernst- Schertzhaffte und Satyrische Gedichte*, Vol. 3 (1732), 30–32. https://www.digitale-sammlungen.de/en/view/bsb10310725?page=50,51. Bayerische Staatsbibliothek Munich.

hymns or poems. Bach used an acrostic in the printed copy of his Musical Offering (BWV 1079) to elaborate the meaning of the word *ricercar*: Regis Iussu Cantio Et Reliqua Canonica Arte Resoluta. The acrostic is commonly used to elaborate a name, with each letter in turn prominently highlighted. The Mylius ode 'Alles mit Gott und nichts ohn' ihn' that Bach set to music, BWV 1127, celebrating the birthday of the Weimar Duke Wilhelm Ernst, includes an acrostic on WJLHELM ERNST. The libretto of an early composition by Bach, Cantata (BWV) 150 'Nach dir, Herr, verlanget mich', also seems to have contained an acrostic, the first letter of every line of three verses spelling the name Doctor Conrad Meckbach, although as a printed version of this text emphasizing the acrostic has not survived, some scholars doubt the observation. Acrostics frequently appear in life mottos. In his *Die bedenckliche und geheimnisreiche Zahl Drey* (page 617 onward), Riederer includes a list of the life mottos of distinguished citizens, male and female, most of which use the initials of the name. For example, the motto of the Leipzig printer Johann Friedrich Gleditsch was "Ich Fürchte Gott" (page 623); the Dresden pastor Hermann Joachim Hahn was "Herr Jesu Hilff," and his wife, Dorothea Sophia Hahn, had the motto "Deo Sit Honor." The life mottos of Bach or members of his family have not been discovered so far, but one can expect that they would follow along these same lines and be created from the letters J.S.B. If he included his life motto in the words of any of his cantatas, it has not yet been detected.

The pictorial poem, or picture rhyme, is a visually symmetrical form. Bach will have seen many of these in published funeral or memorial materials, and in collections of poetry. Figure 1.3a shows a picture poem by Männling in the form of a heart. The heart symbol is used instead of the final word "Hertz" to complete the rhyme "ohn' Schertz, mein Hertz." Several times in his cantata scores Bach uses the heart symbol in place of the word "Hertz," for example in the score of Cantata (BWV) 199/8, soprano aria "Wie freudig ist mein Hertz" (Figure 1.3b).

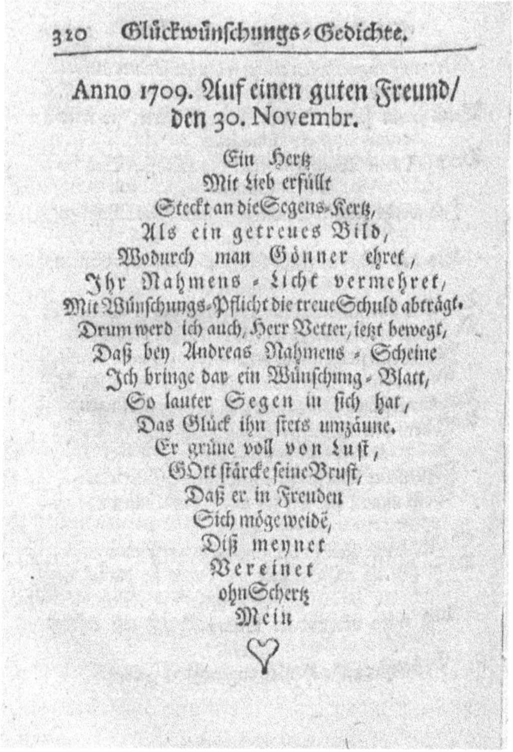

320  Glückwünschungs-Gedichte.

Anno 1709. Auf einen guten Freund/
den 30. Novembr.

Ein Hertz
Mit Lieb erfüllt
Steckt an die Segens-Kertz,
Als ein getreues Bild,
Wodurch man Gönner ehret,
Ihr Nahmens - Licht vermehret,
Mit Wünschungs-Pflicht die treue Schuld abträgt.
Drum werd ich auch, Herr Vetter, ietzt bewegt,
Daß bey Andreas Nahmens - Scheine
Ich bringe dar ein Wünschung - Blatt,
So lauter Segen in sich hat,
Das Glück ihn stets umzäune.
Er grüne voll von Lust,
GOtt stärcke seine Brust,
Daß er in Freuden
Sich möge weidē,
Diß meynet
Vereinet
ohn Schertz
Mein
♥

**Figure 1.3a** Celebratory heart-shaped picture poem "To a Good Friend." J. Chr. Männling, *Poetischer Blumen-Garten* (1717), 320. https://www.digitale-sammlungen.de/en/view/bsb11432965?page= 358,359. Bayerische Staatsbibliothek Munich.

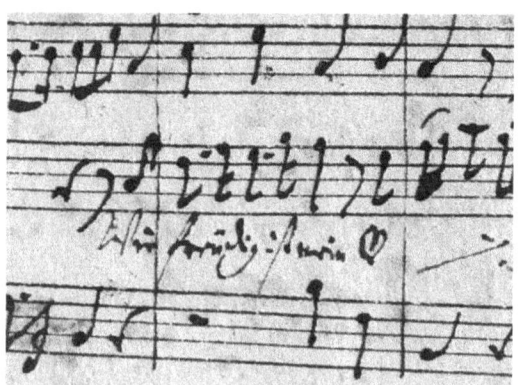

**Figure 1.3b** Bach's use of a heart symbol in Cantata 199/8. DK-Kk mu 6701.0731 Weyses Samling (C I, 615). https://www.bachdigital.de/ receive/BachDigitalWork_work_00000249.

Another very common symmetrical technique in poetry is the head form (Haupt-Ode or Kopf-Ode), where the first line of a stanza is repeated as the last line. This can be seen in the opening verse of Cantata (BWV) 82 (Chapter 6). The form is also used by Mylius in his congratulatory poem for Duke Wilhelm Ernst in 1713, in which each stanza has eight lines, and all of the aria's twelve stanzas are identically structured, their first and last line being the Duke's motto "Alles mit Gott und nichts ohn ihn." This form is used alongside the acrostic on the name Wjlhelm Ernst described above. Combining several creative techniques gave poems many meanings beyond the obvious sense of the words. Bach's setting of the Mylius poem to music (BWV 1127), which he copied into the printed text pamphlet, was unknown until it was discovered in 2005. We have no idea how many other songs Bach wrote for similar congratulatory occasions, whether to celebrate a birthday, name day, or funeral.

## Bach's Domestic Circumstances and the Cantatas

Bach's compositions would have been profoundly different had it not been for the members of his household, both male and female. The careers and progress of his sons and male pupils are well documented. There was a veritable hive of industry each week in the Leipzig household when it was time to copy the vocal and instrumental parts of the cantatas to meet the deadline of the first rehearsal. Bach's pupils and sons were involved in this process, and sometimes too were the womenfolk of the household. All apprentice composers learned their art from copying parts. Copying involved setting out a page neatly, selecting the width of a rastrum to rule the five-lined staves, and knowing how many bars would fit on each sheet of very expensive paper. Not infrequently the surviving parts of the church cantatas are hastily written by a copyist, with orthographic clarifications by Bach. One can imagine the bustle around the working table.

Traditionally the role of the women in Bach's life has been overlooked in the histories. This is largely because after his death, his image was molded first by his sons and male students, and then by the adulation of largely male scholars, who transformed him into a hero of their imaginings. He became a mighty Christian icon, the fifth evangelist, a composer of stern and complex music far removed from traditional feminine sensibilities. Whereas we know now that he encouraged the women in his household to develop their talents, and that he accepted a job in the forward-looking city of Leipzig where women had greater legal rights, and where his status would enable his wife and daughters to enjoy the company of cultured and educated citizens. Because women were ever-present as Bach composed the cantatas, I will give some details here and in the following chapters.

In October 1707 Johann Sebastian Bach married his second cousin, Maria Barbara Bach (1684–1720), a local girl five months his senior. A year later the young couple moved from Mühlhausen to Weimar where, under the protection of the pious Duke Wilhelm Ernst, they established a secure home for their children. First to be born was Catharina Dorothea (1708–1774). At about this time Maria Barbara's unmarried sister, Friedelena Margaretha Bach (1675–1729), moved in. Scarcely afforded a mention in traditional Bach biographies, Catharina Dorothea and Friedelena Margaretha provided decades of domestic stability throughout the unpredictable circumstances of life in the Bach household, enabling Bach to focus on music. They helped with the family move from Weimar to Cöthen in 1717, they witnessed and oversaw the final sickness, death, and burial of their sister and mother in 1720, and they stood by the younger children, regardless of their own sorrow, until brother-in-law and father Bach returned from a trip to Carlsbad with his employer Prince Leopold of Anhalt-Cöthen. Both must have felt the challenge of accepting and even celebrating Bach's remarriage seventeen months later to Anna Magdalena Wilcke/Wülcke (1701–1760), who by virtue of the age difference could have been

Catharina Dorothea's elder sister. Friedelena remained unmarried, living with the family until her death in 1729. Catharina Dorothea similarly remained unmarried, serving as an older sister to the toddlers, an extra pair of hands for Aunt Friedelena, and after Bach's death in 1750, a companion to her stepmother, Anna Magdalena.

Numerous myths and romantic ideas have distorted the reputation of Bach's second wife, Anna Magdalena. We know for certain that she was twenty years old and a professional singer when she married Sebastian in 1721. It is most likely that she was independent-spirited, and yet chose to marry. Although domestic life cannot always have been harmonious, the maiden aunt and oldest daughter must have helped create a smooth-running operation that gave Anna Magdalena extra time to pursue an elegant social life, to continue singing, and assist her husband with copying music when necessary.

## How to Refer to the Church Cantatas

Bach rarely created a title page for his church cantatas, nor did he arrange his works into Opus numbers, although given the indication "Opus 1" on the 1731 title page of the *Clavier Übung*, it seems he may have been planning to use Opus numbers for his published keyboard works. We tend to refer to Bach's cantatas today by their BWV number, BWV being the abbreviation for Bach-Werke-Verzeichnis, whereas the title pages of Bach's scores suggest that he referred to his cantatas by the opening incipit, for example, 'Nun komm der Heyden Heyland'. In this volume I have chosen to use the following format for the first mention, "Cantata (BWV) 147, Title-Incipit," and thereafter simply "Cantata 147." This formula gives the reader the information necessary to access reference materials.

The trend for referring to the cantatas with a number began in 1879 with the Bach Gesellschaft thematic index, where thirty-one cantatas were given the numbers used in the Bach Gesellschaft edition, rather than a cumbersome repetition of thirty-one titles. A second thematic catalogue, Volume 46, was published in 1899 when the edited cantata series was complete. Although the aim to publish the complete works of J. S. Bach had been fulfilled within fifty years, the younger generation saw a need to take the mission forward. A New Bach Society (the Neue Bach Gesellschaft) was proposed and formed with the goal to make the works of J. S. Bach widely known and performed in churches. At this time, they referred to the cantatas by the number used in the Bach Gesellschaft edition as well as by their title. But once the Bach-Werke-Verzeichnis, compiled by Wolfgang Schmieder, was published in 1950 there was no going back.

The Schmieder catalog adopted the numbers that each of Bach's works had been assigned in the Bach Gesellschaft series, and the BWV numbers became standard. This went hand in hand with the commissioning and publication of the New Bach Edition (Neue Bach Ausgabe), and with new research that caused the chronology of Bach's church cantatas to change. The new edition was published from 1954 and completed in 2007, throughout which period the editorial policy was to order the cantatas by the church calendar rather than by BWV number. To this day the New Bach Edition remains the most up-to-date scholarly edition. There was one final attempt to make the numeration of Bach's works reflect the chronology of the composition and first performance of Bach's cantata. This was introduced by Bach scholars Hans-Joachim Schulze and Christoph Wolff, who devised a genre-based catalog system published as *Bach Compendium*, but however excellent the ideal, it was too late. BWV numbers had become inextricably associated with each composition in the minds of performers and listeners.

The most recently updated and fully revised BWV catalog was published by Breitkopf in 2022, using a decimal numbering system to differentiate early and later versions of church cantatas, and new BWV numbers for works formerly listed in various appendices. The printed version was produced for reference libraries, and the core information about every composition by Bach is on the constantly updated open access database https://www.bach-digital.de with live links to zoomable original manuscripts and early copies, enabling anyone with internet access to explore high resolution images of Bach's original scores and parts. These are privileged resources that Bach researchers in the nineteenth and twentieth centuries could never have dreamed of.

## Listening to Bach's Church Cantatas

Story is an important component in all creative endeavors. Behind every musical composition there are many narratives working together to form a coherent whole. The stories I am mostly interested in in this book are those that Johann Sebastian Bach was working with when he composed his cantatas, whether they were the actions in the prescribed Bible readings, or scenarios that suggested themselves to Bach as he worked with the free poetry texts. Although he rarely, if ever, chronicled reasons for composing a specific cantata, he did leave clues in his scores, in the vocal and instrumental parts, and in the musical notation. There are also external clues in surviving documents relating to the poetry he used, the circumstances and context of his domestic life, work duties, and social activities. Studying and piecing these together can help deepen our understanding of Bach's music, and specifically his church cantatas.

Bach did not always start with the poetic text and then interpret it in his composition. Sometimes a musical phrase or melodic shape held an overall meaning for him. For example, he had used the melodic shape of the opening of Cantata (BWV) 82 in earlier compositions, and he would use it again to create a similar musical effect to different words, as discussed in Chapter 6. Similarly, motifs had by Bach's time become tropes with meanings, such as a descending chromatic bass signifying a lament. And then there were musical associations that reminded Bach and his congregations of well-known hymn tunes. Unbidden, the hymn melodies could bring emotional or topical meaning to his congregational listeners, although centuries later we can easily miss these allusions. Bach's own mind was full of such musical associations, and he could play with their allusiveness: they were part of his musical vocabulary.

Bach was working within a tradition, rather than in isolation. He was responding to different styles of music he had heard, to different fashions at the court, at the opera, through traveling musicians, and to what he read. There was of course no recorded music for him to study—his internal musical world was stimulated by "listening to" scores that he owned or copied that translated into sounds and sensations in his body. This ability, a well-known experience for many musicians, was the result of hours and hours of musical training, whether at the keyboard, or singing, or in instrumental practice. The sounds he imagined as he read the scores were as clear as if he was hearing them with his ears.

There are as many ways to respond to Bach's church cantatas as there are individuals. The many different elements in music make it impossible to suggest the best or a better way to listen. There are numerous inroads that will attract those from different educational, social, and philosophical backgrounds. One can, for example, focus on the spiritual, the dramatic, the theological, the theatrical, or the beauty of the poetry; or on musical elements such as the technicalities of the harmony, the construction, the instrumentation, the melodies, the bass, the inner voices, the vocal effects, the historical accuracy, the emotional effects of individual moments or of the whole; all of which can be in either or both text and music. As a reader, performer, or listener you have the power to take from my ideas anything that is helpful, and to discard the rest. The only "right" way to receive the music of Bach is yours.

## Suggestions for Further Reading

The classic understanding of Bach's church cantatas is by Alfred Dürr (Oxford, 2005), 3–74, with deeper coverage of their theological contexts in Robin A. Leaver (2021) and Martin Petzoldt, translated Braatz, https://www.

bach-cantatas.com/Articles/Leipzig-Churches-Petzold.pdf. See Michael Maul (2012) for a study of St. Thomas School; Markus Rathey (2023), Tanya Kevorkian (2007) and (2022), and Andrew Talle (2017) for the social contexts of women; Heide Wunder (1998) and Merkel and Wunder (2007) for the status of women; Bettina Varwig (2023) on the body and music; and Stephen Rose (2011) on the status of musicians. For the significance of compositional choices in Bach's time see David Yearsley (2002), Mark A. Peters and Reginald L. Sanders (2018), and Tatlow (2015) and (1991).

# 2
# Music for a Mühlhausen Occasion
## 'Gottes Zeit ist die allerbeste Zeit'

It is not known when Bach composed Cantata (BWV) 106 'Gottes Zeit ist die allerbeste Zeit' (God's Time Is the Very Best Time"). There is no trace of the original draft or score, and there are no documents, letters, diaries, or receipts to suggest who commissioned the work, when it was first performed, or why Bach composed it. The earliest known version is a copy of the score made in 1768 by an unknown scribe, who gave it the title *Actus Tragicus*.

The musical style of Cantata 106 and the form of its libretto suggest that Bach wrote it sometime between 1706 and 1709, a period that saw him based in Arnstadt, Mühlhausen, and Weimar. Over the past 150 years 'Gottes Zeit' has been classified as a funeral cantata based on textual evidence (discussed below). This has led to the search for plausible funerals that could help give an exact occasion and date for its composition. Furthermore, if the original purpose for the cantata was known, it would strongly influence the way it is performed and understood. With the idea of death, tragedy (from the title "Actus Tragicus"), and a funeral in mind, modern performers have tended to set a somber mood, with body language and facial expressions communicating sorrow. And yet there is very little evidence that Bach wrote it for a funeral. Imagine how differently it could sound if the performers thought it was composed to encourage a living, breathing believer! The motet-like continuous structure of 'Gottes Zeit' certainly suggests an early work: it differs from Bach's later cantatas, which tend to separate movements with recitatives. And some scholars might prefer not to classify it as a "cantata" at all. For our purposes, however, I will continue the tradition, and include this beloved work among the most popular of Bach's church cantatas. In this chapter I will explore evidence to suggest several different scenarios for its composition, with some comments on how it has been constructed. To begin, though, I will introduce the work, with its opening instrumental Sonatina, a second movement made up of six through-composed sections of different time signatures and speeds, a third movement for gambas and two solo voices, and the fourth and final movement, a choral setting of the "Gloria."

## Movement by Movement

### First Movement: Sonatina

The cantata opens with a twenty-bar instrumental Sonatina in the home key of E♭ major. The basso continuo begins by establishing a regular pulse with repeated eighth notes that change pitch every four notes. The gambas then join the regular eighth-note movement, adding the warmth of their bow strokes to the pulsing sonorities. They then introduce an all-important four-bar melody containing musical ideas that will recur throughout the cantata. This instrumental foundation creates a reassuring and meditative atmosphere over which the two recorders breathe intertwining lines of dissonances and resolutions to create a single, mesmeric melody with very little forward momentum. The Sonatina comes to rest with a pause over the final chord, after the bass has repeated the pitch E♭ for three bars. Three groups of instruments performing in contemplative unity may be understood as a sonic image of the three-in-one God. It is composed in a key requiring three flats, although according to traditional practice, the copyist wrote only two in the key signature. Although we cannot know if Bach had this image in mind, something special can be sensed by player and listener here, whether caused by its threefold-ness or its unity or something else.

## Second Movement, Section 1

Gottes Zeit ist die allerbeste Zeit    God's time is the very best time

As the listener wonders if there is any rhyme or reason for the Sinfonia's melodic line, Bach breaks the mood with the words "Gottes Zeit ist die allerbeste Zeit." Starting with an inverted triad and remembering that the triad drew its name from the Holy Trinity (God, Father, and Holy Spirit), the singers animate the performing space with their message that the very best timing is God's. Instead of the repeated pitches and gentle bow strokes of the Sinfonia, every single eighth note now has a different pitch. This short section takes the piece to the first beat of bar 27. Twenty-seven main pulses have been heard since the cantata started; this threefold-ness ($3 \times 3 \times 3 = 27$) of each bar-pulse may be subliminally reinforcing the fundamental message: "God's time is the very best time."

## Second Movement, Section 2

| | |
|---|---|
| In ihm leben, weben und sind wir, | In him we live, move, and are (have our being), |
| solange er will. | as long as he wills. |

Suddenly the time signature changes to a triple meter. For thirty-three bars the listener is seized by an impulse to dance. The irrepressible energy of this section exudes the joy and gift of life. The voices move as pairs with an imitative entry on "In ihm leben" ("In him we live"), followed by the word "weben" (literally, "weave," translated as "move"), which is captured in a repeated stepwise up-and-down motion. This stepwise figure was first heard in the wordless recorders in the Sinfonia and is now transformed into a dance of life. The voices unite on the words "und sind wir" ("and have our being"), which lead to the final phrase "so lange er will" ("as long as he wills"). The first time "lange" ("long") is sung, Bach uses a shock tactic: all voices but the sopranos are silenced. We hear and feel the breath of the sopranos as they sustain a B♭ for ten long beats—a length suitable for the perfect will of God. The music runs immediately into the next line of text.

## Second Movement, Section 3

| | |
|---|---|
| In ihm sterben wir zur rechten Zeit, | In him we die at the proper time, |
| wenn er will. | when he wills. |

The dancing stops and the music changes into a slow common time with four pulses to every bar. Life and death are starkly contrasted. "In ihm sterben wir" is set to a melody strongly reminiscent of the opening gamba phrase in the Sinfonia: repeated notes on the same pitch are followed by two three-note pairs that take the melody down a fourth. This striking motivic resemblance allows the listener to realize retrospectively that the wordless gamba phrase was an expression of "In him we die." As the movement progresses the pain of death is expressed in chromatic steps given to the word "sterben" (to die), and even more strikingly, in the anguished and angular tritone "sterben wir" ("we die") sung by the sopranos, which rounds off with a small stepwise up-and-down motion to "zu rechter Zeit" ("at the right time"). Harmonically this seven-bar section has an unsettling effect as it moves away from the home key. Something entirely new is about to happen.

## Second Movement, Section 4

| Ach Herr, lehre uns bedenken, | Oh Lord, teach us to reflect |
| dass wir sterben müssen, | that we must die, |
| Dass wir klug werden. | so that we might become wise. |

The text now moves from acclamation-like statements to a prayerful plea, taken from Psalm 90:12. Bach sets this for the solo tenor supported by the comforting sounds of recorders and gambas. The phrase "Ach Herr, lehre uns bedenken" ("Oh Lord, teach us to reflect") is sung four times; the phrase "dass wir sterben müssen" ("that we must die") twice, and only once does the phrase give the reason why: "auf dass wir klug werden" ("so that we might become wise"). Knowing how easy it is to forget death when fully enjoying the dance of life, Bach may have chosen to vary the numbers of repetitions to emphasize the importance of reflecting on death.

## Second Movement, Section 5

| Bestelle dein Haus! | Put your house in order; |
| denn du wirst sterben | for you will die |
| und nicht lebendig bleiben. | and not remain living. |

The urgency to prepare for death is further impressed on the listener by the surprising change to a fast triple 3/8 time, as the bass proclaims the prophetic words of Isaiah, "Bestelle dein Haus!" ("Put your house in order!"). There are no soothing gambas in this section. The unison recorders are startled into arpeggiated sixteenth-note motion, playing throughout the sixty bars of this section like a flock of starlings taking flight. The bass soloist imitates this arpeggiated motion on the word "lebendig" ("living"), which creates an almost frantic effect as if the singer is living on an edge that will inevitably lead to death. This breathtaking effect gives way to a three-part choral **fugue** in the common time used also for the Sinfonia and opening chorus, and now raised a tone to the key of F minor. It is to be the most complex section of the work.

## Second Movement, Section 6

| Es ist der alte Bund: | It is the old covenant: |
| Mensch, du musst sterben! | Man/Woman, you must die! |

The fifty-five bars of this section combine three contrasting texts, and three entirely different musical ideas. The uncompromising and unmerciful text "Es ist der alte Bund: Mensch, du musst sterben" ("It is the old covenant: Man/Woman, you must die") is adapted from Sirach 14:18. Bach chose to set this black-and-white theological principle in a rigid fugal form, with its structural logic and inevitability. The three lower voices reiterate the message in a phrase that includes the uncomfortable tritone, just heard in Section 3 on "sterben." After fifteen bars, the message has definitely hit home. The atmosphere is somber. And this is when the soprano enters, piercing the fugal darkness in a moment of pure radiance, speaking directly and personally to the Savior of the new covenant: "Ja, komm, Herr Jesu, komm!" ("Yes, come, Lord Jesus, come!"). These words from Revelation 22:20 are the penultimate phrase of the New Testament, in response to the risen Jesus, the Alpha and Omega, who says that he will return soon. Jesus encourages all believers to respond to his message with the invocation "Come." Revelation 22:17 reads: "The Spirit and the bride say, 'Come!' And let the one who hears say, 'Come!' " The soprano's response is a superlatively affirmative and unqualified "Yes, come, Lord Jesus, come," with "Ja" ("yes") repeated over and again, in fact thirty-seven times. The instruments accompany the soprano with the first half of a familiar chorale, also in the first person "I," the first verse of which is "Ich hab mein Sach' Gott heimgestellt, er machs mit mir, wie's ihm gefällt" ("I have left my concerns with God; He does with me as he pleases"), and the second verse "Mein Zeit und Stund ist, wann Gott will; ich schreib ihm nicht vor Maß noch Ziel" ("My time and hour are as God wills, I have not set him any limits"). But as the instruments have no words, this allusive chorale text may or may not have come into the minds of Bach's listeners. Hidden within the soprano melody, for those with eyes to see and ears to hear, is also the opening of the penitential chorale "Herzlich tut mich verlangen" ("Heartily do I long"), which Bach was to use almost two decades later as the famous passion chorale "O Sacred Head, sore wounded," integral to his St. Matthew Passion, BWV 244. The three ideas converge toward the end of the movement: the three lower voices are released from the legalism of their fugal development, and as they sing the final "sterben" ("to die") they combine in a long stepwise upward motion and meet the soprano, who takes over with one last iteration of "Yes, come, Lord Jesus, come," embellishing the word "Jesus" with fourteen notes. The final, vulnerable, unaccompanied "Lord Jesus" is followed by measured silence, notated as rests, and further stillness that mark the end of this intense second movement.

With a short break after the instrumental Sonatina, the music and text can be seen as a continuously constructed 150 bars "of varying time signatures" (see Mizler in Chapter 1, "Mapping Out the Score") in paired and beautifully proportioned sections of 20 + 40 (7 + 33) + 30 (7 + 23) + 60 bars. This consecutive 60–30–60 pattern is followed by the 55 bars of Section 6, and its silence before Movement 3, which in performance is traditionally quite lengthy—instinctively measuring about five bars. Proportioning music into 1:1 and 1:2 was meaningful, used purposefully to bring compositions into beautiful order (see Chapter 1, "A Creational Theology of Music"), to move the listener, and to honor and imitate the perfection of God and his creativity. As Bach's original score is missing, we cannot know how accurate the earliest surviving copy is, so this observation about its proportioned structure is offered as a suggestion.

It has been said that Bach intended the ending of the second movement to represent the soul ascending to heaven, with its rising vocal parts, the pulsating heartbeat in the continuo ceasing, and the soprano walking into paradise. This imagery works particularly well if Bach composed the work for a funeral, the concept being that the deceased person is seen entering heaven. It can also be seen as an illustration of what happens when the heart stops beating, which is relevant if the cantata was for a living person preparing for his/her own death.

## Movement 3, Section 1

| | |
|---|---|
| In deine Hände befehl ich meinen Geist; | Into your hands I commend my spirit; |
| du hast mich erlöset, | you have redeemed me, |
| Herr, du getreuer Gott. | you faithful God. |

After the silence at the end of the second movement it is hard to anticipate what will be heard next. Bach chooses the sound of two solo voices (alto and bass) accompanied by two gambas, with a continuo group, most likely made up of two instruments, a keyboard, and a cello. Melodically the movement opens with a striking stepwise two-bar ascent that spans an octave and a fifth, and that rounds off with the repeated stepwise up-and-down motion first heard in the recorders in the Sinfonia and then associated with the words "leben und weben" in Movement 2, Section 2. The shape of this ascent is repeated in various guises throughout the section. Bach devotes sixteen bars to "In deine Hände befehl ich meinen Geist" ("Into your hands I commend my spirit"), with the phrase "Into your hands" repeated nine times. This leads to the affirmation "Du hast mich erlöset, Herr, du getreuer Gott" ("You have redeemed me, Lord, you faithful God") in the next eight bars. "In deine Hände" is repeated four times, each time emphasized melodically and rhythmically with a unison repetition of four notes and its downward sighing motif following the natural rhythm of the words. The second half of the text "Herr, du getreuer Gott" ("Lord, you faithful God") is also repeated four times.

The prominent use of groups of two in this twenty-four-bar section may be a deliberate allusion to "Jesus," the second person of the Trinity who spoke these very words before he died on the Cross. The listener understands that it is Jesus who has redeemed "me" and into whose hands "I" commend my spirit. This potentially emblematic interpretation is further strengthened by the number of bars allocated to Movement 3 as a whole—70 bars, 70 being the numerical value of "Jesus" (9 + 5 + 18 + 20 + 18) in the simplest number alphabet. (See Chapter 1, "Symmetrical Forms in Free-Texted Verse").

## Movement 3, Section 2

| | |
|---|---|
| Heute wirst du mit mir im Paradies sein. | Today you will be with me in Paradise. |

Jesus also spoke the words "Heute wirst du mit mir im Paradies sein" ("Today you will be with me in Paradise") to the repentant thief as they hung side by side on their respective crosses: Luke 23:43. Bach gives the phrase to the bass, as he often did when Christ's voice is heard (*Vox Christi*). In this scene Jesus, the bass, addresses the Christian soul, who is sung by the alto, commending his/her spirit into God's hands. The musical and narrative texture increases in complexity as the alto takes up Martin Luther's paraphrase of Simeon's hymn of praise "Mit Fried und Freud ich fahr dahin," reminding the listener of Simeon's consolation when he recognized the baby Jesus in the Temple as being the long-awaited Savior: "In peace and joy I now depart, According to God's will; I am consoled, my heart and mind; Gentle and quiet. As God has promised me: Death has become my sleep."

As the gamba lines interlace around the bass voice singing Jesus' words, and the slow-moving chorale is heard in the alto voice, there is a gradual buildup of intensity reaching a peak in the final bar that ends with the highest note for the bass soloist. The alto takes over, clearing the soundscape and literally toning down the atmosphere with a stepwise descent. The gambas continue their unifying role with a sequence that enables the listener to focus on the final phrase of the chorale: "Wie Gott mir verheissen hat; der Tod ist mein Schlaf worden" ("As God has promised me: Death has become my sleep"). The movement ends with the perfection of a unison note C (1:1) played by the second gamba and continuo, as if in peaceful sleep.

## Movement 4

| | |
|---|---|
| Glorie, Lob, Ehr', und Herrlichkeit, | Glory, praise, honor, and splendor, |
| Sei dir, Gott Vater und Sohn bereit, | be to you by name, God Father, and Son, |
| Dem Heilgen Geist mit Namen! | and Holy Spirit! |
| Die göttlich Kraft macht uns sieghaft | The divine power makes us victorious |
| Durch Jesum Christum. Amen | through Jesus Christ. Amen |

As God's time is the best, whether in life or death, there can be only one fitting response in conclusion: a joyful song glorifying the Triune God, Father, Son, and Holy Spirit. The text is one of the versions of the Gloria included by Johann Olearius (1611–1684) in his book of daily prayers (see below), recalling the worship song of the angels in Revelation 7:12, which Bach would have read in his German Bible as: "Amen, das Lob und der Preis, und die Weisheit, und die Danksagung, und die Ehre, und die Macht, und die Stärke sei unserm Gott in alle Ewigkeit, Amen" ("Amen: Blessing, and glory, and wisdom, and thanksgiving, and honor, and power, and might, be unto our God for ever. Amen"). A similar form of the Gloria was first formulated by Adam Reusner in Verse 7 of his 1533 hymn "In dich hab' ich gehoffet, Herr." As settings of the Gloria frequently end sections of the liturgy or Psalms, it would be easy to see the inclusion of this final movement as formulaic. But this would be short-sighted. The words are a clear conclusion to the overall message of the cantata.

This version of the Gloria is in two parts, the second part beginning at "Die göttlich Kraft" ("the divine power"). Bach however divides his two-part musical setting at a different point, reserving the musical shift in tempo, texture, and rhythm for the final words "durch Jesum Christum, Amen" ("through Jesus Christ, Amen") for which he chose imitative style: the melody is heard in unison, first in the tonic, then at the fifth, again at the tonic, and again at the fifth, creating a horizontal expression of the 1:2 proportions inherent in these pitches. The altos singing the phrase first, followed by the sopranos at the fifth, then the basses, and finally the tenors at the fifth, creating a life-affirming ending to the cantata. The listener is helped to sense the joy of being alive, and of living confidently, even while knowing that death is inevitable, all because there is victory over death "through Jesus Christ"!

## Ways of Understanding Cantata 106

Given that Bach's original score and the instrumental and vocal parts are lost, the earliest surviving copy of this work holds the best evidence of Bach's intentions. Held in the Berlin State Library under the call mark *P 1018*, the score specifies the instruments and voices used today: two recorders, two gambas, basso continuo, and soprano, alto, tenor, and bass voices. The anonymous scribe wrote at the end "Sc: Lipsiae. 1768 / M. Oct:," indicating that it was copied in Leipzig in October 1768. It was once thought to be in the handwriting of Christian Friedrich Penzel (1737–1801), but it is now understood to be in the hand of Anon 421, a scribe who, so far, has not been identified.

The cantata has been well loved since the nineteenth century and much has been written about it. Ideas about its purpose and origins have been repeated so many times that they stand almost as facts in scholarly literature and on internet sites, the standard account being that it is a funeral cantata composed while Bach was organist in Mühlhausen in 1707–1708. Its text consists of an assortment of direct citations from the Bible, and with two non-biblical phrases about time: "Gottes Zeit ist die allerbeste Zeit" ("God's time is the very best time"), and "In ihm sterben wir zu rechter Zeit" ("In him we die at the right time"). Numerous details have been used to support the funeral cantata narrative, for example, the suggestive phrase "Actus Tragicus" written on the cover of the 1768 score, and the choice of chorale melodies. Many have assumed that "Actus Tragicus" means "tragic act," which is both a misunderstanding of "Tragicus" and a false understanding of the Lutheran view of death in Bach's time. Furthermore, there is no evidence that the title originated with Bach. Several scholars have suggested that the phrase "Gottes Zeit ist die allerbeste Zeit" might have been the life motto, or *Devise*, of the person who had died. When thinking afresh about this cantata it is important to remember that many of these fondly held stories about its history and origins are unsubstantiated.

One of the earliest and most enduring views is that it was composed for the funeral of Tobias Lämmerhirt (1639–1707), brother of Bach's mother Maria Elisabeth née Lämmerhirt. Bach's Uncle Tobias was a furrier, master craftsman, and councilor in the city of Erfurt, where he died on 10 August 1707. Tobias and his wife Martha Catharina had made a joint will, earmarking the sum of 50 florins each to J. S. Bach and his brother, Johann Jacob (1682–1722). On the death of Martha Catharina fifteen years later, in March 1722, the will was still valid, although it is not known how much remained in the estate and how much Bach received. *The New Bach*

*Reader* (1998) states (page 95) that he received the princely sum of 550 thaler, whereas on page 490 note 82 Christoph Wolff in *The Learned Musician* (2000) states that "Bach's share came to about 50 florins, but it was not paid out to him until 1722." Whatever the sum, the fact that Tobias remembered his late sister's children in his will suggests that he felt protective toward them and might even have kept in regular contact. We know that Bach's first-born child, Catharina Dorothea, took the name Catharina after Martha Catharina Lämmerhirt, who served as godmother at the child's baptism on 29 December 1709. Unfortunately, there are no surviving letters or diaries to confirm the more everyday meetings between the young Bachs and the Lämmerhirts. Nor are there any surviving printed funeral materials for either Tobias or his wife. Given his relationship to Bach, and his social standing as a town councilor, Tobias Lämmerhirt could have commissioned and paid for a musical setting of some of his favorite biblical texts, for example for a festive celebration, such as a significant wedding anniversary or birthday. But would it make sense to commission a funeral composition that he would never hear? Although this was the model for the aristocracy and royalty for state funerals, it seems to be a double-edged compliment, less likely within a family.

Another candidate whose funeral has been mentioned as a possible occasion for the composition of Cantata 106 is Dorothea Susanna Tilesius, née Eilmar, the sister of Pastor Georg Christian Eilmar (1665–1715), one of Mühlhausen's most senior clergymen, and the wife of a Mühlhausen councilor, Johann Adolph Tilesius (1668–1728). She died on 1 June 1708, leaving four children between the ages of four and eleven. She was just thirty-four years old when her death brutally interrupted an active life. Given her age and childbearing status, hers was most likely to have been yet another case of maternal mortality. Pastor Eilmar also lived in Mühlhausen. He was a theological advisor, professional colleague, neighbor, and by all accounts, a friend to Bach and his family. Bach's relationship with Eilmar lasted beyond his period of service in Mühlhausen, with records showing that he was one of three godparents at the Weimar baptism of Catharina Dorothea, alongside Martha Catharina Lämmerhirt.

The connection between the Bachs and Eilmars is particularly important when it comes to the practice of commissioning or asking Bach to compose cantatas. On the score of Cantata (BWV) 131, 'Aus der Tiefen rufe ich, Herr, zu dir' (Out of the Depths, Lord, I Cry to You) Bach wrote: "Auff begehren Tit: Herrn D: Georg: Christ: Eilmars in die Music gebracht von Joh: Seb: Bach Org: Molhusino" ("At the request of Mr. Dr. Georg Christ: Eilmar, set to music by Joh: Seb: Bach, Organist of Mühlhausen"). There are just two surviving autograph scores of any of Bach's known early cantatas: the score of Cantata (BWV) 71 'Gott ist mein König' (God Is My King) and the score of Cantata 131. Together these two works provide verifiable samples of Bach's handwriting and his compositional style from his period as organist in Mühlhausen. That Pastor Eilmar requested Bach to compose a cantata is also important. Eilmar regularly wrote poems and devised personalized texts for funerals and festive occasions (see Chapter 1), as can been seen from several surviving occasional prints. He no doubt wrote many more occasional poems that have since been lost. He might even have compiled the text for Cantata 131, in addition to asking Bach to compose the music. And this in turn opens the possibility that Eilmar might have done the same for Cantata 106. However, no documentary evidence to support these ideas has yet been found.

Given the funerary practices in Mühlhausen, and the elevated social status of Dorothea Tilesius as both wife of a town councilor and close relative of a senior Mühlhausen pastor, it is highly likely that the sermon preached at her funeral, and the dedicatory poems written in her honor, would have been printed, and under normal circumstances these would show which biblical texts, chorales, and concerted music, if any, were used at her burial and memorial services. Unfortunately, no such pamphlets have so far been discovered. She was buried on 3 June 1708, just two days after her death. This short window between her death (perhaps sudden) and her burial makes it unlikely that Bach would have composed Cantata 106 from scratch as well as prepare a performance for a public burial service. There would have been more comfortable time, though, to commission and compose a musical setting for the customary memorial celebration for the life of an eminent citizen, usually held a month or so after the burial, which for Dorothea Tilesius would have been just before the Bach family left Mühlhausen for Weimar. In this scenario, Cantata 106 would have been commissioned and composed for a church celebration in her honor in June or July 1708, with text compiled and music requested by her brother Pastor Eilmar. However, this is still working on the premise that the cantata was composed for a funeral or memorial service.

Another Mühlhausen citizen has recently been added to the list of funerals for which the cantata might have been composed. Elderly Mühlhausen councilor Adolph Strecker died at 10 P.M. on 13 September 1708 at the age of eighty-four years, and was buried three days later, on 16 September a couple of months after the Bach family had moved to Weimar. As a well-to-do councilor, Strecker would have had the appropriate wealth and status to commission music for his own funeral, had he been interested in doing so. But there is no surviving record of his having commissioned creative work, nor have I found any music dedicated to him. Strecker's funeral was held at the Blasius Church in Mühlhausen, and the sermon was preached by Superintendent Johann Adolf Frohne (1652–1713). As was customary, a revised version of the sermon was printed after the event, and in this case was dated 20 December 1708. Like Uncle Tobias, councilor Strecker was elderly, with plenty of time to commission music and texts for his funeral. He chose Romans 8:17–18 for the text on which his funeral sermon was to be preached. This bears no resemblance to the texts in Cantata 106. The title Superintendent Frohne chose for Strecker's funeral sermon includes the words "Zeit und Ewigkeit," which might suggest a link to the "Zeit" of Cantata 106, although more likely to have been an allusion to a well-known annual cycle of sermons by theologian and orientalist Martin Geier (1614–1680), *Zeit und Ewigkeit*, a copy of which Bach also owned.

## Clues Indicating the Possible Purposes of 'Gottes Zeit'

### (a) The text in Olearius, *Betschule,* Leipzig, 1664

The primary clue to the purpose of Cantata 106 can be found in its selection of texts. In one of the most dynamic Bach discoveries of the 1980s, Renate Steiger (1934–2006) recognized much of the cantata's libretto in a widely circulated book of private prayers: Johann Olearius; *Christliche Bet-Schule* (*Christian Prayer School*), on page 128 of the first edition (1664). This is one and the same Johann Olearius who wrote the amplified *Biblische Erklärung* (1681) that Bach owned. The *Christian Prayer School* is a comprehensive and systematic guide to personal devotion, with prayers for every stage of daily life. It was well known in Mühlhausen, first published in 1664 and followed by several expanded editions. Despite having more than 800 printed pages divided into three "books," this small and chunky volume was designed to fit into a pocket or handbag. Its first "book" is devoted to dutiful preparation for prayer, the second focuses on how to pray, and the third is to help the devout intercessor express gratitude. "Book" 2 is ordered into thirteen different prayer categories or classes, the third of which focuses on common daily prayers, and is divided into seven subcategories. It was on the very first page of the seventh category that Steiger recognized the texts from Cantata 106. The prayers in this category are headed: "3. Common Daily Prayer[s]/ and Exercises for [the purpose of] True Godliness 7. When Contemplating a Blessed End" ("3. Die allgemeinen Täglichen Gebet[e]/ und Übungen der wahren Gottseligkeit 7. Bey

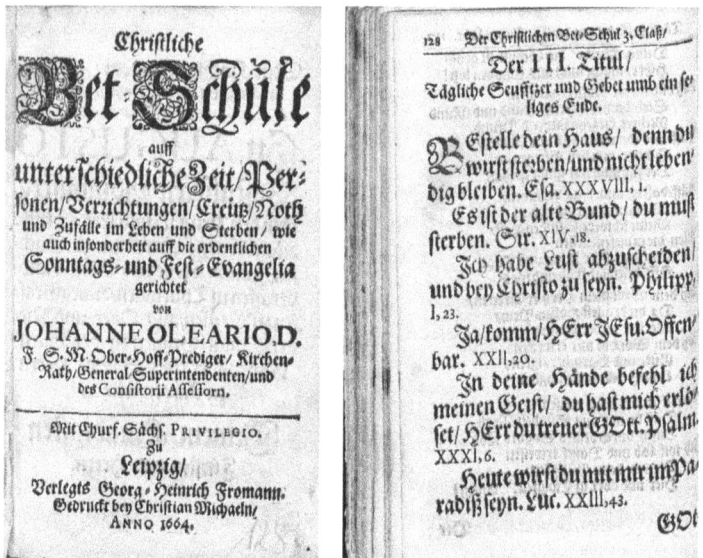

Figure 2.1a and 2.1b  Title page and page 128 of Johann Olearius, *Christliche Bet-Schule* (1664). 1st ed. http://dx.doi.org/10.25673/opendata2-20708. Halle (Saale) Universitäts- und Landesbibliothek Sachsen-Anhalt.

Betrachtung eines seligen Endes"). The phrase "Exercises for True Godliness" ("Übungen der wahren Gottseligkeit") is a quotation from 1 Timothy 4:7b. The prayers in Section 7 are devised to train the living believer in daily righteousness, and to contemplate his/her own mortality. The short title of this section is printed in the header: "Daily sighs and prayers for a blessed end" ("Tägliche Seufftzer und Gebet umb ein seliges Ende"), again emphasizing that this section is devised for the living believer in their daily contemplative practice. Figures 2.1a and 2.1b show page 128 in the 1664 edition.

Missing from this page, but used as a text in Cantata 106, is verse 12 of Psalm 90: "Oh Lord, teach us to reflect that we must die" ("Ach Herr, lehre uns bedenken daß wir sterben müssen"). Additionally, there are two free-texted phrases that do not appear in either

Olearius or in the Bible, but which nonetheless capture biblical principles. The first is "God's time is the very best" ("Gottes Zeit ist die allerbeste Zeit"), and the second "In him we die at the right time, when he wills" ("In ihm sterben wir zur rechten Zeit, wenn er will"), which mirrors and complements the structure of the phrase from Acts 17, "In him we live, and move and have our being, as long as he wills." These free-texted phrases are by David von Schweinitz (see below).

Several of the biblical verses printed on page 128 of the prayer book can also be found elsewhere in the volume, under different headings. Not surprisingly Olearius lists some of them in Book 2, Section 12, which is devoted to daily prayers for the final moments of life, where he also includes "In deine Hände befehl ich meinen Geist, du hast mich erlöset, Herr du getreuer Gott" (page 712) and "Heute wirstu mit mir in Paradies sein" (page 713). The verse "Bestelle dein Haus" also appears in Section 12.2, "The last will and testament of a Christian, which is to be repeated every day" ("Testament und leetzer Wille eines Christen welches täglich zu wiederholen"), on page 718. It is important to realize here that even prayers concerning death are designed as daily prayers for the living believer.

Some scholars have claimed that the text of the final movement of Cantata 106 'Gloria, Lob, Ehr, und Herrlichkeit' is a modified version of the seventh verse of the chorale "In dich hab ich gehoffet, Herr" by Adam Reusner (1533). But Bach used neither the melody nor the adapted verse of Reusner's hymn in this cantata, whereas he does use the exact form of the Gloria text found in Olearius, Section 12.1, page 714. Whoever compiled the text for Cantata 106 certainly knew this prayer book well.

*Christliche Bet-Schule* was written to aid the individual in private daily devotions at all stages of life. Relevant to understanding Cantata 106 are the following points: (a) the prayers were for the living; (b) they were daily prayers to be prayed as a reminder and as a reflection on mortality; (c) some of the same verses appear in different sections, including for the sick and dying; (d) if prayed daily they may have become favorite verses of reassurance; and (e) the verses were not set to music in the prayer book. Rather than thinking that Cantata 106 was composed for a funeral, I suggest that this prayer book context strongly intimates that Cantata 106 was commissioned for a devout believer in need of regular encouragement that the timing of death is God's gift, not the choice of the individual, and that death will happen at absolutely the best time.

The emphasis on the daily need to prepare for death can be found in many devotional publications of the time. Reflecting on Isaiah 38:1, "Bestelle dein Haus, denn du wirst sterben," August Pfeiffer writes the following. It is from his second sermon for the Purification of Mary, 2 February (Figure 2.2):

> **Bestelle dein Haus, denn du wirst sterben, Isaiah 38:1.** Every one of us can usefully use this same death verse daily, not just as an expression of lip-service, but in our actions so that we make the best use of our time. (Unum est necessarium) **Only one thing is necessary (Luke 10:42)** and it is in fact good that you prepare your house, and even better, that you prepare your soul, and can depart as a servant of God like Simeon.

Figure 2.2 Detail from August Pfeiffer, *Apostolische Christen-Schule* (1704), 242. https://digital.slub-dresden.de/werkansicht/dlf/59217/262. Sächsische Landesbibliothek, Staats- und Universitätsbibliothek Dresden.

## (b) The chorale "Mit Fried und Freud ich fahr dahin"

Another clue lies in the chorale "Mit Fried und Freud ich fahr dahin," heard in Movement 3, Section 2. The alto sings the chorale verse and melody, as the bass sings a countermelody on the words "Today you will be with me in Paradise." The chorale "Mit Fried und Freud" is Martin Luther's German paraphrase of Simeon's song, the Nunc dimittis, described in Luke 2:22–40. Simeon had been told that he would not die until he had met the Savior, and when Mary and Joseph brought the baby Jesus into the Temple, he was moved to sing this song of praise. As Martin Luther's paraphrase was often sung at funerals, its presence has been used to strengthen the notion that Cantata 106 was for a funeral. However, the Song of Simeon also regularly featured in services throughout the church year, and the entire story is the specified for the festival of the Purification of Mary. Bach includes the chorale in his purification Cantatas (BWV) 83 and 125 for 1724 and 1725.

Simeon is joyful because he has seen the Savior who will bring salvation to every human being, past, present, and future. Just like Olearius's prayers for a blessed end, Simeon's hymn is an affirmation of the wisdom that comes from an awareness of personal mortality and salvation. Bach uses the chorale as the basis of Cantata (BWV) 125 'Mit Fried und Freud ich fahr dahin', a cantata for the feast of Purification, 2 February 1725, as well as in the opening movement of Cantata (BWV) 95 'Christus der ist mein Leben', composed for the Sixteenth Sunday after Trinity, 12 September 1723. Following this line of evidence, its inclusion in Cantata 106 might indicate that the cantata was composed to celebrate the Purification of Mary, an idea further strengthened by the fact that the opening text of Cantata 106 is part of a mediation for this festival (see (f) below). Taken together these clues do little to suggest that Cantata 106 was composed for a funeral.

## (c) The chorale melody "Ich hab' mein Sach' Gott heimgestellt"

In the movement "Es ist der alte Bund," Bach introduces the well-known chorale melody to "I have left my affairs with God" ("Ich hab' mein Sach' Gott heimgestellt") by Johann Leon, first published in 1589. The words of this chorale have again suggested to many that Bach designed Cantata 106 for a funeral. The chorale is played by the instrumental group in short sections, while the soprano solo sings "Ja, komm, Herr Jesu, komm." Bach made a clear differentiation between the lower voices singing "Es ist der alte Bund" and the instrumental chorale: in fact, these two different ideas are never heard together. The overall theme of the chorale is trust in God in every area of life. The second of its twelve verses describes God's timing and God's will, which fits the theme of 'Gottes Zeit ist die allerbeste Zeit' particularly well.

| | |
|---|---|
| Mein Zeit und Stund ist, wann Gott will; | My time and hour will be when God wills; |
| Ich schreib ihm nicht vor Maß und Ziel. | I do not tell him what measure and goal I have. |
| Es sind gezählt all Härlein mein, | Every hair on my head is numbered, |
| Beid groß und klein; | Both long and short, |
| Fällt keines ihn den Willen sein. | Not a single one falls unless he wills it. |

The imagery of the chorale comes from a combination of Jesus' teaching on worry: Matthew 10:30, "Nun aber sind auch eure Haare auf dem Haupte alle gezählt" ("Realize even the hairs of your head are all numbered"), and his teaching about God's protection if a believer remains faithful: Luke 21:17–18, "And you will be hated by all for my name's sake. But not a hair of your head will perish." Even though heard without words, the presence of this chorale reinforces the message of the cantata: God's time is the best. Don't worry about anything. God is in charge. Again, its presence does not necessarily indicate a funeral.

### (d) The phrase "Actus Tragicus"

The phrase "Actus Tragicus" on the title page of the surviving score of Cantata 106 is probably one of the most common reasons why the funeral narrative remains. The score was copied out a good sixty years after the original composition, and eighteen years after Bach's death. As Bach's original score is lost, we do not know how close the copy is to Bach's original, or who added the title "Actus Tragicus," "a tragic act/ceremony." Markus Rathey explains that the term "Actus Tragicus" was used for humanistic school dramas in the late eighteenth century, whereas the term "Trauer Actus," "a funeral act/ceremony," was more common for Lutheran funerals. Additionally, it is important to remember that a Lutheran funeral in Bach's time was not a tragedy in the modern sense. Even though, naturally, there was deep sorrow when a loved one died, the grief was matched by rock-solid confidence in the joyful prospect of union with Christ and reunion with predeceased, believing family members and friends (see Chapter 6). Furthermore, death and resurrection were often portrayed as triumphant and joyful. If the term "Actus Tragicus" came originally from Bach, the tragedy must have been referring to something other than a funeral ceremony—perhaps even referring to the physical endurance and suffering of the person for whom the cantata was commissioned.

### (e) The significance of the choice of viola da gamba

Bach's choice of two gambas is yet another element that has been used to support the notion that Cantata 106 was for a funeral. This is because the viola da gamba and other instruments such as the recorder with soft timbres were often called upon for funerals. However, the mellifluous sound of the gamba was also popular as a solo instrument, and in ensembles in non-liturgical, occasional music, such as the 1679 celebratory aria by Johann Arnold Vockerodt (Vokkerod) for the lawyer, councilor, and politician Conrad Meckbach (1637–1712) when he was elected to be mayor of Mühlhausen for the first time on 8 January 1679.

In art and music, the gamba is also associated with royalty. Bach used the gambas in his 1727 ode 'Lass Fürstin, lass noch einen Strahl' Cantata (BWV) 198, composed on the death of the Electress Christiane Eberhardine (1671–1727). The primary association here is between the gamba and royalty, and not the gamba and her funeral, although the two are combined in this 1727 ode. Bach also used the gamba as a solo instrument in "Komm süsses Kreutz" in the St. Matthew Passion, and in "Es ist vollbracht" in the St. John Passion, both of which can also be seen as a reference to royalty of Christ rather than to His death. Another view of the gamba is seen in poetry of the time. One of Bach's librettists, the renowned Christian Friedrich Hunold (1680–1721), who used the pen name Menantes, composed an "Ode on the Viola Gamba" (Figures 2.3a and 2.3b) at about the same time as Bach composed Cantata 106. His ode was subsequently published as part of a collection of poetry in 1713, in a section of "Galant and Mixed Poetry" ("Galante und vermischte Gedichte") rather than in the section devoted to funeral odes and poems. He describes the gamba as another instrument of King David, able to banish sadness, with sounds that inspire grace to cast out dark storm clouds, to make the weather pleasant, that create an image of virtue, bring great joy, inspire new strength and energy, that are friendly and reassuring, and that can banish sorrow like no other treasure on earth. Bach's choice of the two gambas in Cantata 106, and of the solo gamba in his passions, may also have been because of its association with virtue, inspiring new strength, and ability to bring great joy.

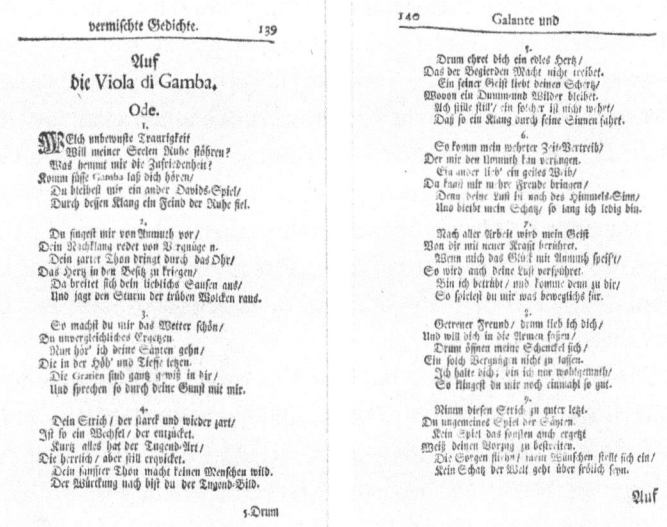

Figure 2.3a and 2.3b *Menantes Academischer Neben-Stunden Allerhand neuen Gedichte* (1713), 139–140. https://opendata.uni-halle.de//handle/1981185920/56071. Halle (Saale) Universitäts- und Landesbibliothek Sachsen-Anhalt.

(f) The phrase "Gottes Zeit ist die allerbeste Zeit"

In Bach literature one can find the idea that the free-texted phrase "Gottes Zeit ist die allerbeste Zeit" might have been the life motto, or *Devise*, of the deceased person for whose funeral the cantata was written. But this seems unlikely to me as life mottos of this period usually used a famous phrase from the Bible or from the classics, and often had an emblematic element, such as an acrostic, to give an additional layer of meaning (see Chapter 1). For example, Pastor Eilmar chose Romans 8:31b: "Si Deus pro nobis, qvis contra nos?" ("If God is for us, who can be against us?"). Or the life motto of one of the Mühlhausen's most senior citizens in Bach's time, Dr. Conrad Meckbach (1637–1712), "Christum Meum Desidero" ("I long for my Christ"), which uses the three first initials of his name: Conrad Meckbach Doctor. As a lawyer Meckbach frequently read and worked in Latin, just as pastor Eilmar worked in Latin, so it is not surprising that they used Latin for their mottos. On the other hand, his wife, Maria Elisabeth Meckbach (1645–1709), was not university-trained, and would have been more fluent in German. Naturally she chose a German motto: "Meines Erlösers Mahlzeichen **G**eben **Z**ierde": "The signs of my savior give glory," which uses the five first initials of her name: **M**aria **E**lisabeth **M**eckbach **g**eborene **Z**incke (Maria Elisabeth Meckbach, née Zincke).

Thanks to a discovery published in early 2025 we now have confirmation that "Gottes Zeit ist die allerbeste Zeit" was not a life motto or *Devise* (Rathey 2024). It was written by David von Schweinitz (1600–1667) as part of a reflection on the gospel reading for the festival of the Purification of Mary and published in his popular *Hundert Evangelische Todes=Gedancken: Das ist Vorbereitung Eines Christlichen Lebens Zum Seligen Sterben* (1664).

**Figure 2.4** David von Schweinitz, *Hundert Evanglisches Todes-Gedancken* (1716), 237. 5th ed. Pred. 2075-c. Courtesy of the Universitätsbibliothek Leipzig.

Figure 2.4 shows the opening twenty-seven words of Cantata 106 in their original context. The unknown compiler of the cantata text clearly knew this popular volume by von Schweinitz. Over the following century it was printed in nine German editions as well as translated into French and Swedish. Its subtitle "Preparation of a Christian Life for a Blessed Death" confirms the notion that von Schweinitz was writing for a living, breathing believer. It was not a funeral text. The phrase "God's time is the very best time", in all its wisdom, could easily have become a favorite daily refrain to encourage someone sick or suffering.

### (g) Payment

How much is a cantata worth? When Bach was in Mühlhausen he composed Cantata (BWV) 71 for the installation ceremony of the new Mühlhausen town council on 4 February 1708. He received 3 Reichsthaler (4 florins, 12 groschen) for this commission. The following year, on 7 February 1709 when he was working in Weimar, the Mühlhausen council paid him 4 Reichsthaler (6 florins, 2 groschen) for the composition of another installation cantata, as well as 2 Reichsthaler (3 florins [gulden] and 1 groschen) to cover return travel costs from Weimar. A year later, on 20 February 1710, he received the same sum (9 florins, 3 groschen including travel expenses) from the Mühlhausen council for the composition of a third piece to celebrate the new town council. Although it is difficult to make an accurate comparison, it seems that 6 florins for the composition of a new cantata would have represented almost one month's salary, a welcome addition to Bach's income. This is compared with the salary he negotiated on 15 June 1707 of 85 florins per year, plus 54 bushels of grain, 2 cords of wood, and 360 fagots of kindling wood, and also compared with the legacy of 50 florins [gulden] in the will of his Uncle Tobias. Although 6 florins was a significant sum for a musician, it would have been comfortably within the means of a benevolent senior clergyman or wealthy businessman.

There is an important piece of social context that should be added to the picture when thinking about the timing of Bach moving to Mühlhausen. On 30 May 1707 there had been a huge fire in the center of the city: it started at 8:30 A.M. and continued to rage until 6 A.M. the next day. In addition to the numerous barns and stables razed to the ground, 300 homes were destroyed. This was the fourth big fire Mühlhausen had experienced in fifty years, the last being in 1689 and from which many families were still only just recovering. On 24 May 1707, a week before the fire, Dr. Conrad Meckbach proposed that Johann Sebastian Bach from Arnstadt should replace the late Johann Georg Ahle as organist of Divi Blasii (St. Blasius Church). Bach negotiated his salary two weeks after the fire. Major repairs were needed in the city. Funds had to be found to house dispossessed citizens and to rebuild the dwellings. The financial challenges for the Mühlhausen councilors and the city's wealthy citizens must have been colossal. Meckbach was a major sponsor, yet in the middle of these challenges he not only brought in Bach as organist, he found funds to commission the building of a new organ too.

The costly reconstruction of Mühlhausen city center calls into question the priority of privately commissioned music, with implications for the dating and composition of Cantatas 106 and even Cantata 131. After the fire, a patron commissioning new compositions must have had great confidence in his investment to include music among other pressing social demands. Negotiations to attract Bach to Mühlhausen predate the fire. This suggests that Meckbach or someone else on the town council had firsthand experience of Bach's art, and that after the fire and after his arrival, there must have been a determination to keep Bach in what had become a city full of ash, ruin, and building works. Meckbach's name appears prominently in the surviving civic documents, and as primary signatory to Bach's contract. Furthermore, Meckbach had the financial means, the political influence, and the cultural interest to commission compositions privately. Bach may even have set the contemplative and encouraging words of Cantata 106 before his move to Mühlhausen, while he was still employed in Arnstadt; equally likely, the commission could have been later. The fact is that the dating of Cantata 106 is largely based on stylistic ground, and without further documentary evidence, it is not yet possible to establish with any certainty the extent of Meckbach's influence upon Bach and his early cantata production.

## For Whom Did Bach Write Cantata 106?

There are many possible scenarios for the commissioning and purpose of Cantata 106.

The evidence presented above persuades me that this work should be released from its traditional funeral narrative. Any one of Tobias Lämmerhirt, Dorothea Tilesius, her husband or brother, or Councilor August Strecker could have commissioned the work: they had the financial means and possibly the interest to ask Bach to set the reassuring text to music. There is, however, a character who has recently been named in Bach literature, who fits all the evidence more perfectly than any other: Maria Elisabeth Meckbach, wife of Dr. Conrad Meckbach, Mühlhausen lawyer, town councilor and mayor, major city benefactor, and patron of the arts. There are many tantalizing details to connect the Meckbachs to Bach.

Conrad Meckbach invited Bach to Mühlhausen. He had commissioned composers and poets to create occasional pieces since the late 1670s. Many of these pieces have survived in print. His name appears as an acrostic in the text to Cantata (BWV) 150 'Nach dir, Herr, verlanget mich' (For You, Lord, I Long), a sentiment also encapsulated in his life motto "Christum Meum Desidero" ("I long for my Christ"), cited above. Minutes from the town council meetings show that Meckbach was very sorry when Bach asked to be released from his Mühlhausen contract to move to Weimar. The Meckbachs, and the textile merchants the Lutteroths, were considered the most prominent and wealthy families in Mühlhausen. Their burial site in the small Creuzkirche was an indication of their supremely high social status. The Meckbachs lived across the street from the entrance to St. Blasius Church, and due to the scarcity of available private dwellings caused by the city fire, it is thought that Bach lived with them when he first arrived in Mühlhausen in June 1707. When Bach was first introduced to the family, probably in 1706, he may well have been struck by how similar the name of his hostess, Frau Maria Elisabeth Meckbach, was to that of his late mother, Maria Elisabeth Bach (1644–1694). The two women would have been the same age, had Bach's mother not passed away twelve years earlier. The similarity between the surnames Bach and Meckbach was noted by Pastor Eilmar in his funeral oration for Frau Meckbach in 1709, when he developed emblematic imagery on the word "Bach" (stream). Even though the Bach and the Meckbach families were poles apart financially and socially, this coincidence of name similarities and with the young bachelor Bach as their respected lodger, could explain one small part of the unlikely friendship and longer-term connection between the two families. After the Bachs moved away from Mühlhausen, the two families kept in touch through their son, Paul Friedemann Meckbach (1674–1731), who traveled to Weimar in November 1710 to be godfather to Wilhelm Friedemann (1710–1784).

Maria Elisabeth Meckbach came from a well-to-do Dresden family, most probably bringing private wealth to the marriage. In the materials for her funeral and memorial services she is referred to as Frau Doktor Maria Elisabeth Meckbach, taking on her husband's educational titles, as would have been the normal at the time. Eilmar was her father confessor. In his eulogy ("Trauer-Rede") at her funeral on 27 January 1709 he gives numerous extraordinary personal details about her godly character, details beyond what is customary in such publications. Eilmar states that she was benevolent and very popular in Mühlhausen among the needy, not only because of her financial and practical gifts but because she prayed for them. She died on 22 January 1709, which was after the Bach family had left for Weimar. We learn that in her final years she was crippled with pain, sometimes bedridden, sometimes able to move, and that the family spent a fortune on doctors, but to no avail. On several occasions her pain was so acute that she asked to be given the last rites. She longed to die, but her body would not allow her to. Her comfort was spending time in prayer and reading devotional literature. Her private bedroom, to which she was often confined, was full of books written by the greatest theologians and mystics, and among these may have been the popular volumes by Olearius and von Schweinitz.

Isaiah 40:31 was the biblical text for her funeral sermon: "But those who hope in the Lord will renew their strength. They will soar on wings like eagles: they will run and not grow weary; they will walk and not be faint." Eilmar states that Frau Meckbach not only chose this verse for her funeral sermon, as was common, she also wrote the sermon herself. This would have been unusual for a pastor, let alone for an untrained lay woman. In the printed sermon ("Christliche Leich-Predigt") preached at her memorial service on Reminiscere Sunday, 24 February 1709, Superintendent Frohne stated: "She loved to go to church and praise God there, and in the last years when the pain of the gout was in remission she could be carried there. But when this was not possible, she held her church services at home, with singing, reading, and praying. cf. Matt 6:6." (Original German in Figure 2.5.) Might the encouraging words in Cantata 106 have been set to music by Bach for his hostess, the wife of his patron?

**Figure 2.5** Detail from the eulogy by Johann Adolph Frohne in honor of Frau Meckbach (1709), 9. Courtesy of the Stadtarchiv Mühlhausen.

The winter of Maria Elisabeth Meckbach's death and funeral coincided with the bitter cold of the little European ice age. At her funeral service there were three pieces of concerted music: two were arias with texts by Eilmar, and one was an unnamed piece accompanied by an instrumental ensemble similar, but not identical, to the ensemble used in Cantata 106: perhaps a combination of instruments favored by this musically sensitive woman. To clarify, I do not think that Cantata 106 was composed for or performed at her funeral. It could very well have been written for her encouragement, while she struggled with pain and disability, set to biblical texts that she loved, and to encourage her preparations for a blessed end, as von Schweinitz put it.

There is no doubt that the devotional texts of Cantata 106 could have been set to music for this privileged and prominent Mühlhausen lady, with instruments befitting a princess. She loved to sing and pray, and Bach wrote a beautiful soprano line that would have resonated deeply with her: "Yes, Yes, come Lord Jesus," ending it with a confident choral "through Jesus Christ. Amen!" Her husband may have commissioned the music to lift her spirits and give her courage to live with her physical pain. It is scored for an ensemble small enough to be used for household devotions, perhaps in her room just across from the church. Were this the case, the cantata might have been commissioned before Bach even moved to Mühlhausen, while Johann Georg Ahle (1651–1706), from whom Meckbach had previously commissioned works, was too unwell to compose anything new. This would also have been before the devastating Mühlhausen fire of 1707 and the resulting costly restoration work that probably took priority over all other expenditure. If Bach had composed and delivered the cantata while he was still in Arnstadt, it could explain why Meckbach was so confident to persuade the city council to bring him to Mühlhausen. The evidence fits, the scenario fits, but we cannot know for sure.

For many listeners and scholars Cantata 106 will always be a funeral cantata. For some it will be a cantata for the festival of

Purification, while others will continue to find its Sinfonia inspirational and joyful, appropriate for a wedding voluntary, or as an intimate piano duet, such as performed by the renowned Hungarian composer György Kurtág (b. 1926) and his wife Márta (1927–2019). Even though we may never know why and when Bach composed this gem, my hope is that it will be released from its funerary bonds, breathe its wisdom into many more generations of the living, and shed light on daily paths wherever they lead, and whenever they end.

## Suggested Further Reading

For life in Mühlhausen in Bach's time see Markus Rathey (2023) and Christoph Wolff (2000). Cantata 106 is examined by Eric Chafe (1991), 91–123, while the meanings of the fugue and of music are discussed respectively by David Yearsley (2002) and Ruth Tatlow (2015). Important source-based insights are given in German by Markus Rathey (2024), Ernst Koch (2021), 55–71, 72–91, Hans-Joachim Schulze (2011), 255–257, and Renate Steiger (1989). For coverage of early theories see Hermann Schmalfuß (1970), 36–43, and Markus Rathey (2006).

# 3

# Advent Music for Weimar and Leipzig

## 'Nun komm der Heyden Heyland'

Cantata (BWV) 61 'Nun komm der Heyden Heyland' (Now Come, Savior of the Heathen) was composed for the first Sunday of the church year, Advent Sunday, 2 December 1714. At this time twenty-nine-year-old Johann Sebastian Bach had a respectable job at the Weimar court. He was husband to his thirty-year-old wife, Maria Barbara, and father to their growing family: Catharina Dorothea, soon to be six years old; Wilhelm Friedemann, aged four; and Carl Philipp Emanuel, a babe in arms. On all fronts this seems to have been a stable period albeit with the usual ups and down of family life.

A year earlier Sebastian had been invited to audition for the post of organist and music director at the Marktkirche (the Market Church of St. Mary) in Halle. The previous incumbent Friedrich Wilhelm Zachow (1663–1712), the teacher of George Frideric Handel (1685–1759), had died and the attractive Halle post was still vacant. Bach's audition and interview resulted in his being offered the job in January 1714, but he did not take it. Maria Barbara was heavily pregnant and perhaps this was a factor in the decision not to relocate to a different region.

On 8 March 1714, a healthy son was born, and his baptism was held three days later at the Weimar chapel court. Their family friend Georg Philipp Telemann (1681–1767), who was by now a famous composer, traveled 250 kilometers from Frankfurt am Main to be godfather to the new baby, adding "Philipp" to the infant's names, which were recorded as Carl Philipp Immanuel (*sic*). The Halle job offer had tangible consequences for Bach and his position in Weimar. It caused the Weimar duke to raise his salary, and to make him Concertmaster, which included sharing responsibility for the chapel music with the Capellmeister, Johann Samuel Drese (1644–1716), and his son, Johann Wilhelm Drese (1677–1745), who was the Vice Capellmeister. Bach's new duties included composing a cantata each month to be performed by the castle musicians in the court chapel. The first of his new cantatas was for Palm Sunday, 25 March 1714, Cantata (BWV) 182 'Himmelskönig sei Willkommen' (Welcome, King of Heaven).

A fortnight earlier, during the baptismal festivities one can imagine that conversations between Bach and Telemann might have included the practicalities of his new role and even exchanges of ideas for inspiring church cantata texts. Over the previous two years Telemann had been providing the concerted music for two Frankfurt churches, as well as maintaining ties with his former employers in Eisenach. His newest project for Eisenach and Frankfurt am Main was an annual cantata cycle with texts by the renowned theologian and pastor Erdmann Neumeister (1671–1756). Telemann thought highly of Neumeister's devotional cantata texts, writing on 28 December 1714 that Neumeister is "the most famous and only good poet in spiritual matters" ("berühmtesten und eintzien guten Poeten in geistlichen Sachen"). For his latest Neumeister cycle, Telemann had taken the extraordinary decision to compose all the cantatas in the French musical style.

This little piece of history is worth mentioning because the Neumeister text that Telemann set for Advent Sunday in the French style is the very same text that Bach used for Cantata 61, and for which he made the extraordinary decision to set the opening movement in the form of a French overture. Even though Neumeister's fourth cantata cycle would not be published in book form until March 1717, documents suggest that he wrote the texts throughout 1713, which enabled Telemann to set them successively from

Advent Sunday 1713 until the end of the church year 1714. This timeline implies that Telemann had already begun to compose his "French Cycle" before the Weimar baptism in March 1714. The coincidence of the Neumeister text and Bach's use of the French overture in his 1714 Advent cantata also allows for the possibility that Telemann brought a copy of some of the unpublished Neumeister texts to Weimar, and perhaps a score or two to show Bach what he was working on. Whatever the precise scenario, we know for sure that these two ambitious and gifted young composers wrote music to the same Neumeister "Nun komm der Heyden Heyland" text, and that both cantatas were performed on the very same date, Advent Sunday, 2 December 1714: Bach's Cantata (BWV) 61 at the Weimar court chapel and Telemann's Cantata (TWV) 1:1175 in his Frankfurt churches, having performed it first a year earlier in Eisenach on Advent Sunday 1713. Whether because of a friendly challenge, a kindly exchange of privileged resources, a baptismal present, or some other reason, the Neumeister text and Bach's choice of the French overture are built into one of Bach's most-loved cantata settings.

## Advent Sunday

The prescribed biblical passages for Advent Sunday were the introductory psalm, Psalm 102; the Epistle of the day, Romans 13:11–14, with its urgent message to wake up, and to behave decently, refraining from sexual immorality and debauchery or jealousy, and to be clothed with the Lord Jesus Christ; and the Gospel of the Day, Matthew 21:1–9, which describes Jesus' entry into Jerusalem on a donkey, a passage also associated with Palm Sunday, the week before Easter. It reads:

> As they approached Jerusalem and came to Bethphage on the Mount of Olives, Jesus sent two disciples, saying to them, "Go to

the village ahead of you, and at once you will find a donkey tied there, with her colt by her. Untie them and bring them to me. If anyone says anything to you, say that the Lord needs them, and he will send them right away." This took place to fulfill what was spoken through the prophet: "Say to Daughter Zion, 'See, your king comes to you, gentle and riding on a donkey, and on a colt, the foal of a donkey.'" The disciples went and did as Jesus had instructed them. They brought the donkey and the colt and placed their cloaks on them for Jesus to sit on. A very large crowd spread their cloaks on the road, while others cut branches from the trees and spread them on the road. The crowds that went ahead of him and those that followed shouted, "Hosanna to the Son of David!" "Blessed is he who comes in the name of the Lord!" "Hosanna in the highest heaven!"

Erdmann Neumeister based his reflective cantata text on these biblical readings and on the recommended chorales of the day, which included Martin Luther's hymn "Nun komm der Heyden Heyland." With many years of theological reading, sermon writing and pastoral practice, Neumeister did not need to slavishly adhere to the words of the set Bible readings. His motivation for weaving the themes into contemplative reflections was to provide devotional aids that helped him and his readers to understand the lessons of that Sunday more deeply. His starting point was the chorale "Nun komm der Heyden Heyland," Martin Luther's German adaptation of the ancient Latin hymn "Veni redemptor gentium" (Come, Savior of the Nations). Indeed, Neumeister published several different poetic reflections for Advent Sunday. The first was published in his third annual cycle of texts, *Geistliches Singen und Spielen* (1711), and was originally written for Telemann and the Eisenach court chapel. The second was published in his fourth annual cycle, *Geistliche Poesien . . . auf alle Sonn = und Fest = Tage durch gantzes Jahr* (1717), which includes the text used by Bach in Cantata 61.

In Neumeister's published text the opening and closing chorale texts are printed in bold and set in larger font (Figures 3.1a and 3.1b). It has six clear sections, which Bach followed by composing a six-movement church cantata organized into twelve sections distinguished by changes of time signature. Unusually for Bach's cantata compositions, the score for Cantata 61 is a **fair copy**, with orthography almost as perfect as in a published score. A ruler was used to draw the bar lines, and there is hardly any correction or blemish in the handwriting. In other words, it was copied out very carefully and precisely. The first movement is in the hand of Johann Lorenz Bach (1695–1773), a distant relative of Bach's who lived with the family as an apprentice or student for two years from late 1714. The remaining five movements are in Bach's own handwriting. The original performing parts are lost.

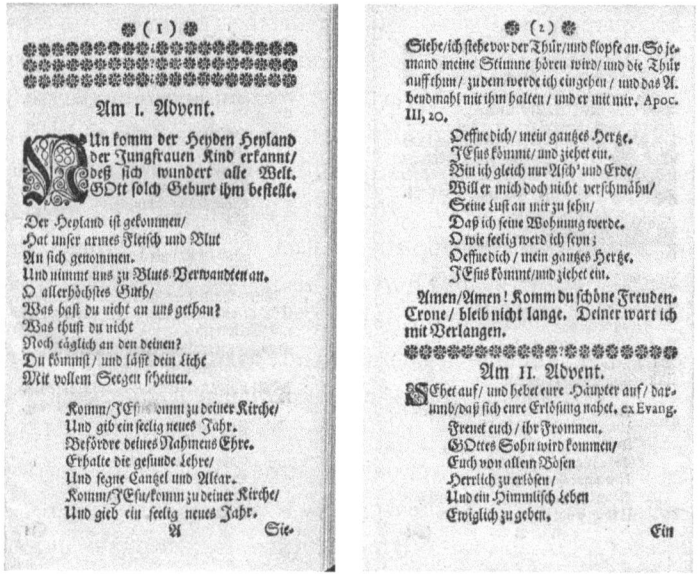

Figure 3.1a and 3.1b   Erdmann Neumeister, *Geistliche Poesien . . . auf alle Sonn = und Fest = Tage durch gantzes Jahr* (1717), 1–2. http://resol ver.sub.uni-goettingen.de/purl?PPN670450324. Niedersächsische Staats- und Universitätsbibliothek Göttingen.

## The Text and Its Theology

Neumeister's text presents a sequence of four theological moments in the salvation story: Jesus, Savior of the pagans and the heathen, arrives on earth as a baby born of a virgin (movements 1 and 2); he is invited into the church (movement 3); he knocks and enters the believer's heart (movements 4 and 5); and he will come in glory at the end of time (movement 6).

An important starting point at the outset of this exploration is to try to grasp how Bach thought about the heathen ("Heyden"). Were the heathen non-Lutheran German-speaking peoples, or foreign visitors to the large German trade and market fairs, or humans from every language-group, race, and nation across the globe? The answer given by August Pfeiffer (1640–1698) in his volume of systematic theology, *Evangelische Christen-Schule*, a volume that Bach owned, is that the heathen includes every human being, past, present, and future. Bach had more books in his library by Pfeiffer than by any other author: he owned nine volumes in addition to several volumes for which Pfeiffer wrote a preface, which suggests that Bach had a predilection for Pfeiffer's style and content. Pfeiffer was a theologian and ordained pastor, who became Arch-Deacon at St. Thomas's Leipzig and then at St. Mary's Lübeck, alongside being professor of oriental languages at the universities of Leipzig and then Lübeck.

Pfeiffer's *Evangelische Christen-Schule* was published first in Leipzig in 1688 and then in several editions until 1724. The page numbers given below all refer to the 1688 edition. Pfeiffer's chapter 2 is devoted to the natural recognition of God and includes the following section from pages 39–40:

> §8 This also explains the inner witness of the heart by the majority, and the approval of all nations. No folk or people has ever been so barbaric, wild, and crude that they lacked a sense of God, religion, or worship (*aliquem numinis sensum & cultum*) or at least a

shadow of these. This clearly shows that even though they did not really know what or who God was, they nonetheless recognized and were convinced in their hearts that there was a God.

In Pfeiffer's opinion every single human on the planet has an innate sense of God and of worship, however faint that sense is. In chapter 31 "The Merciful Calling of God," he grapples with the logic of how God's love of the world can be squared with the salvation story, and how the heathen is included in God's plan. In doing so he is critical of the hard-line beliefs of the Calvinists, who say (page 723, §11) "if only all heathens were as clever and could think like us. But most of them are barbaric, dumb, rude people who have probably never been enlightened."

Pfeiffer then criticizes the Dutch Calvinist missionary endeavors to convert the indigenous peoples of the Gold Coast along the Gulf of Guinea. To support his point, Pfeiffer cites chapter 21 of a report by the explorer Pieter de Marees (fl. 1602), which shows that the indigenous people both worshipped their deity and believed in the afterlife. Pfeiffer states that he values and respects these beliefs as evidence of the merciful calling of God. He asks why the Calvinists should undertake such a perilous and potentially fatal sea voyage just to insult the Ghanaians by trying to teach them what they already knew! De Marees's reports were translated from the original Dutch into German by Levinus Hulsius (1550–1606) and so available to Pfeiffer and his contemporaries. They describe the very worst kind of colonialism in the name of religion. With today's sensibilities, it is refreshing to read Pfeiffer's respect for the world communities, and to realize that Bach too could have read this. Pfeiffer continues the section by stating that there are wise and reasonable humans in every place and time in whose heart God has written his natural laws, writing on pages 724–725:

> §12 For man has a soul, which foretells of a divine judgment and another life after it. . . . Besides if such an American or other

barbarian uses his natural light correctly, and desires to know the right way of honoring God, he will have every opportunity to do so. God's hand is not shortened to bring such a man to the knowledge of the truth, and we would rather trust divine goodness too much than too little, even though this is not the usual method of salvation.

Pfeiffer understands that God's dispensation of grace, based on love, covered all peoples from every corner of the world. His writings are full of similarly inclusive respect for the heathen in all lands and times. Possibly signaling a vote of confidence in Pfeiffer's writing, Bach chose to bequeath Pfeiffer's books to his children.

Pfeiffer's gentle and kind theology of grace for all humans is not explicit in Neumeister's text for Cantata 61, but it is implied. Here is the cantata text in everyday English:

> Now come, Savior of the heathen, known as child of the virgin. The world is amazed that God ordained such a birth. The Savior has come; he has taken on flesh and blood like us, and we have become family. O most high Good, what have you not done for us; what do you continue to do for your own every day! You come and shine your light with full blessing. Come to your church, Jesus, and grant a blessed new year. Promote the honor of your name; support healthy teaching and bless pulpit and altar. "Look I stand at the door and knock. If anyone hears my voice and opens the door, I will go in and keep the Lord's supper with him, and him with me." Open yourself my whole heart; Jesus is coming and will enter. Even though I am just dust and earth he will not reject me, he will look upon me with delight, that I might become his home. O how blessed and happy I will be! Amen! Amen! Come, you beautiful crown of joy, Don't delay. I am longing for your arrival.

In the light of Pfeiffer's writings, the phrase "Nun komm der Heyden Heyland" can be understood to embrace every single person on the planet. The heathen (not just the Lutherans) will also be amazed that the Savior took on the flesh and blood of humanity. God is referred to as the most-high Good, because highest Goodness is a quality recognized in the heart of natural man. The text then becomes a prayer specifically for the church at the start of a new church year, and moves onto the response of the individual—a believing soul, made of dust and earth—who opens his/her heart and invites the Savior in.

What this text suggested to Bach can probably best be seen in his musical choices. He would have spent as long as possible considering the text, thinking which voices and combination of instruments would best suit each of the six sections. Ideas for musical textures, time signatures, characters, themes and fragments of melodies will have suggested themselves as Bach gained a sense of the whole, that is, if he made a deep study of the text before setting it to music, as the famous composer Agostino Steffani did (see Chapter 1). Bach would look for a coherent textual thread, decide how long the cantata could take to fill the allotted time before the sermon, and then plot out the movements. He would know which singers and instrumentalists he had to hand at the Weimar court. Some of the musical material was given: the chorale theme, "Nun komm der Heyden Heyland," and the final section of the hymn "Wie schön leuchtet der Morgenstern." The remainder could be as free as he wished.

## Does Bach's Musical Setting Reflect Pfeiffer's Inclusive Theology?

Bach could have made many different musical choices in setting Neumeister's text. Eric Chafe sees the overall tonal plan of this cantata as representing "anticipation and hope in the events surrounding the coming birth of Christ," moving as it does from its opening in A minor to the relative C major (movements 2 and 3), and then to the dominant key of E minor (movement 4) and its relative G major (movements 5 and 6). The emotional effect of this optimistic, rising minor-major motion may be one way in which Bach expressed the inclusive view of salvation he may have read in his Pfeiffer volumes.

Another overall formal choice that may also reflect Bach's theology is the length of sections in the cantata. There are two striking sections with fifty-two bars. As the number 52 spells out "Jesu" (9 + 5 + 18 + 20) in the common number alphabet (see Chapter 1), Bach may have thought it fitting to use this number-letter device as one of his points of invention. The first fifty-two bar section is in the middle of the opening movement; a lively "gai" section in 3/4 meter to the words "Des sich wundert alle Welt" ("Of this all the world marvels"). The second fifty-two-bar section is in the fifth movement, set to the words of the believer as he/she invites the Savior in: "Open yourself, my whole heart." Furthermore, as Jesus' birth revealed the Godhead to be three-in-one, it would be quite natural had Bach also used the number three as a fundamental source of inspiration when he structured this cantata that celebrates the arrival of Jesus. The consecutive number of bars suggests he might indeed have done so: the cantata has 297 written bars, 297 being 99 (33 × 3) × 3. But these numbers, although intriguing structurally, cannot necessarily be detected by the listener. I will now look at Bach's musical choices movement by movement and try to identify any audible evidence that might suggest he was mirroring Pfeiffer's inclusive view of salvation.

### 1. Chorus

| | |
|---|---|
| Nun komm, der Heyden Heyland, | Now come, Savior of the heathen, |
| Der Jungfrauen Kind erkannt, | Known as child of the virgin; |
| Des sich wundert alle Welt, | Of this, all the world marvels: |
| Gott solch Geburt ihm bestellt. | God ordained him such a birth. |

For the opening movement Bach's chose the three-sectioned slow-fast-slow form of the French overture, with its distinctive dotted rhythm in the slow sections (see discussion of Telemann and his

"French Cycle" above). This is a highly unusual choice for a church cantata. In opera the French overture was associated with the entrance of the King. In this church cantata, the King is not earthly, but rather the Heaven-sent Savior and deliverer who takes on "our flesh and blood." Given the Gospel reading, we see the Savior entering Jerusalem on a humble donkey, rather than on a proud charger or in a splendid chariot.

There is theological and musical inclusivity in the very opening entries of 'Nun komm der Heyden Heyland'. The sopranos sing the phrase first, and then the altos. After a short instrumental interlude, the tenors sing it next, and finally the basses. One might understand this to illustrate every corner of humanity recognizing the arrival of the Savior, who is "known as the child of the virgin," words that are sung by all voices together. As mentioned above, the central section in 3/4 is a joyful dance, with exactly fifty-two bars, perhaps an emblematic reference to "Jesu". The feeling of joy in the royal entrance, though, is not dependent upon any hidden allusion. The main focus is the Savior of the heathen, that is, Jesus. It is Jesus who is being celebrated as the new church year is ushered in on Advent Sunday. And it is Jesus, the Savior of the whole world, that God loved so much (John 3:16; see Chapter 7), which causes the chorus to sing together: "of this, all the world marvels: God ordained him such a birth."

2. Tenor recitative

| | |
|---|---|
| Der Heyland ist gekommen, | The Savior has come; |
| Hat unser armes Fleisch | Has taken on our wretched flesh |
| Und Blut an sich genommen | And blood upon himself; |
| Und nimmet uns zu Blutsverwandten an. | And takes us on as blood relatives. |
| O allerhöchstes Gut, | Oh Most-High possession, |
| Was hast du nicht an uns getan? | What have you not done for us? |
| Was thust du nicht | What do you not |
| Noch täglich an den Deinen? | Still daily do for your own? |
| Du kommst und läßt dein Licht | You come and let your light |
| Mit vollem Segen scheinen. | Shine with full blessing. |

The choice of recitative form for tenor solo here is reminiscent of opera, particularly with its naturalistic rhythm for the line "Was hast du nicht an uns getan?" before it moves into a lyrical arioso on the phrase "Du kömmst und läßt dein Licht." Bach divides the ten lines of Neumeister's text for this movement into two sections. He could have divided it after line 4, or after line 6, but instead he divides it after line 8, allocating nine bars of *secco* recitative to the first eight lines of text, and nine bars of Arioso to the final two lines of text. Furthermore, these two nine-bar sections follow on directly from the fast nine-bar section that concludes the first movement. Each of these nine-bar sections is separated by a double bar and distinguished by a change in speed. If Leibniz was correct (see Chapter 1), the listener will sense the symmetry of these three consecutive nine-bar sections, unaware that s/he is counting. In terms of theological emphasis, Bach decided to single out the last two lines of text, setting it as a nine-bar lyrical Arioso with solo cello: "You come and let your light shine with full blessing." This phrase is repeated three times, and the cello ends the movement with a stepwise octave descent, seeming to paint the blessing falling down upon "us."

3. Tenor aria

| | |
|---|---|
| Komm, Jesu, komm zu deiner Kirche | Come, Jesus, to your church |
| Und gib ein selig neues Jahr! | And grant a blessed new year. |
| Befördre deines Namens Ehre, | Promote your name's honor, |
| Erhalte die gesunde Lehre | Uphold the sound teaching, |
| Und segne Kanzel und Altar! | And bless pulpit and altar. |

As if multiples of three have not been clear enough so far, Bach now chose to follow the nine-bar sections with a tenor aria in 9/8, a time signature with three sets of three eighth notes per bar. The descending stepwise "blessing" cello figure is heard again, although now unmistakably in the major key, perhaps expressing the welcome invitation "Come, Jesus, to your church." In addition to the triple time, Bach chose a three-part texture (unison strings, continuo, and voice) for this movement, as well as the common da capo form with its three clearly defined and aurally recognizable sections, which is most probably another nod towards the trinitarian implications of the arrival of Jesus.

The text of this movement is a prayer specifically for the church itself, and we can assume Neumeister intended it for the German Lutheran church on this first Sunday of the church year. The request is that there would be sound teaching, a blessing on the preacher through the pulpit, through the sacrament of the Word, and on those ministering at the altar in the sacrament of the Eucharist, that Jesus' name will be honored. Besides the triple meter, instrumentation, and structure, there are no other strong characterizations or emphases in the musical setting, and this allows the text to speak for itself "for those with ears to hear." It also creates a great contrast to the next movement.

4. Bass recitative

| | |
|---|---|
| Siehe, ich stehe vor der Tür und klopfe an. So jemand meine Stimme hören wird und die Tür auftun, zu dem werde ich eingehen und das Abendmahl mit ihm halten und er mit mir. | Look, I stand before the door and knock. If anyone hears my voice and opens the door, I will go in and have supper with him, and he with me. |

The almost pantomimic musical characterization of this short ten-bar movement is clear from the very first sounds of plucking strings, which Bach uses to recreate the image of gentle knocking. The phrase "Behold I stand at the door and knock" is recorded in Revelation 3:20 and spoken by Jesus. From Martin Luther's time onward, Jesus's direct speech—the *Vox Christi*—had been emphasized in services, not least during the institution of communion. Seventeenth-century Lutheran composers used different devices to make Jesus' words stand out. Some set them realistically, for single male voice, others used multi-voiced movements or a particular style of writing that stood out from the rest of the piece. In this movement Bach chose a kind of realism, assigning Jesus' works to a bass voice, accompanied by pizzicato strings, and their onomatopoeic expression of "Klopfe" ("knock"). This highly unusual effect contrasts with the remainder of the sonorities in the cantata and alerts the listener to something profound. After the prayer in movement 3 that Jesus would come to the church, the words "Behold I stand at the door and knock" emphasize the personal rather than communal nature of Jesus' invitation. The Savior of the Universe is heard to be knocking on your door, and not just in the third person, but as "I." Not only does the listener hear the knocking, s/he hears the invitation "I will go in and have supper with him, and he with me." The bass soloist is silent, and the knocking continues for the final **cadence**. There is no sense either in Neumeister's text, or in Bach's music, that Jesus' invitation is exclusive. Rather, the listener with any religious persuasion or humanistic perspective will find this movement welcoming, possibly disturbing, and yet inclusive.

From this point onward, the text develops into an intimacy that is associated with the mystic union of the Eucharist or holy communion, with its enactment of the consummation of Bride (Jesus) and Bridegroom (the church) at the holy wedding. The widely circulated and frequently reprinted communion prayer book *Himmlisches Freuden-Mahl* (1683) by Johannes Rittmeyer (1636–1698) includes an illustration of Revelation 3:20 (Figure 3.2a). The reader sees Jesus literally knocking on the door of the human heart, waiting to be invited in. This picture precedes the first page of the first chapter, which has the heading "How one must prepare oneself before coming to Holy Communion" ("Wie man sich bereiten und anschicken muß ehe man zum Heil. Nachtmahl kömt").

80  BACH'S CHURCH CANTATAS

**Figure 3.2a and 3.2b** Johann Rittmeyer, *Himmlisches Freuden-Mahl Der Kinder Gottes auf Erden* (1713), Facing pages 1 and 122. Pred. 1913-b. Courtesy of the Universitätsbibliothek Leipzig.

5. Soprano aria

| | |
|---|---|
| Öffne dich, mein ganzes Herze, | 5. Open yourself, my whole heart; |
| Jesus kömmt und ziehet ein. | Jesus comes and enters in. |
| Bin ich gleich nur Staub und Erde, | Even though I am but dust and earth, |

| | |
|---|---|
| Will er mich doch nicht verschmähn, | He will, nevertheless, not disdain me; |
| Seine Lust an mir zu sehn, | He will look upon his delight in me, |
| Daß ich seine Wohnung werde. | That I may become his dwelling-place. |
| O wie selig werd ich sein! | O how blessed will I be! |

In movements 2 and 3 the tenor recitative is followed by a tenor aria, and so one might expect the bass recitative of movement 4 to lead into a bass aria, but it does not. Bach chooses a high soprano for the following aria. The words of movement 5, together with the soprano voice, clarifies that the bass of movement 4 was the voice of Christ, and that we are now hearing a personal response to Jesus' knocking. Neumeister's text is a delightful piece of rhyming verse showing the inner dialogue of the faithful soul, from a first trembling almost self-encouraging response in section one, through a rehearsal of the rational arguments in the middle section, to the third section which is a da capo repeat of the opening section. Following the form of Neumeister's text, Bach sets this movement in three sections, with identical music in triple time for the first and third sections, and the central section in common time. The vulnerability, perhaps anxiety, of Bach's soprano is emphasized by the trills on "ganze" and "Herze," giving the melody of the first section a tremulous quality above the angular continuo line. The central section ends with a joyful sixfold reiteration of the phrase "O wie selig" ("O how blessed [will I be]"). When the third section is heard, the plea of the believing soul is far more assured and confident about opening his/her heart, with the trills now sounding like moments of joy and blessedness.

In a section on penitential prayer, Rittmeyer includes an illustration Figure 3.2b of Jesus sweeping out the heart to make it a worthy dwelling place, a pictorial representation of Psalm 51:12 (51:10 in modern editions), "Create in me a clean heart and renew a right spirit within me." Reminiscent of the text of movement 5, the rhyme beneath the picture reads:

| | |
|---|---|
| Jesu kehre selbst und fege, | Jesus himself returns and sweeps |
| Was dir misfällt aus dem wege | What you dislike out of the way |
| Mach mein Herz von Sünde rein | Make my heart clean from sin |
| Las es deine Wohnung sein. | Let it be your dwelling place. |

Bach makes just a few minor alterations to Neumeister's poetry in the soprano aria. The words "Asche und Erde" ("ashes and earth") are changed to "Staub und Erde" ("dust and earth") in line 3. It may seem to be a tiny change, but both versions hold important allusions. Neumeister was following Luther in using "Asche und Erde," words that Abraham spoke in Genesis 18:27: "Now that I have been so bold as to speak to the Lord, though I am nothing but dust and ashes": they show the humility of Abraham before God. Bach's use of "Staub," on the other hand, brings with it the allusion of the tiniest particles and, according to usage of the time, refers to the leftovers after grain has been harvested and threshed, the dust being something only pigs could eat in the winter harvest, and which was totally useless after the summer harvest. These allusions suggest that in choosing "dust" Bach may have been emphasizing the sinful, worthless nature of humankind, underlining the extraordinary paradox that Jesus could delight in entering the "I" of the human heart.

### 6. Chorale

| | |
|---|---|
| Amen, amen! | Amen, amen! |
| Komm, du schöne Freudenkrone, | Come, you beautiful crown of joy, |
| Bleib nicht lange! | Tarry not long! |
| Deiner wart ich mit Verlangen. | I wait for you with longing. |

Neumeister chose to end his meditation with the last two lines of final verse of Philipp Nicolai's "Wie schön leuchtet der

Morgenstern," which Bach set exactly as Neumeister had imagined. The resulting partial rendition of the instantly recognizable text and melody caused some consternation among Bach scholars until Markus Rathey demonstrated in 2002 that the practice was part of a tradition in central German church music. In 2011 Kerala Snyder pointed out that Dieterich Buxtehude (1637–1707) had set the same words in his *Die Hochzeit des Lamms* (BuxWV 128) for the Lübeck Abendmusik in 1678, and that Buxtehude might have shown Bach some of his old scores in 1705 when he famously visited Buxtehude in Leipzig. Whatever the provenance, Bach understood Neumeister's cue, and rounded off Cantata 61 with an ecstatic fourteen-bar movement with joyful strings in full flight, and the chorus singing the segment of familiar melody. As it comes to an end, the chorale descends to the tonic, the keynote, G, while Bach asks the violins to ascend not just one but two octaves until they reach a glorious high G—among the highest notes he ever wrote for violinists, to accompany "I wait for you with longing!" What better way to set the final words of the New Testament: Revelation 22:20, where Jesus says: "Surely I am coming quickly." "Amen. Even so, come, Lord Jesus!"

The cantata was performed a second time nine years later, on Advent Sunday 28 November 1723, during Bach's first year in Leipzig. Unfortunately, the performing parts have not survived to give more detailed information about any modifications or adaptations he might have made to suit the new acoustics or congregation. However, we do have a record in his handwriting of the occasion itself (Figure 3.3). Bach carefully wrote down the running order of the elements of the Leipzig service on the reverse side of the title page of the score, showing that he was still fairly new to the role of Thomaskantor. According to his description the first part of the cantata was performed between the Gospel reading and the intonation of the Credo before the sermon, and the second part performed after the sermon, after the words of institution but before or during the administration of communion.

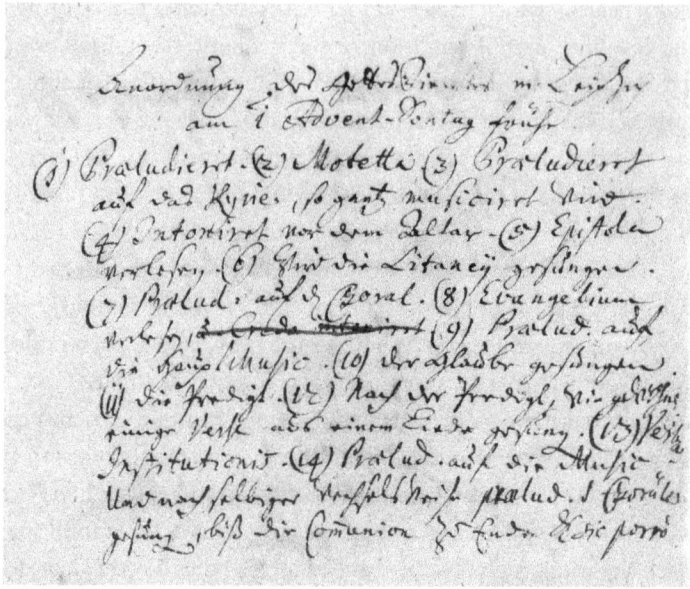

**Figure 3.3** Bach's handwritten description of the Leipzig order of service, inside the cover of Cantata 61. https://digital.staatsbibliothek-berlin.de/werkansicht?PPN=PPN845728342&PHYSID=PHYS_0098&DMDID=DMDLOG_0044. Staatsbibliothek zu Berlin, Preussischer Kulturbesitz. In English translation, Figure 3.3 reads: "Order of the Divine Service in Leipzig on the First Sunday in Advent: Morning. (1) Preluding. (2) Motet. (3) Preluding on the Kyrie, which is performed throughout in concerted manner. (4) Intoning before the altar. (5) Reading of the Epistle. (6) Singing of the Litany. (7) Preluding on the Chorale. (8) Reading of the Gospel. (9) Preluding on the principal music [the cantata]. (10) Singing of the Creed. (11) The sermon. (12) After the sermon, as usual, singing of several verses of a hymn. (13) Words of institution. (14) Preluding on the music. After the same, alternate preluding and singing of chorales until the end of the Communion, and so on."

In English translation, Figure 3.3 reads:

> Order of the Divine Service in Leipzig on the First Sunday in Advent: Morning. (1) Preluding. (2) Motet. (3) Preluding on the Kyrie, which is performed throughout in concerted manner. (4) Intoning before the altar. (5) Reading of the Epistle. (6) Singing of the Litany. (7) Preluding on the Chorale. (8) Reading of the Gospel. (9) Preluding on the principal music [the cantata]. (10) Singing of the Creed. (11) The sermon. (12) After the sermon, as usual, singing of several verses of a hymn. (13) Words of Institution. (14) Preluding on the music. After the same, alternate preluding and singing of chorales until the end of the Communion, and so on.

## Listening Today

There are very many different features in this cantata to capture the attention of the listener, whatever the style of performance. Something I like to listen out for is the spirit of the aria "Open yourself, my whole heart." A technically perfect rendition by a trained soprano soloist can give this aria a self-assurance and confidence that can gainsay the vulnerability integral to such a plea. I find it easier to experience the spiritual anxiety when it is sung with less assurance and polish, for example when performed by a child soloist. Should it not be terrifying to have the Creator of the world knocking on the door of your heart? Even understanding that the knocking is motivated by love and grace, how many of us would remain standing? How many of us dare to open the door? When confronted by such a cosmic invitation, surely most of us would recognize our inner trembling child, whether our response be terror, reluctance, or a courageous welcome? When all is said and done, though, if the listener can engage with the text and music, regardless of her/his religious persuasion, and if the transformative elements of Cantata 61 are allowed to work in the listener, then Bach's goal for his music and for this cantata will have been fulfilled.

## Suggestions for Further Reading

For more on the context and nature of Bach's early cantatas see Christoph Wolff (1995). Further discussion of Cantata 61 can be found in Eric Chafe (1991), 125–149, and more on *Vox Christi* settings in Bach's music in Mark Peters (2008), Chapter 3. Robin A. Leaver discusses Rittmeyer's emblems and communion practises in Bach's time in "Emblematic Jesus", *Discussing Bach* 2 (July 2021).Kerala Snyder (2011), 69–95, discusses Buxtehude's Abendmusik. For those comfortable with German, further details on the tradition of the final chorale form of Cantata 61 can be found in Rathey (2002), 105–117.

# 4

# Music for Winter and Summer

'Hertz, und Mund, und That, und Leben'

## The Six-Movement Weimar Cantata

Cantata (BWV) 147 'Hertz, und Mund, und That, und Leben' (Heart and Mouth and Deed and Life) was first composed in Weimar, in the version sometimes referred to as (BWV) 147a or 147.1. It was to be performed in the court chapel on the Fourth Sunday of Advent, 20 December 1716. The six-movement libretto was written for the occasion by Weimar court poet, Salomo Franck (1659–1725), and published in 1717 in his *Evangelische Sonn- und Fest-Tags-Andachten*. This was Franck's third cycle of cantata texts, which, in common with the earlier two, were dedicated to the reigning duke Wilhelm Ernst of Saxony, and written specifically to be set to music for use in the Weimar court chapel. For each of his collections, Franck chose a specific textual form. In his cycle for the church year 1715–1716, for example, each cantata text included recitatives between the arias, whereas there are no recitatives in his collection for 1716–1717, to which Cantata 147.1 belongs. It has an opening chorus, "Hertz, und Mund, und That, und Leben," four arias "Schäme dich, O Seele nicht," "Hilff, Jesu, hilff," "Bereite dir Jesu," and "Laß mich der Ruffer Stimmen hören," and a closing chorale "Dein Wort laß mich bekennen," for which Franck gives only the first line.

The few bits of evidence that can be gleaned from the surviving musical materials suggest that Bach composed and possibly performed the cantata in 1716 in the six-movement version stipulated by Franck (Figures 4.1a and 4.1b). Bach's complete Weimar score has not survived, but what we do have today is a clean

## Auf den vierten Advent-Sonntag.

**Chor.**

Hertz, und Mund, und That, und Leben
Muß von Christo Zeugniß geben,
Ohne Furcht und Heucheley,
Daß er GOtt und Heyland sey.

**Aria 1.**

Schähme dich, o Seele, nicht,
Deinen Heyland zu bekennen,
Soll er seine Braut dich nennen,
Vor des Vaters Angesicht!

Denn wer ihn auf dieser Erden
Zu verläugnen sich nicht scheut,
Soll von ihm verläugnet werden,
Wenn er kommt zur Herrligkeit!

**Aria 2.**

Hilff, JESU! hilff, daß ich auch dich bekenne,
In Wohl und Weh! in Freud und Leyd!
Daß ich dich meinen Heyland nenne,
In Glauben mit Gelassenheit.
Daß stets mein Hertz von deiner Liebe brenne!

**Aria 3.**

Bereite dir JESU, noch heute die Bahn!
Beziehe die Höhle
Des Hertzens, der Seele,
Und blicke mit Augen der Gnade mich an.

**Aria 4.**

Laß mich der Ruffer Stimmen hören,
Die mit Johanne treulich lehren,
Ich soll in dieser Gnaden-Zeit
Von Finsterniß und Dunckelheit
Zum wahren Lichte mich bekehren.

**Choral.**

Dein Wort laß mich bekennen ꝛc.

**Figure 4.1a and Figure 4.1b** Salomon Franck, *Evangelische Sonn- und Fest-Tages Andachten.* (1717) Harvard University, pages 7 and 8 respectively. https://hdl.handle.net/2027/hvd.32044040177537.

copy of the later score written in several stages. The handwriting and watermarks show that Bach wrote out the first movement in Weimar, and that he copied the remaining movements in Leipzig at various times; movements 2–5 in 1723, and the end of movement 5, movements 6, 7, 8, and 9 sometime between 1727 and 1732. We do not know if Bach made a fair copy of the cantata when he was in Weimar. There is also the possibility that he composed only the first movement in Weimar. It has been suggested that he stopped writing out a complete score, or even stopped composing it after the first movement, because of some frustrating circumstances among the musicians at the Weimar court.

The story goes like this: until 30 November 1716, Johann Samuel Drese was the court Capellmeister to Duke Wilhelm Ernst, (1662–1728). Drese's son, Johann Wilhelm, was Vice Capellmeister, and Bach was the court Concertmaster. Between them these three senior musicians provided a new cantata every week for the court chapel. From 1714 onward Bach was responsible for composing a new cantata every month. The post of Capellmeister became vacant when the elder Drese died on 1 December 1716. Possibly because he wished to compete for the vacant position, Bach then stepped up his cantata productivity and seems to have composed a new cantata every week for the next three Sundays in Advent. These were Cantatas (BWV) 70.1 for the Second Sunday of Advent, 186.1 for the Third Sunday, and 147.1 for the Fourth Sunday of Advent. But his extra effort did not land him the job. Given the tradition of nepotism, it is no surprise that the younger Drese was appointed Capellmeister in his father's place, leaving Bach in second position for his remaining years at Weimar.

Although we cannot know how it felt from the inside, one can imagine that it was hard for the talented and diligent Bach to have no living father from whom to inherit a prestigious position. The circumstances might justifiably discourage many an artist, but Bach, it seems, took active steps to move forward and out of this irksome situation. He accepted an opportunity to present the Good Friday passion service at the Gotha court chapel on 26 March 1717, standing in for the very sick Capellmeister Christian Witt (c. 1660–1717), who died two weeks later. Although this did not lead to a new position, Bach had made it known that he was available, and by August 1717 he had signed a contract to become Capellmeister at the Calvinist court of Prince Leopold of Anhalt-Cöthen (1694–1728).

By all accounts Bach seemed to be very happy in the Cöthen court job until circumstances changed, and he decided it was time to move on. Once more the Bach family was to be uprooted and this time move to the cosmopolitan city of Leipzig, where Bach had been appointed the Cantor of St. Thomas Church. From the moment of his installation in May 1723 he had to provide music for all the main weekly Sunday services and for feast days, which put cantata composition back as a top priority.

Composing a cantata from scratch was a time-consuming process. It would save time if he reused earlier musical materials and, even better, if he could freshen up church cantatas that he had already in his portfolio. This was not always as easy as it might sound because of differing church traditions. In Leipzig there was a fasting, or "closed," season (*tempus clausum*) when there was no concerted music in services after the First Sunday in Advent, which made his Weimar cantatas for the later weeks of Advent redundant. He had to think how to turn this to his advantage. Shortly after their move to Leipzig Bach saw a way of reusing the materials from his Weimar cantata for the fourth week in Advent. There was a thematic overlap between the role of John the Baptist in the anticipation of Christ at Advent and the anticipation of Christ at the summer celebration of the Visitation, held every year on 2 July. In 1723 the Visitation festival fell on a Friday, which made the preceding week super pressurized, as it was necessary to provide a cantata for both Friday 2 and Sunday 4 July. This would be the ideal occasion to rework his already impressive and festive Weimar cantata 'Hertz, und Mund, und That, und

Leben". With some deft alterations to Franck's libretto, Bach saw a way to expand his Weimar materials by adding recitatives based on the Gospel text for the Visitation and transforming Franck's six-movement Advent Cantata into a much longer ten-movement Cantata (BWV) 147 divided into two parts. The first part was to be heard before the sermon, and the second during communion. As far as the Leipzig congregation was concerned, this magnificent music was brand-new from start to finish.

## The Ten-Movement Leipzig Cantata

Among the readings prescribed in the Leipzig liturgy for the Visitation were Isaiah 11:1–5, Romans 12:9–16, and the Gospel text from Luke 1:39–56. The recommended hymns included "Jesu, meiner Seelen Wonne" (Dresden hymnal) and the German translation of the Magnificat, "Meine Seel erhebt den Herrn" (Leipzig and Dresden hymnals).

The prescribed Gospel reading tells the story of young Mary as she paid a visit to her cousin Elizabeth:

> At that time Mary got ready and hurried to a town in the hill country of Judea, where she entered Zechariah's home and greeted Elizabeth. When Elizabeth heard Mary's greeting, the baby leaped in her womb, and Elizabeth was filled with the Holy Spirit. In a loud voice she exclaimed: "Blessed are you among women, and blessed is the child you will bear! But why am I so favored, that the mother of my Lord should come to me? As soon as the sound of your greeting reached my ears, the baby in my womb leaped for joy. Blessed is she who has believed that the Lord would fulfill his promises to her." And Mary said: "My soul glorifies the Lord and my spirit rejoices in God my Savior, for he has been mindful of the humble state of his servant. From now on all generations will call me blessed, for the Mighty One has

done great things for me—holy is his name. His mercy extends to those who fear him, from generation to generation. He has performed mighty deeds with his arm; he has scattered those who are proud in their inmost thoughts. He has brought down rulers from their thrones, but has lifted up the humble. He has filled the hungry with good things, but has sent the rich away empty. He has helped his servant Israel, remembering to be merciful to Abraham and his descendants forever, just as he promised our ancestors." Mary stayed with Elizabeth for about three months and then returned home.

The story provides the context for Mary's exultant hymn of praise, known as the "Magnificat," Mary's Canticle, or Mary's song. The Magnificat has been an integral part of church liturgy for centuries, and countless composers have set it to music. Bach too had composed a setting of the Magnificat in E flat, (BWV) 243.1, which may have been performed for the first time on 2 July 1723. This is not to be confused with Bach's more famous revised Magnificat in D major, (BWV) 243, that would not be heard in Leipzig until a decade later. A Magnificat setting, though, could not replace the prescribed cantata in the Leipzig church service. Bach had no alternative but to create a cantata, a reflective setting of text and music, that would communicate the sentiments of Mary's profound song of joy and help the congregation to apply its teachings to their lives.

Comparing Franck's 1717 text to the libretto in Bach's 1723 score, there are no changes to the opening chorus, "Hertz, und Mund, und That, und Leben" nor to the aria "Hilff, Jesu, hilff, das ich auch dich bekenne," although its position changed from being the second aria to becoming the third; Bach, or his poet, altered four words in the first aria "Schäme dich, o Seele, nicht" and seven words in the aria "Bereite dir Jesus, noch heute die Bahn." The most radical alteration, though, was to the fourth aria, which retained the meter and rhyme scheme of Franck's original but was entirely rewritten to make it suitable for the feast of the Visitation. For the same reason Bach also exchanged the chorale that Franck originally stipulated, "Dein Wort laß mich bekennen," with two verses from "Jesu, meiner Seelen Wonne."

## Movement by Movement

1. Chorus

| | |
|---|---|
| Hertz, und Mund, und That, und Leben | Heart and mouth and deed and life |
| Muss von Christo Zeugnis geben | Must bear witness to Christ, |
| Ohne Furcht und Heucheley, | Without fear and hypocrisy, |
| Dass er Gott und Heiland sey. | That He is God and Savior. |

The text of the opening chorus "Hertz, und Mund, und That, und Leben" has a regular meter and rhyme scheme. The syllables of its four lines have a two-part pattern 8877, and the last words of each of its four lines form the rhyme scheme AABB, reinforcing the bipartite pattern of the syllables. Although Bach does not disturb this two-part textual division, he did not choose a two-part musical form. Instead, he created a crystal-clear ABA form noticeable even to a first-time listener: an eight-bar instrumental *ritornello* (A), a fifty-bar setting of Franck's four lines (B), and a return to the opening eight bars (A). Rather than writing out the eight bars again, Bach indicated the return to the opening eight bars with the abbreviation **D.C.** (*da capo*), giving eight bars rest for the voices. The prominent triadic trumpet figure may have been designed to represent the trinitarian nature of Christ (see Chapter 1, "Meaning in Music").

The musical spirit of this movement is upbeat and positive, illustrating its life-affirming phrase: "Heart and mouth and deed and life must bear witness to Christ . . . that He is God and Savior." Entering after the instrumental introduction are the sopranos, who sing the melody to the first line of text, with "Leben" ("life") given special attention with fifty-five notes woven in stepwise figuration across three bars. The altos then enter in **imitation** at the fifth, with an even longer emphasis of "Leben," extending over five bars with no fewer than ninety-one notes! This pattern is repeated for the imitative tenor and bass voices who again sing many notes to "Leben." The "Leben" figuration was first heard in the opening trumpet line and is heard again when the instrumental A section returns. The tangible energy of this "breath of life" figure is reminiscent of the power of the trumpeters and singers in 2 Chronicles 5:13 when "The trumpeters and musicians joined together to praise and thank the Lord. . . . And the house of the Lord was filled with the cloud of the glory of God." When Bach was reading this page in his Calov commentary some years later, he was moved to write in the margin beside verse 13: "Where there is devotional music, God with his grace is always present" (Figure 4.2). Perhaps he had experienced this manifestation of God's grace during performances of Cantata 147.

In Leipzig at this time Bach had the reputably excellent trumpeter Gottfried Reiche (1667–1734) at his disposal. We also know that many of Anna Magdalena's relatives were professional trumpeters, and it is quite possible that one or other of Bach's in-laws were in Leipzig in July 1723, available and willing to supplement the orchestral forces. Her father, Johann Caspar Wülcke, was a court trumpeter at Weißenfels, and her brother a court trumpeter in Zerbst, while her three sisters were connected to court trumpeters through marriage. One can imagine that family members would have been particularly keen to visit Leipzig at this time, as Anna Magdalena had recently given birth to her first baby, Christiana Sophia Henrietta. Regardless of who was playing the trumpet parts on that 1723 feast day, the trumpet sonorities most definitely add a spirit of celebration to the cantata.

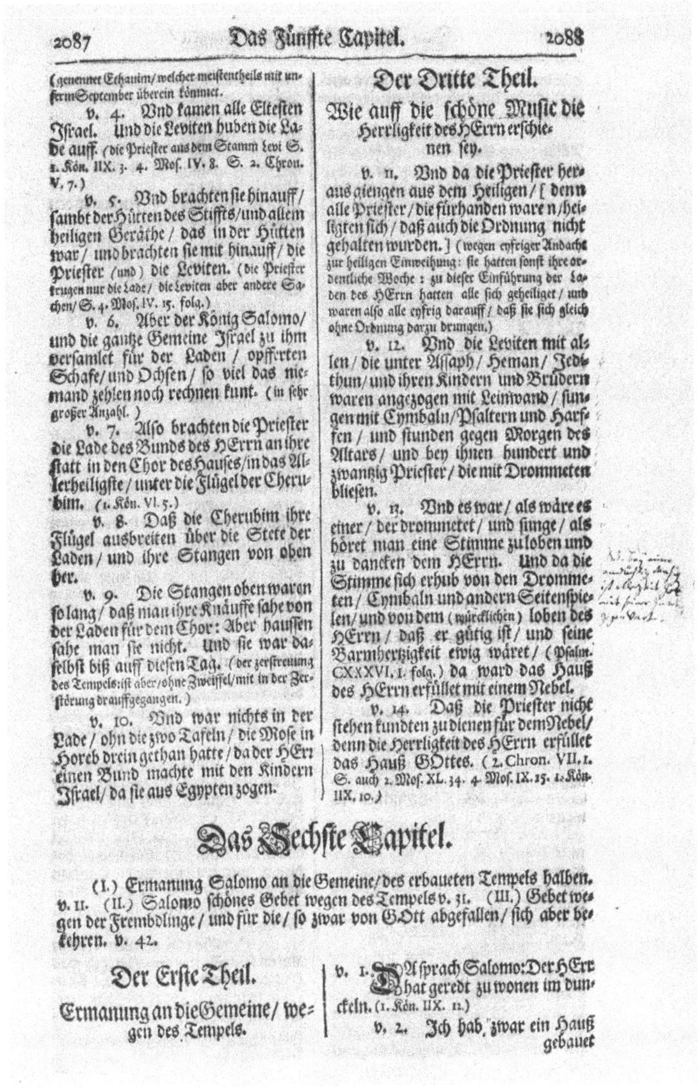

2087 Das Fünffte Capitel. 2088

(genennet Ethanim/ welcher meistentheils mit unserm September überein kömmet.

v. 4. Vnd kamen alle Eltesten Israel. Und die Leviten huben die Lade auff. (die Priester aus dem Stamm Levi S. 1. Kön. IIX. 3. 4. Mos. IV. 8. S. 2. Chron. V. 7.)

v. 5. Vnd brachten sie hinauff/ sambt der Hütten des Stiffts/ und allem heiligen Geräthe/ das in der Hütten war/ und brachten sie mit hinauff/ die Priester (und) die Leviten. (die Priester trugen nur die Lade/ die Leviten aber andere Sachen/ S. 4. Mos. IV. 15. folg.)

v. 6. Aber der König Salomo/ und die gantze Gemeine Israel zu ihm versamlet für der Laden/ opfferten Schafe/ und Ochsen/ so viel das niemand zehlen noch rechnen kunt. (in sehr großer Anzahl.)

v. 7. Also brachten die Priester die Lade des Bunds des HErrn an ihre statt in den Chor des Hauses/ in das Allerheiligste/ unter die Flügel der Cherubim. (1. Kön. VI. 5.)

v. 8. Daß die Cherubim ihre Flügel ausbreiten über die Stete der Laden/ und ihre Stangen von oben her.

v. 9. Die Stangen oben waren so lang/ daß man ihre Knäuffe sahe von der Laden für dem Chor: Aber haussen sahe man sie nicht. Und sie war daselbst biß auff diesen Tag. (der zerstreuung des Tempels: ist aber/ ohne Zweiffel/ mit in der Zerstörung drauffgegangen.)

v. 10. Vnd war nichts in der Lade/ ohn die zwo Tafeln/ die Mose in Horeb drein gethan hatte/ da der HErr einen Bund machte mit den Kindern Israel/ da sie aus Egypten zogen.

Der Dritte Theil.

Wie auff die schöne Music die Herrligkeit des HErrn erschienen sey.

v. 11. Vnd da die Priester heraus giengen aus dem Heiligen/ [denn alle Priester/ die fürhanden waren/ heiligten sich/ daß auch die Ordnung nicht gehalten wurden.] (wegen eyfriger Andacht zur heiligen Einweihung: sie hatten sonst ihre ordentliche Woche: zu dieser Einführung der Laden des HErrn hatten alle sich geheiliget/ und waren also alle eyfrig darauff/ daß sie sich gleich ohne Ordnung darzu drungen.)

v. 12. Vnd die Leviten mit allen/ die unter Assaph/ Heman/ Jedithun/ und ihren Kindern und Brüdern waren angezogen mit Leinwand/ sungen mit Cymbaln/ Psaltern und Harffen/ und stunden gegen Morgen des Altars/ und bey ihnen hundert und zwantzig Priester/ die mit Drommeten bliesen.

v. 13. Vnd es war/ als wäre es einer/ der drommetet/ und sünge/ als höret man eine Stimme zu loben und zu dancken dem HErrn. Und da die Stimme sich erhub von den Drommeten/ Cymbaln und andern Seitenspielen/ und von dem (würcklichen) loben des HErrn/ daß er gütig ist/ und seine Barmhertzigkeit ewig wäret/ (Psalm. CXXXVI. 1. folg.) da ward das Hauß des HErrn erfüllet mit einem Nebel.

v. 14. Daß die Priester nicht stehen kundten zu dienen für dem Nebel/ denn die Herrligkeit des HErrn erfüllet das Hauß GOttes. (2. Chron. VII. 1. S. auch 2. Mos. XL. 34. 4. Mos. IX. 15. 1. Kön. IIX. 10.)

Das Sechste Capitel.

(I.) Ermanung Salomo an die Gemeine/ des erbaueten Tempels halben. v. 11. (II.) Salomo schönes Gebet wegen des Tempels v. 31. (III.) Gebet wegen der Frembdlinge/ und für die/ so zwar von GOtt abgefallen/ sich aber bekehren. v. 42.

Der Erste Theil.

Ermanung an die Gemeine/ wegen des Tempels.

v. 1. DA sprach Salomo: Der HErr hat geredt zu wonen im dunckeln. (1. Kön. IIX. 12.)

v. 2. Ich hab zwar ein Hauß gebauet

**Figure 4.2** Calov's commentary on 2 Chronicles 5:4–14 with Bach's marginal comment beside verse 13. The facsimile of Bach's Calov Bible. Courtesy of Dingeman van Wijnen.

## 2. Tenor recitative

| | |
|---|---|
| Gebenedeiter Mund! | Blessed mouth! |
| Maria macht ihr Innerstes der Seelen | Mary makes her innermost soul |
| Durch Dank und Rühmen kund; | Known by thanks and glorifying. |
| Sie fänget bey sich an, | She begins with herself, |
| Des Heilands Wunder zu erzählen, | To tell of the Savior's wonders, |
| Was er an ihr als seiner Magd gethan. | What He has done to her as his maidservant. |
| O menschliches Geschlecht, | O human race, |
| Des Satans und der Sünden Knecht, | Servant of Satan and of sin, |
| Du bist befreit | You are freed |
| Durch Christi tröstendes Erscheinen | By the consoling advent of Christ |
| Von dieser Last und Dienstbarkeit! | From this burden and servitude. |
| Jedoch dein Mund und dein verstockt Gemüte | Yet your mouth and your stubborn disposition |
| Verschweigt, verleugnet solche Güte; | Keeps quiet, denies such goodness; |
| Doch wisse, dass dich nach der Schrift | But know that in accordance with Scripture |
| Ein allzu scharfes Urteil trifft! | You will meet an all too harsh judgment. |

Each of the three recitatives that Bach added in 1723 is scored for a different solo voice and obbligato instrument. The structure of each of the new recitatives is similar, with the first half focusing on the Gospel story or part of the Magnificat, and the second half speaking directly to the listener. After encouraging the congregation to bear witness to Christ freely with "heart and mouth and deed and life" in the opening movement, the first recitative "Gebenedeiter Mund!" ("Blessed mouth") warns of the harsh consequences of denying the

Savior. The recitative explaining Mary's place in the story is sung by the tenor in standard quasi-improvised speech patterns, with a background sonority of the sustained strings of two violins and viola. Due to this simple texture, the embellishment above "Christi" (of Christ) stands out clearly: "You are freed in the consoling advent of Christ."

3. Alto aria

| Schäme dich, o Seele, nicht, | Do not be ashamed, o soul, |
| Deinen Heyland zu bekennen, | To profess your Savior, |
| Soll er dich die seine nennen | If he is to call you his own |
| Vor des Vaters Angesicht! | Before [God] the father's face! |
| Doch wer ihn auf dieser Erden | But whoever is unafraid |
| Zu verleugnen sich nicht scheut, | To deny him on this earth |
| Soll von ihm verleugnet werden, | Will be denied by him |
| Wenn er kommt zur Herrlichkeit. | When He comes in glory. |

Taking up the theme of the consolation of Christ, Bach sets the next movement for the alto voice and the oboe d'amore with its mellifluous sonorities. The oboe d'amore, literally the oboe of love, is pitched a minor third lower than the more common oboe, and has a distinctively warmer and darker sound, ideal for expressing reassurance and kindness. Three words in this aria were changed from Franck's original: line 3 became, "Soll er dich die seine nennen" ("If he is to call you his own") instead of "Soll er seine Braut dich nennen" ("If he is to call you his bride"), taking away any resonance with the Bride/Bridegroom story of Advent. Bach lends particular emphasis to two phrases in the aria through the use of running sixteenth notes: the first is "Vor des Vaters Angesicht!" (literally, "Before the Father's face"), and the second "zur Herrlichkeit" ("in glory"), with the sixteenth notes at the end passed from the continuo, to the voice, and then to the d'amore. Since the soul here is being inspired to profess Christ and assured of the subsequent reward of salvation in Glory, I suspect these sixteenth notes are a musical gesture to express encouragement.

## 4. Bass recitative

| | |
|---|---|
| Verstockung kann Gewaltige verblenden, | Stubbornness can blind the powerful |
| Bis sie des Höchsten Arm vom Stuhle stösst; | Until the arm of the Most High casts them from their throne; |
| Doch dieser Arm erhebt, | But in contrast this arm, |
| Obschon vor ihm der Erden Kreis erbebt, | Though the earthly globe trembles before it, |
| Hingegen, die Elenden, | Lifts up the miserable/exiled, |
| So er erlöst. | Whom it [God's arm] redeems. |
| O hochbeglückte Christen, | Oh highly fortunate Christians, |
| Auf, machet euch bereit, | Up, make yourselves ready; |
| Itzt ist die angenehme Zeit, | Now is the acceptable time; |
| Itzt ist der Tag des Heils: | Now is the day of salvation: |
| Der Heiland heisst | The Savior bids |
| Euch Leib und Geist | You equip body and spirit |
| Mit Glaubensgaben rüsten, | With gifts of faith; |
| Auf, ruft zu ihm in brünstigem Verlangen, | Up, call to him in ardent desire, |
| Um ihn im Glauben zu empfangen! | To receive him in faith. |

The second recitative "Verstockung kann Gewaltige verblenden" ("Stubbornness can blind the powerful") is sung by a bass soloist supported by the continuo line (*secco* recitative) and a text loosely drawn from the second half of Mary's song. The scrunching and disturbing dissonance describing "stubbornness" ("Verstockung") provokes the listener to get up, get ready, and call out to the Savior.

## 5. Soprano aria

| | |
|---|---|
| Bereite dir, Jesu, noch itzo die Bahn, | Prepare the highway for you Jesus, even now; |
| Mein Heyland, erwähle | My Savior, choose |

| | |
|---|---|
| Die gläubende Seele | My believing soul |
| Und siehe mit Augen der Gnade mich an! | And look upon me with eyes of grace. |

The fifth movement is an aria for soprano and solo violin. Figure 4.3 shows that in bar 19 Bach had written "Beziehe die" from the original Franck setting, before striking it through and replacing it with "Mein Heyland, erwähle die glaubende Seele." The dance-like solo violin sounds wordlessly for ten bars in triplet motion before the soprano sings. It is not until we hear "Bereite dir, Jesu, noch itzo die Bahn" ("Prepare the highway for you, Jesu, even now") that we understand the violin's dance to be part of preparing the pathway for Jesus. With all the loveliness of a flower girl strewing rose petals before a bride, the violin and soprano create an atmosphere of purity, and the unspoken desire to be seen as lovely by someone who adores them.

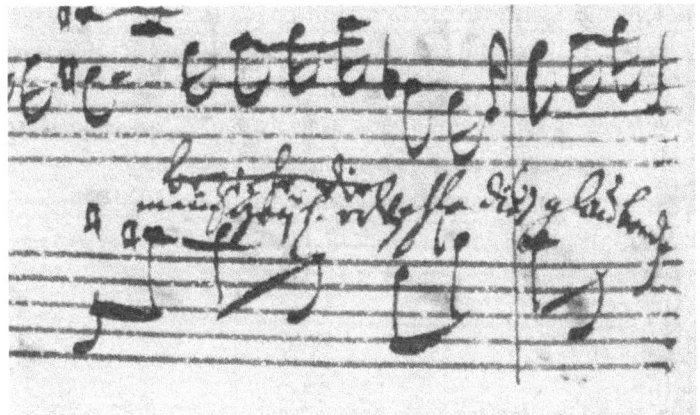

Figure 4.3  Bach striking through the original Franck text and correcting it to "mein Heyland, erwähle . . ." https://digital.staatsbibliothek-berlin.de/werkansicht?PPN=PPN84777578X&PHYSID=PHYS_0012&DMDID=DMDLOG_0001.
Staatsbibliothek zu Berlin, Preussischer Kulturbesitz.

Franck described this as "the beauty of the believing soul longing to be looked upon by the Savior with the eyes of grace."

## 6. Chorale

| | |
|---|---|
| Wohl mir, dass ich Jesum habe, | It is well with me that I have Jesus; |
| O wie feste halt ich ihn, | Oh, how fast I hold him, |
| Dass er mir mein Herze labe, | That he might refresh my heart |
| Wenn ich krank und traurig bin. | When I am ill and sad. |
| Jesum hab ich, der mich liebet | I have Jesus, who loves me |
| Und sich mir zu eigen gibet; | And gives himself to me, to be my own; |
| Ach drum lass ich Jesum nicht, | Ah, thus I will not let Jesus go, |
| Wenn mir gleich mein Herze bricht. | Even if my heart breaks |

The triplet motion of the solo violin of the preceding soprano aria moves seamlessly into the triplet motion of the chorale setting that ends Part 1 of the cantata. The chorale arrangement of verse 6 of the hymn "Jesu, meiner Seelen Wonne" by Martin Jahn (c. 1620–c. 1682) refers to Mary's trust: "Ach drum lass ich Jesum nicht, / Wenn mir gleich mein Herze bricht" ("I will not leave Jesus even if my heart should break"). The chorale is sung in four parts, with its melody strengthened by the trumpets, and woven together with sections of flowing orchestral episodes with the oboes leading the flow. This memorable setting will be heard again as the final chorale of the cantata, to a verse that gave rise to the popular title "Jesu, Joy of Man's Desiring."

## 7. Tenor aria

| | |
|---|---|
| Hilff, Jesu, hilff, dass ich auch dich bekenne | Help, Jesus, help that I too may profess you |
| In Wohl und Weh, in Freud und Leid, | In weal and woe, in joy and sorrow; |
| Dass ich dich meinen Heiland nenne | That I may call you my Savior |

| Im Glauben und Gelassenheit, | In faith and serenity |
| Dass stets mein Herz von deiner Liebe brenne. | That my heart may ever burn with your love. |

The second part of the cantata was designed to be sung after the sermon and during communion. It begins with an aria for tenor with no obbligato instrument, accompanied simply by a continuo line consisting of low string instruments and keyboard. The bass strings play in unison, introducing the opening four-bar melody. The tenor sings the opening four notes "Hilff, Jesu, hilff" ("Help, Jesus, help"), which is then imitated by the continuo section. The clarity of these simple melodic lines with one note per syllable is broken when Bach starts to emphasize particular words. First to be embellished is "meinen Heyland nenne" ("name my Savior"). In his best handwriting, Bach gives this phrase exactly sixty-five stepwise notes over six whole bars. As "Heyland" has a total of 65 (8 + 5 + 23 + 11 + 1 + 13 + 4) in the common number alphabet, he may have been using the number of notes to literally "name my Savior". The second and third embellishments are both on the word "brenne" ("burns"). The first "brenne" is given fifty-five notes of mostly stepwise triplet motion. The number value of "brenne" happens to be 55 (2 + 17 + 5 + 13 + 13 + 5). Bach may have been adding an extra layer of emblematic meaning to these prominent words, but one cannot be sure. The second time "brenne" is embellished, it is given an angular rhythm and note pattern. These different musical images of fire can be understood to represent the fire of Jesus' love burning in the believer's heart. The devotional invocation J. J. ("Help, Jesus!") that Bach frequently wrote at the start of a cantata score is absent on the first page of the score of Cantata 147. Perhaps the words of this movement "Help, Jesus, Help" were sufficient.

In 1711 Franck had published a very different text for the Fourth Sunday of Advent in his *Geist- und Weltliche Poesien* (1711), based on Matthew 10:32 (*sic*) (Figure 4.4). Its two verses cover ideas and phrases that Franck would develop six years later, when he wrote his reflection for the Fourth Sunday in Advent, the text for Cantata 147.1.

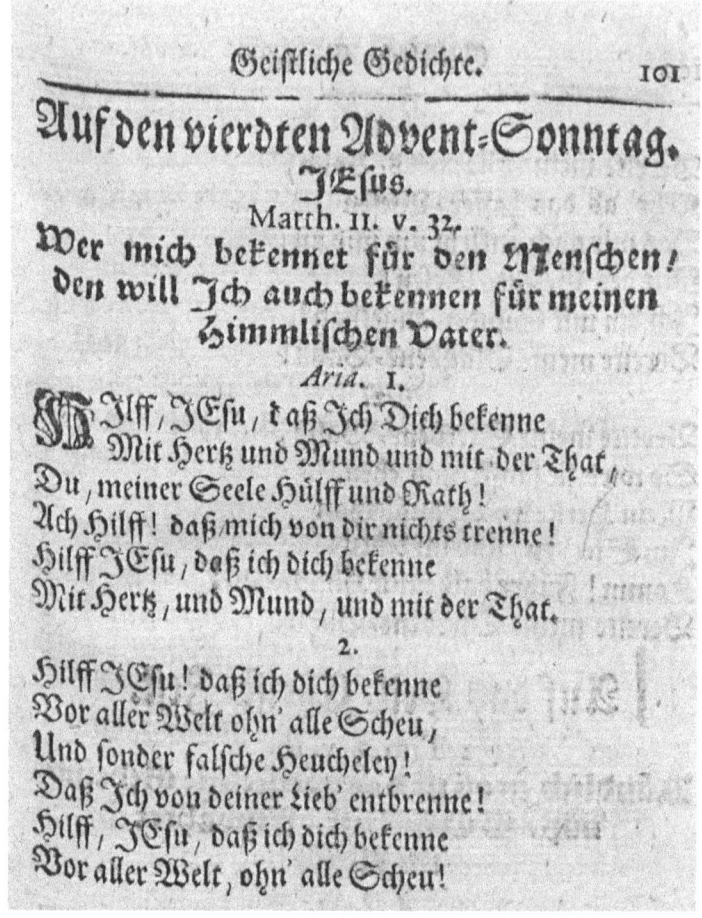

**Figure 4.4** Salomo Franck, *Geist- und Weltliche Poesien* (1711), 101. Aria for the Fourth Sunday of Advent. https://opendata.uni-halle.de//handle/1981185920/49948. Halle (Saale) Universitäts- und Landesbibliothek Sachsen-Anhalt.

There are numerous echoes of Franck's 1711 setting in his 1717 text, including the phrase "Mit Hertz und Mund und mit der That" that would be developed into "Hertz, und Mund, und That, und Leben"; the phrase "Hilff, Jesu" that would become a complete aria; the idea of "falsche Heucheley" to become "Ohne Furcht und Heucheley" in 1717; and "Jesu ... daß ich dich bekenne ... ohn' alle Scheu" that would feed into the image of "Deinen Heyland zu bekennen . . . sich nicht scheut." This comparison illustrates the flexibility a poet had toward texts and reflects the light touch Bach or his poet would have applied when he/they felt that a word in a text was not quite right.

8. Alto recitative

| | |
|---|---|
| Der Höchsten Allmacht Wunderhand | The miraculous hand of the most almighty |
| Wirkt im Verborgenen der Erden. | Acts in the hidden place of the earth. |
| Johannes muss mit Geist erfüllet werden, | John has to be filled with Spirit: |
| Ihn zieht der Liebe Band | The bond of love clothes him |
| Bereits in seiner Mutter Leibe, | Already in his mother's womb, |
| Dass er den Heiland kennt, | So that he knows the Savior, |
| Ob er ihn gleich noch nicht Mit seinem Munde nennt, | Even though he [John] does not yet Call him (Jesus) by name with his mouth; |
| Er wird bewegt, er hüpft und springet, | He (John) is stirred, he skips and jumps |
| Indem Elisabeth das Wunderwerk ausspricht, | As Elizabeth proclaims the wonderwork, |
| Indem Mariae Mund der Lippen Opfer bringet. | As Mary's mouth brings lip praise offering. |
| Wenn ihr, o Gläubige, des Fleisches Schwachheit merkt, | When you, O believers, note the flesh's weakness, |
| Wenn euer Herz in Liebe brennet, | When your heart burns in love, |
| Und doch der Mund den Heiland nicht bekennet, | And yet the mouth does not profess the Savior, |
| Gott ist es, der euch kräftig stärkt, | God is the one who powerfully strengthens you; |
| Er will in euch des Geistes Kraft erregen, | He wants to stir up in you the power of the Spirit, |
| Ja, Dank und Preis auf eure Zunge legen. | Yes, put thanks and praise on your tongue. |

The third recitative, "Der Höchsten Allmacht Wunderhand," is for alto solo accompanied by two oboes da caccia that weave a warm texture around the vocal line. The alto describes the meeting of Mary and Elizabeth, and how the baby John leaps and jumps in Elizabeth's womb as Mary arrives. There is unmistakable delight in the music to "Er wird bewegt, er hüpft und springet" ("He is stirred, he skips and jumps"), which must surely reflect the humor and pride of Bach's experience of fatherhood. Within the past months he had witnessed the kicking *in utero* of their healthy baby, and the comeliness of his second wife, twenty-three-year-old Anna Magdalena, experiencing the wonders of pregnancy for the first time. The oboe da caccia, literally a hunting oboe, is pitched a fifth below the common oboe. These instruments add a mellowness to the sonorities of the movement that seems to create a mood of joyful mystery.

9. Bass aria

| | |
|---|---|
| Ich will von Jesu Wundern singen | I want to sing of Jesus' wonders, |
| Und ihm der Lippen Opfer bringen, | And bring him the lip offering of praise, |
| Er wird nach seiner Liebe Bund | In accordance with the covenant of his love, |
| Das schwache Fleisch, den irdischen Mund | he will powerfully conquer weak flesh, |
| Durch heilges Feuer kräftig zwingen. | the earthly mouth by holy fire. |

The final aria of the cantata is a solo bass voice singing a song of praise in the first person: "Ich will von Jesu Wundern singen" ("I want to sing of Jesu's wonders"). An exultant trumpet line boosts the joy as it introduces the melody before the bass sings. The words "Opfer" ("offering of praise") and "heilges Feuer" ("holy fire") are emphasized with a striking vocal sixteenth-note movement, which is also heard in the instruments. This creates a hymn of praise with trumpets reminiscent of the opening chorus, and the episode described in 2 Chronicles 5:13.

10. Chorale

| | |
|---|---|
| Jesus bleibet meine Freude, | Jesus remains my joy, |
| Meines Herzens Trost und Saft, | The consolation and sap/blood of my heart; |
| Jesus wehret allem Leide, | Jesus bars all sorrow; |
| Er ist meines Lebens Kraft, | He is the power of my life, |
| Meiner Augen Lust und Sonne, | The desire and sun of my eyes, |
| Meiner Seele Schatz und Wonne; | The treasure and bliss of my soul; |
| Darum lass ich Jesum nicht | Thus I will not let Jesus |
| Aus dem Herzen und Gesicht. | Out of heart and sight. |

The cantata ends with a reiteration of the chorale setting heard at the end of Part 1, although this time with verse 17 of Martin Jahn's hymn "Jesu, meiner Seelen Wonne" ("Jesus, Delight of My Soul"). Such an optimistic and reassuring musical setting must have helped his congregation renew their heart's allegiance to Jesus. The words have since become inextricably linked to this iconic musical setting, known in English as "Jesu, Joy of Man's Desiring," of which countless instrumental and vocal arrangements continue to inspire generations of listeners beyond the context of this cantata.

## Hearing the Cantata as a Story

When Bach expanded his Weimar cantata, he did more than make an adaptation of already good music; he created something entirely new. In Leipzig he had a different narrative to play with—the story of the two pregnant cousins and Mary's social visit. It is a peculiarly female festival. Bach would have appreciated the moral and spiritual support that Mary's visit gave to her kinswoman Elizabeth as he revised the cantata in Leipzig, because Anna Magdalena was expecting their first child and was most probably separated from her parental family. This story of young motherhood was very close to home. Although it is difficult to pinpoint gender sensibilities in music, I wonder if Bach's response can be detected in the lyrical trumpet writing, which skillfully avoids macho triumphalism.

Of all the Bach cantatas I know, Cantata 147 is one of the most theatrical. I can imagine the two main characters, Elizabeth and Mary, and their supportive husbands (even though not mentioned in Luke 1), acting out events as the cantata progresses. The four protagonists seem to be portrayed in the different sounds of the characterful arias: the younger maiden, Mary, in the soprano solo; the more mature Elizabeth, past the days of childbearing and yet six months pregnant, in the alto solo; Joseph, the concerned father-to-be, in the tenor; and the doubting elderly priest Zechariah, whose muted tongue would be released after his son's birth, in the bass solo. Zechariah's aria is accompanied by trumpets and oboes. His story six months earlier was truly dramatic. Angel Gabriel appeared to him when he was serving in the Temple, to tell him that his wife Elizabeth would bear him a son, and that this son, to be named John, would have a vital role in the redemption of Israel (Luke 1:5–25). But Zechariah doubted the angel and was struck dumb, and would remain so, until the first part of the angelic prophecy had come to pass with the birth of the baby. At the time of the Visitation, Zechariah was still unable to speak, learning the hard way the cost of stubbornness ("Verstockung") and the virtues of faith. The two verses from Jahn's hymn "Jesu, meiner Seelen Wonne" affirm the faith of the believer. These too befit the story's four characters as they aspire to live through the coming events with confidence in God.

The keys in which the arias are composed are related and seem to link the couples: the arias for soprano and tenor (Mary and Joseph) are in the related keys of D minor and F major respectively; the arias for alto and bass (Elizabeth and Zechariah) in the related keys of A minor and C major respectively. These pairings create a unity across the cantata as well as within the storyline.

Even though Bach did not indicate characters in his score, I like to listen as if he had.

1. **Reflection** "[Let your] heart and mouth and deed and life bear witness that Christ is God and Savior."
2. **Joseph (tenor), singing about Mary**: "Blessed mouth! Mary makes her innermost soul known by telling the Savior's wonders."
3. **Elizabeth (alto), pregnant late in life**: "Do not be ashamed, O soul, to profess your Savior."
4. **Zechariah (bass), struck dumb because of his unbelief**: "Stubbornness can blind the powerful. The Savior bids you equip body and spirit with gifts of faith."
5. **Mary (soprano), a virgin yet willing to be mother of the Savior**: "My Savior, choose my believing soul and look upon me with eyes of grace."
6. **Reflection**: "I will not let Jesus go, even if my heart breaks."

Part 2, sung after the sermon, and during communion:

7. **Joseph (tenor), who considered breaking off his engagement to Mary because of the pregnancy**: "Help, Jesus, help that I too may profess you in joy and sorrow, in faith and obedience."
8. **Elizabeth (alto), six months pregnant, feeling her baby jumping in her womb, pregnant against all odds**: "The wonder-working hand of the Most High, Even though [John] does not yet know the savior he is stirred, he skips and jumps!"
9. **Zechariah (bass), dumb because of his disbelief:** "I want to sing of Jesus' wonders and bring him the offering from the lips."

10. **Reflection:** "Jesus remains my joy. The consolation of my heart. He is the protection of my life, the desire and sun of eyes. The treasure and bliss of my soul. I will not let Jesus out of heart and sight."

## More Thoughts on the Final Chorale

Besides the addition of the recitatives, the one big musical change to the Weimar cantata was to the final chorale. Bach chose "Jesu, meiner Seelen Wonne" whereas the chorale that Salomo Franck prescribed at the end of his six-section text for the Fourth Sunday of Advent (Figure 4.1b) is "Dein Wort laß mich bekennen" ("Let Me Confess Your Word"). This is the first line of the sixth verse of the hymn "Ich danke dir, lieber Herre" ("I thank you, dear Lord"), a chorale text written by Johann Kohlroß (1487–1560) and invariably categorized in the hymnals of the period as a morning hymn. Of Bach's three surviving harmonizations of Kohlroß's hymn, the only one thought to date from Weimar is the sixteen-bar setting, BWV 348. Another setting of this hymn that Bach could easily have known, due to the contemporary practice of exchanging music, is Cantata (GWV) 1163/16 by Christoph Graupner (1683–1760). Graupner composed it for the Twenty-Second Sunday after Trinity on 8 November 1716 for a cantata based on a text by Georg Christian Lehms. The opening movement is a chorale setting of "Dein Wort laß mich bekennen" for four voices, in C major with a 12/8 time-signature, with strings accompanying in a rippling quaver movement, notated as thirty-three bars (Figure 4.5).

This recalls the triplet motion in common time, C, of Bach's setting of the verses of Jahn's "Jesu, meiner Seelen Wonne" that has become famous as "Jesu, Joy of Man's Desiring." Might Graupner's setting have suggested the idea of triplet motion with a 12/8 time signature for Bach's 1716 chorale setting of "Dein Wort laß mich bekennen"? If so, no such setting by Bach has survived. Might Graupner's setting have suggested the idea of a triplet motion chorale setting at the end of the expanded version of Cantata 147? It is not possible to say,

Figure 4.5 The rippling instrumental motion of Graupner's setting of "Dein Wort laß mich bekennen," Cantata (GVW) 1163/16. https://tudigit.ulb.tu-darmstadt.de/show/Mus-Ms-424-25. Courtesy of the Universitäts- und Landesbibliothek Darmstadt.

but it is interesting to see how the musical idea for "Jesu, Joy of Man's Desiring" might have been spawned in Weimar.

The chorale melody Bach used in Cantata 147 is published in Schemelli's *Gesangbuch* (1736) as number 142, set to Jahn's words "Jesu, meiner Seelen Wonne," and classified as a communion hymn. Even though today the melody is associated with the words "Jesu, Joy of Man's Desiring," it was the phrase "Werde Munter, mein Gemüthe" that would have arisen unbidden in the minds of the congregation in Bach's time. It is difficult to rethink our responses when a melody has such strong associations and memories. The final chorus of Cantata 147 might suggest the pastoral, the warmth of spiritual comfort of Jesus close to the believer, but for Bach's listeners the associations were entirely different. They sang the melody at Advent to different words, and as a morning hymn in their private devotions to yet others. Bach may have had yet another image in mind when he composed the flowing triplet motion in G major. In the Visitation Cantata 147, I can hear it at the end of Part 1 as a joyful meeting of a courageous young girl going to meet her older cousin for companionship and encouragement, and at the end of Part 2, as a portrayal of two faithful women touched by the hand of God, whose offspring would go on to alter the course of global history and eternity: the flow of oboes portraying the simplicity of their faithful actions, their human frailty yet courage to move forward while not knowing how things would pan out, and still with the strength to dance to words that affirm the comfort of Jesus' presence.

"Jesu, Joy of Man's Desiring" was made popular in the twentieth century through the piano solo and piano duet arrangements by Dame Myra Hess (1890–1965) that continue to warm the hearts and souls of music lovers. The chorale setting, and the cantata itself, was clearly much loved by the Bach family too. Unlike the majority of Bach's Leipzig cantatas, this was not put on one side to gather dust after its first performance in Leipzig's St. Thomas and St. Nicholas churches on that Sunday in the summer of 1723. Markings in the score show that Bach performed it again sometime between 1728 and 1733, and evidence from some additions to the oboe d'amore part indicate that it was heard at least once more between 1735 and 1739. The handwriting on the wrapper around the score is by Bach's son, J. C. F. Bach (1732–1795), who wrote the title "Festo Visitationis Mariae," and the much older C. P. E. Bach (1714–1788), who wrote "von J. S. B" ("by J. S. B."), as if overseeing the work of his younger brother. The first movement, "Hertz, und Mund, und That, und Leben," was also performed again after Bach's death, when W. F. Bach (1710–1784) incorporated it into his own Pasticcio Cantata (BR-WFB F20).

The traditional view that Bach composed the whole six-movement cantata in Weimar has recently been revised (published in the 2022 BWV catalog and on Bach Digital), the new hypothesis being that as only the opening chorus survives from Weimar, Bach may not have composed the entire cantata there in 1716. The ten-movement cantata, though, is still thought to date to 1723 because of the complete set of parts, even though the handwriting shows that Bach copied movements 6–9 and an oboe d'amore part sometime between 1727 and 1732, and even though no text booklet of this cantata has survived from 1723. Similar questions have been raised about the Weimar versions of two Leipzig cantatas with texts by Salomo Franck, originally dating from Advent 1716: 'Wachet! Betet! Betet! Wachet', Cantata (BWV) 70.1 or 70.a, and 'Ägre dich O Seele nicht', Cantata (BWV) 186.1 or 186.a. Research will continue to evolve and sourced-based hypotheses refined as new documents are discovered. Above all, though, the music that has survived will continue to speak, regardless of its precise genesis.

As multiple layers of history and significance resonate within a melody and a composition, what is understood by one generation of listeners may be lost to the next. Obviously, there cannot be just one way of hearing and understanding a work, nor a "correct" way to listen to this cantata. It is equally fine to imagine the characters as I have suggested, or simply to let the performance flow and move you as it will. If this cantata stirs a heart, and mouth, and actions, indeed inspires any individual life to greater deeds, then it has served the purpose of both poet and composer.

## Suggestions for Further Reading

For further details on Cantata 147 see Hans-Joachim Schulze and James A. Brokaw II on https://doi.org/10.21900/wd.21 and Alfred Dürr (2005), 86–90 and 670–680. Bach's annotations in his Calov Bible are discussed in Robin A. Leaver (1985), and in Albert Clement ed. (2022). The transmission of "Jesu, Joy of Man's Desiring" is the focus of Ruth Tatlow, "Famous Movements," in *The Cambridge Companion to the Bach Cantatas* (forthcoming). Dame Myra Hess can be seen performing it on https://youtu.be/yaCg_nC2W5s. More on GWV 1163/16 can be found at https://christoph-graupner-gesellschaft.de/details-einer-kantate?GWV=1163/16.

# 5

# Pastoral Music for a Leipzig Springtime

## 'Du Hirte Israel, höre'

Bach composed Cantata (BWV) 104 'Du Hirte Israel, höre' (You, Shepherd of Israel, Hear) for the Second Sunday after Easter, 23 April 1724, toward the end of his first year in Leipzig. Today this Sunday is called Shepherd Sunday, but in Bach's day it was still known as Misericordias Domini after its ancient Latin introit, Psalm 89, which begins "Misericordias Domini in aeternum cantabo" ("I will sing of the Lord's great mercies forever").

The original score of this cantata is lost, although some of the vocal and orchestral parts have survived. Also surviving is a copy of one of the booklets sold to the Leipzig congregation, which contained the texts set to music for the Easter festival days and the following two Sundays in 1724. Its title page reads:

*Texte | Zur Leipziger | Kirchen=Music, | Auf die | H. Oster= Feyertage, | Und die beyden folgenden | Sonntage Quasimodogeniti | und Misericordias Domini. | 1724. || Leipzig, | Gedruckt bey Immanuel Tietzen.*

[Texts to the Leipzig Church Music/Cantatas for the Holy Easter Holidays, and the two following Sundays, Quasimodogeniti and Misericordias Domini. 1724. Leipzig. Printed by Immanuel Tietz.]

## The Cantata Text

Cantata 104 is one of the most joyful, gentle, and pastoral church pieces that Bach composed. It is immediately accessible to a first-time listener. Its libretto begins and ends with direct quotations: the first movement citing Psalm 80:1, and the final movement citing the hymn transcription by Cornelius Becker of the opening of Psalm 23 (see below). The central four movements of Cantata 104 are all free texts written by an anonymous poet. It is not known if they were written specifically for Bach's setting. The Gospel reading prescribed for the day, John 10:11–16, was most probably the focus of the sermon on 23 April 1724:

> Jesus said: "I am the Good Shepherd. The Good Shepherd lays down his life for the sheep. The hired hand is not the shepherd and does not own the sheep. So when he sees the wolf coming, he abandons the sheep and runs away. Then the wolf attacks the flock and scatters it. The man runs away because he is a hired hand and cares nothing for the sheep. I am the Good Shepherd; I know my sheep and my sheep know me—just as the Father knows me and I know the Father—and I lay down my life for the sheep. I have other sheep that are not of this sheep pen. I must bring them also. They too will listen to my voice, and there shall be one flock and one shepherd."

When preparing to select the libretto and compose the music, Bach would have done some deep thinking around the themes in the Psalm, the Gospel, and Epistle readings for the day. He had friends and colleagues with reference books, as well as a small library of his own from which to draw inspiration. Among the books listed in the inventory of his possessions after his death is a volume of sermons by Martin Geier for each Sunday and festival day in the church year, written from the perspective of time and eternity (*Zeit und Ewigkeit*). There were also volumes by Heinrich Müller (1631–1675) and by August Pfeiffer (1640–1698), whose theological reflections tended to be personal and devotional. He also owned copies of Luther's German Bible that had been amplified with interleaved comments and annotations by Johann Olearius (1611–1684) (*Biblische Erklärung*) and, after 1733, the volumes by Abraham Calov (*Die Bibel*), known as Bach's "Calov Bible."

## Pfeiffer on the Good Shepherd

Among the collections in Bach's library was a volume of sermons by August Pfeiffer that had originally been preached in Meissen and

Figure 5.1 August Pfeiffer, *Gazophylacion Evangelicum: Evangelische-Schatzkammer* (1686), 430. https://digital.slub-dresden.de/werk ansicht/dlf/173512/456. Sächsische Landesbibliothek, Staats- und Universitätsbibliothek Dresden.

then published as *Evangelische Schatzkammer* (1686). If Bach had turned to the sermon for Misericordias Domini Sunday, he would have noticed two emblematic pictures and accompanying mottos, to which Pfeiffer refers throughout his sermon (Figure 5.1). The first emblem shows a hired shepherd about to run away. The text surrounding the image reads: "Ein Miedling ist vezagt, Läufft, eh man Ihn noch jagt!" ("A hired hand loses heart. Run, before someone hunts him!") The second is of a shepherd defending his flock, with his staff aimed at a wolf, and the words: "Wer bleibt, der ist ein Hirt! Den Jesus loben wird!" ("He who remains is a [true] Shepherd. Praise be to Jesus!"). The two images and their mottos are followed by a prayer: "Das walte Jesus Christus, der oberste Bischoff und Erz-Hirt unserer Seelen, hochgelobet in Ewigkeit. Amen" ("May the chosen Lord Jesus, the highest Bishop and archshepherd of our souls, be highly praised in eternity. Amen").

Pfeiffer wrote about God as the Good Shepherd in many of his publications, including in his Christian handbook *Evangelische Christen-Schule* (1688). Because the idea of the Good Shepherd has gathered numerous romantic and idyllic connotations within different church traditions since Bach's day, I will include a lengthy quotation, in English translation, of Pfeiffer's section on the lost sheep to show what Bach and his librettist could have read. The ideas are familiar, but subtly different from those one might hear today.

The section is printed in a chapter devoted to the image of God, in which Pfeiffer draws on three different parables to illustrate different aspects of God. The first is the parable of the lost sheep, the second the parable of the lost coin, and the third the parable of the lost son, or the prodigal son. It is in the first that Pfeiffer illustrates how God is like a good shepherd, drawing on many different biblical passages about sheep and shepherds. Sometimes the citation is an allusion, sometimes a word or two, and sometimes a complete biblical phrase. He weaves the shepherd verses into a complete theology from the innocence of Eden, through the temptation and fall of Adam and Eve, the subsequent total depravity of humankind, the essential sacrifice of Christ for the grace and redemption of the trusting soul, to the end of life when the elect will be shepherded into the joy of heaven.

This is a selection in English translation from pages 154–158 (1688 edition):

> §2 For the first parable Jesus describes a shepherd who has lost a sheep and who searches diligently for it, and when he has found it, carries it with joy on his shoulders, saying to his friends and neighbors: Rejoice with me, for I have found my sheep who was lost. In this we can see our original state as sinners, and the subsequent state of grace: before the fall, with Adam as our father, we humans were originally wise, pure, and devout sheep, wandering in a state of innocence, free from any constraint or direction, surrounded by the Shepherd of the Holy Angel, and enjoying the delicious, rich pastures of paradise. Our parents (Adam and Eve) could not cope with these good pastures for long, but fell for the cunning deception of the disguised serpent's hissing to make them hanker after better pastures by eating from the forbidden tree, to become educated men-gods like God Himself. God have mercy! They ate themselves and us, which brought misfortune and temporal and eternal death! Adam, a mangy sheep, infected the whole human race: Through one man sin entered the world, Romans 5:12, and death through sin, and in this way, death came to all people, because all sinned. Therefore, we are now by nature left like sheep without a shepherd, Matthew 9:36, confused and lost Sheep, Psalm 119, last verse, oppressed Sheep, Isaiah 53:7, and, just like sheep who run away from their shepherd, caught in the jaws of the wolf, Zechariah [13:]7. Therefore, in this dreadful state we should (had there not been salvation) be in hell like sheep who deserve eternal death, Psalm 49. The eternal son of God alone was sent to the

world from the bosom of his heavenly Father, from the spectacular heights of his Majesty, as a man to be to us a true shepherd, to release and redeem us poor sheep condemned to hell, not with perishable gold and silver, but with his holy, divine blood, 1 Peter 1[:18]. Through his excruciating suffering, this true shepherd offered himself freely to be punished Zechariah 13[:7], solely so that his sheep might forever be unpunished. All the blows, pains, welts, and wounds were inflicted on Him so that we might have peace, Isaiah 53:6, and He allows us access to this expensive redemption through the Word and sacrament. He calls to us: Repent you apostates, Jeremiah 3 [:12]; Come to me all you who are weary and heavily laden, and I will revive you, Matthew 11 [:28]. If we do not ignore or reject his voice, he will faithfully care for us, as he said: I will search for my sheep personally, and will seek them out; just as a shepherd seeks out his flock when his sheep have been scattered abroad, so will I seek out my sheep. . . . I will lead them to the best pasture . . . time and again I will seek the lost, and I will bring back the strays, and I will bind up the crippled, and I will strengthen the weak, and I will protect the fat and the strong, as is right and just, Ezekiel 34:11 onward. He washes us in the holy waters of baptism so that we will be like clean sheep that come out of the washing place, Song of Solomon 6:5. He gives us food and drink in the holy communion, where he lets us share his food and drink from his cup, as 2 Samuel 12:3 puts it. He hides us from all calamities and from hell itself through his blood-dripping wounds. He protects us against all ravening wolves, so that we his sheep can say: The Lord is my Shepherd, so I will lack nothing. He leads me to green pastures, and so on Psalm 23:1, and at the last he will carry us with joy to the shepherd of the chosen ones in heaven.

The use of sheep and shepherd imagery softens the judgmental blow that often hangs over essays about God. Here the blow falls heavily on Adam—"our parent"—while "we," the sheep, are granted mercy and grace. Although there is no evidence that Bach's librettist based his rhyming text on Pfeiffer's commentary, they share a common theological understanding of God and Jesus as the shepherd of mankind, and they both use a similar technique of drawing imagery and allusions from biblical verses. Pfeiffer's progression from the first man in creation, through salvation, to the welcome into heaven at life's end was familiar to all Lutherans in Bach's time. This shared knowledge allowed the cantata librettist to move straight into a devotional response to the familiar shepherd narratives. Reading the cantata text in everyday continuous prose, rather than in the more usual layout of verses and movements, gives a fresh insight into the way Bach might have read the text of Cantata 104.

> Hear and appear oh shepherd of Israel, you who lead Joseph like a sheep, you who are enthroned upon the Cherubim. The highest shepherd cares for me. What use are my worries? Why, the shepherd's loving kindnesses are new every morning! Therefore, calm yourself, my heart, God is faithful. If my shepherd is hidden too long, and if the wilderness makes me too anxious, my weak steps still hurry forward. My mouth cries to you, my shepherd, and through your Word [the Bible] you help me to believe and say "Abba, Father." Yes, this Word is the food of my soul, a refreshment to my heart, the pasture that I call my delight, a foretaste of heaven, indeed, my everything. Dear Good Shepherd, gather up us poor and straying ones, let our path soon end, and lead us into your sheepfold. You happy flock, Jesus' sheep, know that the world itself is a heavenly kingdom. You can taste Jesus' goodness here and now, and still hope for faith's reward after death's sweet sleep. The Lord is my faithful shepherd to whom I entrust myself completely. He leads me, his little sheep, to a meadow of beautiful green pastures, to fresh waters that powerfully revive my soul through his blessed Word of grace.

Note that the cantata text is spoken by an individual ("I" and "me") who addresses Jesus directly and reacts with personal reflections. In Bach's musical setting we hear this individual as a tenor and as a bass, which is an interesting choice when half of his congregation would have been female. But it was the tenor and bass voices Bach chose—his older, more stable, and stronger soloists. A company of mixed voices, including soprano and alto, sing the opening chorus and the concluding chorale based on Psalm 23.

## Bach's Musical Response, Movement by Movement

### 1. Chorus

| | |
|---|---|
| Du Hirte Israel, höre, | You, shepherd of Israel, hear. |
| der du Joseph hütest wie der Schafe, erscheine, | You who lead Joseph like sheep, appear |
| der du sitzest über Cherubim. | You who are enthroned upon the Cherubin. |

The cantata opens with a joyful twenty-four-bar instrumental introduction with strings and three oboes in a triple time, in dancing triplet motion. The chorus enters, singing words from Psalm 80:1–2, addressing the Good Shepherd who leads the people of Israel from his celestial throne. Even though in several Bibles of the time this psalm has the heading "Prayer that God would save his church from its miserable state," Bach's setting of verses 1–2 contains no sense of desperation about the miserable state of the church. The closest it gets to desperate pleas are the recurring invocations "hear" and "appear," which stand out clearly because they are repeatedly set as two emphatic eighth-note chords. The spirit of this movement seems to be far more related to the Gospel reading for the day, John 10:11–16, than to the Psalm. John 10:14 reads: "I am the Good Shepherd. I know my sheep and my sheep know me."

The pastoral idyll created by the flowing motion in the strings is interrupted by "hear" ("höre") and "appear" ("erscheine"). The oboes join the voices, and the listener recognizes the two-note "hear-appear" figure as having been first heard in the opening instrumental introduction. Perhaps Bach was aiming to evoke an image of carefree sheep enjoying the sounds and scents of an Arcadian hillside, with little thought of imminent death or danger that might be lurking around any corner. The vulnerable sheep need to know that the strong shepherd of their souls, the shepherd of Israel, will hear and appear when danger arises. The interjections are heard at least thirty-four times across the movement of 114 bars, leaving a lasting musical memory of this movement: "You, shepherd of Israel, hear, appear!"

2. Tenor recitative

| | |
|---|---|
| Der höchste Hirte sorgt vor mich, | The highest shepherd cares for me, |
| Was nützen meine Sorgen? | What use are my cares? |
| Es wird ja alle Morgen | Indeed, every morning |
| Des Hirten Güte neu. | The shepherd's loving kindnesses are new. |
| Mein Herz, so fasse dich, | My heart, then, take a grip on yourself, |
| Gott ist getreu. | God is faithful. |

Bach sets the opening words of this rhyming verse in the quasi-spoken form of a recitative, with the tenor as "me": "God is faithful, his mercies are new every morning." The voice is supported by the lightest of instrumental continuo lines, ensuring that the text is heard by everyone in the congregation. Bach reserves the musical action and emphasis for the final phrase "God is faithful" ("Gott ist getreu"). The continuo line breaks into eighth notes, and the tenor's lyrical melody on "getreu" ("faithful") is decorated and repeated three times, perhaps in reference to the threefold perfection of God's nature.

## 3. Tenor aria

| | |
|---|---|
| Verbirgt mein Hirte sich zu lange, | If my shepherd is hidden too long |
| Macht mir die Wüste allzu bange, | If the wilderness makes me too anxious, |
| Mein schwacher Schritt eilt dennoch fort. | My weak steps still hurry forward. |
| Mein Mund schreit nach dir, | My mouth cries to you, |
| Und du, mein Hirte, wirkst in mir | And you, my shepherd, work in me |
| Ein gläubig Abba durch dein Wort. | A believing "Abba" through your Word. |

The text of this aria repeats the longing wish expressed in the opening chorus that the shepherd will hear and appear, with the added anxiety of what would happen if "my" shepherd is "hidden" ("verbirgt"). What will I do if he does not appear, as "I" had requested in the opening chorus, and how long will it be before he appears, and how anxious will "I" feel in the meantime? Two oboes play almost nonstop, throughout the aria. The part writing is impeccable, but the relentless, reedy sonorities in this particular key of B minor are not ingratiating for the oboes of the time and create a mildly irritating and unrestful atmosphere. Bach works with the rhyme scheme of the first two lines, "lange" ("long") and "bange" ("anxious") embellished with sighing two- and three-bar phrases. The listener experiences the literal length of "lange" and the even greater length of the anxiety in "bange." The next prominent effect is "my mouth cries" ("schreit") when Bach gives the tenor an octave leap to a high F sharp, followed by a demanding decorated top A and G. This is guaranteed to resound throughout the church building, and to challenge the vocal abilities of the tenor soloist, embodying the cry for help. The first two lines are then repeated to a modified melody, with "lange" and "bange" taking even longer than they had the first time around. The aria ends with the opening six-bar instrumental *ritornello*. Interestingly, Bach chose not to emphasize the arguably more significant phrase "A believing 'Abba' through your Word." Instead, his focus is to help the congregation empathize with "my cry and the anxiety" when the Shepherd is hidden.

4. Bass recitative

| | |
|---|---|
| Ja, dieses Wort ist meiner Seelen Speise, | Yes, this Word is the food of my soul, |
| Ein Labsal meiner Brust, | A refreshment to my breast, |
| Die Weide, die ich meine Lust, | The pasture, that I call my delight, |
| Des Himmels Vorschmack, ja mein alles heiße. | A foretaste of heaven, indeed my all. |
| Ach! sammle nur, o guter Hirte, | Ah! Gather up, O Good Shepherd, |
| Uns Arme und Verirrte; | Us poor and straying ones; |
| Ach lass den Weg nur bald geendet sein | Ah, let our path soon be ended |
| Und führe uns in deinen Schafstall ein! | And lead us into your sheepfold! |

Next comes a rhyming verse that Bach sets as a bass recitative, using it to raise the brightness of the music to D major. This musical device creates a sense of optimism. In twelve short bars, the listener senses the comfort of being led by the Good Shepherd into the safety of the sheepfold.

5. Bass aria

| | |
|---|---|
| Beglückte Herde, Jesu Schafe, | Happy flock, Jesus's sheep, |
| Die Welt ist euch ein Himmelreich. | The world is to you a heavenly realm. |
| Hier schmeckt ihr Jesu Güte schon | Here you already taste Jesus' goodness |
| Und hoffet noch des Glaubens Lohn | And still hope for faith's reward |
| Nach einem sanften Todesschlafe. | After a sweet sleep of death. |

The dominant mood of this bass aria is the joyful innocence of the pastorale. It comments on Jesus' goodness to those who fall asleep in faith and wake up in the heavenly kingdom. There is no judgment or fear, either in the words or in their musical setting. The reassuring and tender sonorities of the upper strings are used to create a memorable, and elegantly constructed melody, with the first violin doubled on the oboe d'amore, the mellow-toned "oboe of love." Bach, the master of melodic permutation, composes a melody for the bass soloist that is a mirror image of the string theme. The contrary up-down motion, known as **melodic inversion**, can be seen in Example 5.1. Both musical lines begin on pitch A; the upper line ascends two triad steps, descends two scalic steps, ascends a third, then descends two scalic steps, while the bass melody does the opposite; the singer begins on pitch A, descends two triad steps, ascends two scalic steps, descends a third, then ascends two scalic steps, before uniting with the other instruments. It is like a photograph of a horizon, with the clouds reflected in the waters of a lake. This musical effect is repeated several times across the movement: an eight-note phrase in symmetrical contrary motion, clear for those with ears to hear. It perfectly captures the 1:1 symmetrical perfection of God's created order (see Chapter 1) and perhaps illustrates in music that heaven is reflected on earth here and now ("The world is to you a heavenly realm").

Example 5.1 Mirror image motion between the solo bass voice and the violins/oboes.

Bach sets the first two lines of text, section A, to thirty-two bars, and then changes the music for the next three lines of text, section B, taking it through the more unstable key of F sharp minor. He uses long high notes to emphasize "hoffet" ("hope"), low notes to color "Tode ("death"), and long notes to accompany "schlafe" ("sleep"). It is a huge relief when the music returns to section A in its optimistic key of D major, and the reassurance that "the world is to you a heavenly realm" ("Die Welt ist euch ein Himmelreich").

The rising tonal progression across the cantata continues to the very end when Bach chooses to set the final chorale in A major, which seems to express the ultimate reassurance of the versified words of Psalm 23.

6. Chorale

| | |
|---|---|
| Der Herr ist mein getreuer Hirt, | The Lord is my faithful shepherd |
| Dem ich mich ganz vertraue, | To whom I entrust myself completely |
| Zu Weid er mich, sein Schäflein, führt, | He leads me, his little sheep, |
| Auf schöner grünen Aue, | To a meadow in beautiful green pastures, |
| Zum frischen Wasser leit' er mich, | To fresh water he leads me |
| Mein Seel zu laben kräftiglich | To revive my soul mightily |
| Durchs selig Wort der Gnaden. | Through his blessed Word of grace. |

This chorale stanza is verse one of Cornelius Becker's versification of Psalm 23:1–3a from his much-loved collection of the Bible's 150 Psalms, which he put into modern rhyming German to help them to be sung more easily to well-known Lutheran melodies (Figures 5.2a and 5.2b). Originally published in 1602, Becker's hymn book was reprinted in numerous editions throughout the seventeenth and into the early eighteenth centuries. Gottfried Vopelius included it

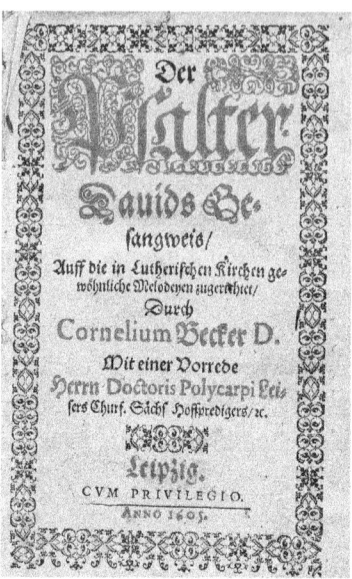

**Figure 5.2a** Title page of one of the many editions of Cornelius Becker's transcriptions of the Psalms, *Der Psalter Davids Gesangweis*, originally published in 1602. https://digital.ub.uni-leipzig.de/object/viewid/0000000188. Universitätsbibliothek Leipzig.

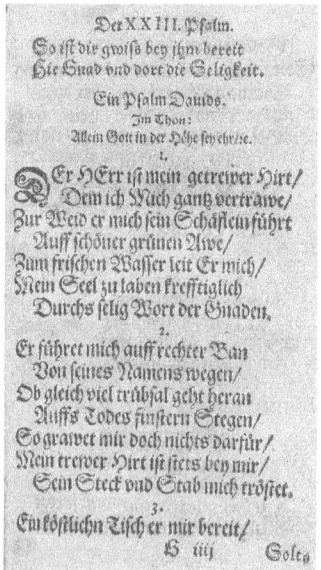

**Figure 5.2b** Two verses of Becker's Psalm 23, n.p. https://digital.ub.uni-leipzig.de/object/viewid/0000000188. Universitätsbibliothek Leipzig.

on page 666 of his *Neu Leipziger Gesangbuch* (1682), used by Bach's Leipzig congregation.

The key sequence across this cantata seems designed to underscore the progression of the text. It opens with the chorus in G major, a key with one sharp; the first aria and subsequent recitative are in B minor and D major respectively, keys with two sharps; and the final chorale is in A major, a key with three sharps. This movement-wise progression through the **circle of fifths** is extraordinary in Bach's cantatas, and I suspect it was a device also aimed to move the listener emotionally, so that without knowing why, personal confidence in the Good Shepherd would increase over the course of the cantata.

## Bach's Life Circumstances as He Wrote about the Good Shepherd

Alongside producing a cantata for every Sunday and feast day of the church year, Bach was very busy at home in the family quarters at the St. Thomas School, where his responsibilities included taking turns to keep order among the boarders, training the choirboys musically, making sure there was enough income to cover the family bills, and looking out for career and educational opportunities for his children.

Cantata 104 was first performed on Sunday, 23 April 1724, during a sunny period in the Bach family household. Having just celebrated their second wedding anniversary on 3 December 1723, Anna Magdalena and Johann Sebastian had been blessed in the early spring of 1723 with a first-born daughter, Christiana Sophia Henrietta. Their first son, Gottfried Heinrich, arrived scarcely twelve months later, on 27 February 1724. Both seemed to be thriving; Christiana was a chatting toddler, and Gottfried at two months looked to become a strong child. We know with hindsight that Gottfried did not develop mentally to full maturity, but in April 1724 this was probably not yet detectable. The twenty-three-year-old Anna Magdalena too seems to have bounced back quickly after the pregnancies. All this was great cause for rejoicing and gratitude when childbirth-related complications were a major cause of infant and maternal mortality. "The shepherd's loving kindnesses are new every morning! . . . God is faithful, faithful, God is faithful," as Bach made his tenor sing so lyrically.

After the excitement of winning the audition and being elected to become the next Leipzig Thomaskantor, there was the settling-in process at the Thomas School. Pastor Christian Weiss, representing Superintendent Salomon Deyling (1677–1755), endorsed the new appointment and Bach was to be answerable to the legal arm of the diocesan consistory. In June 1724 Deyling reported to the consistory, probably at Bach's request, that the non-musical teaching duties (Latin) would be carried out by a substitute and not by Bach himself. To everyone's relief this potentially problematic stipulation was accepted. The children from Bach's first marriage were also settling down in Leipzig. His eldest daughter, Catharina Dorothea (1708–1774), would have been helping Anna Magdalena with domestic duties as well as learning social graces, particularly dancing and singing; twelve-year old Wilhelm Friedemann (1710–1784) and nine-year old Carl Philipp Emanuel (1714–1788) were enrolled into their respective classes at the St. Thomas School, while eight-year old Johann Gottfried Bernhard (1715–1739) seems to have waited a further year before becoming a pupil there.

At the same time that Bach was reflecting on and composing Cantata 104, he was working on his Passion according to St. John. The text booklets for Good Friday 1724 had been printed, giving St. Thomas Church as the location, whereas Deyling, who was the Superintendent of the Leipzig churches, wanted the new passion to be performed first at St. Nicholas. The consistory met on 3 April 1724, just four days before the St. John Passion was to be performed. Disaster was averted and a quick resolution found: the council agreed to pay for a flyer to be reprinted with the correct location, the choir gallery at St. Nicholas would be rearranged to make space for the musicians, and the harpsichord would be repaired. These are typical of the time-consuming frustrations that Bach faced, recognizable to many a composer and performer producing a complex world première. By comparison, preparations for Misericordias Domini, just two Sundays later, must have felt like a walk in the park.

Anna Magdalena was still singing professionally at this stage, invited occasionally to travel away from Leipzig to give guest performances. The Cöthen court accounts show that Bach and his wife were paid for performances on 18 July 1724, when Gottfried was almost five months old, and on 15 December 1725, when their third child, Christian Gottlieb (1725–1728), was eight months old. As far as we know, Anna Magdalena was excluded from performing in her husband's church cantatas in Leipzig because she was a woman. However, it is heartening to know that she could, to some extent, continue her singing career elsewhere.

Bach was to compose two more cantatas for Misericordias Domini. The next was Cantata (BWV) 85 'Ich bin ein guter Hirt', performed on Sunday, 15 April 1725, and for which Bach's original score and parts have all survived. It was based on the same Bible readings as Cantata 104, and once again it is not known who wrote the libretto. Like Cantata 104, Cantata 85 also had six movements, used the first verse of Cornelius Becker's versified Psalm 23, included two oboes, and had a movement in triple time. Despite these similarities, the two cantatas sound entirely different. On the first page of the full score of Cantata 85, above the first line of music, Bach wrote: "J. J. Dominica Misericordias Domini Ich bin ein guter Hirt." The first movement opens with an aria for solo bass, "I Am a Good Shepherd," in the voice of Christ, *Vox Christi*. The second movement is for solo alto, "Jesus Is a Good Shepherd," and the third movement is for solo soprano, "The Lord Is My True Shepherd," from the first verse of Becker's adaptation of Psalm 23, which had been set a year earlier as the final movement of Cantata 104. The soprano is given a lilting melody usually associated with "Allein Gott in der Höh' sei Ehr." Bach had improvised upon this melody endless times at the keyboard, and he was to publish three settings of it in 1735 in the third part of his *Clavier Übung*, which is, as its title page reads, a collection "consisting of various preludes on the catechism and other hymns for the organ." A recitative for tenor then follows. It takes up the theme of the images from Pfeiffer's treasury (Figure 5.1), focusing on the faithless hireling who sleeps or runs away, leaving the sheep unprotected. This is followed by a tenor aria in triple movement, affirming the power of love. The progression runs from Jesus' statement ("I am a Good Shepherd"), through the factual "Jesus is a Good Shepherd" to the more personally affirmative "The Lord is my true Shepherd." On 14 April 1725, the very day before Misericordias Domini, Christian Gottlieb was born. Perhaps during those anxious hours of labor, the reassuring phrase "Ich bin ein guter Hirt" and music from the newly composed cantata came unbidden to the watching parents.

By summer 1725 the honeymoon period of Bach's Leipzig job was very definitely over, and sources suggest that the financial strains of living in a cosmopolitan city were beginning to tell. Bach submitted requests for payment for the university church services, eventually taking his case against the university to the Elector of Saxony, who was also the King of Poland, with three letters dated 14 September 1725, 3 November 1725, and the most extensive one dated 31 December 1725. There is also a letter to his former schoolmate Georg Erdmann (1682–1736), showing how delighted Bach was to receive greetings from his friend by word of mouth. They had exchanged news, and updates on their respective movements since late teenage days, and had been out of touch until 28 October 1730, when Bach turned to Erdmann to explore the possibility of moving away from Leipzig. Documented circumstances suggest that the years between 1725 and 1730 had been particularly demanding for Bach. The family continued to increase in size; little

Elisabeth Juliana Frederica arrived a month before Misericordias Domini Sunday, on 5 April 1726, and this was the same year that Bach decided to perform eighteen cantatas by his Meiningen relative Johann Ludwig Bach (1677–1731) rather to compose his own.

In 1726 Misericordias Domini Sunday fell on 5 May, when the Leipzig congregations heard J. L. Bach's 'Und ich will ihnen einen einigen Hirten erwecken', for which Bach wrote out the score and had the parts copied. There was a creative exchange system of music-for-hire in central Germany at the time, and it is possible that the two Bach relatives availed themselves of this service for a period. Alternatively, it may have been a private arrangement, whether as an exchange, or a goodwill gesture by this Meiningen relative grateful to have his works performed in the prestigious central Leipzig city churches.

We do not know which cantatas Bach performed on the Shepherd Sunday for the next four years. It was not until 1731 that he set his hand to compose a new shepherd cantata: 'Der Herr ist mein getreuer Hirt', Cantata (BWV) 112, which turned out to be his last cantata for Misericordias Domini. It was composed for 8 April 1731 and is quite different from Cantatas 104 and 85. It is a chorale cantata based on a versification of Psalm 23. This time the versification of the psalm was not by Becker, but from a five-verse hymn, possibly by Wolfgang Meuslin (1497–1563), which had been in the Lutheran hymnals since 1530s. Rather than transforming the chorale verses into recitative and aria texts, as was the case for his 1724/1725 chorale cantatas, the text for Cantata 112 sets the five chorale verses unaltered to a melody by Nikolaus Decius (1485–1541). In the second movement Bach introduced the mellow sounds of oboes d'amore in compound time. He also used two horns in the first chorus, which is unexpected and has caused some scholars to suggest that this movement was an adaptation of a previously composed piece with a different text and for another occasion (see Chapter 1), although this cannot be verified.

Why Bach didn't repeat his Cantatas 104 and 85 in the intervening years is an intriguing question. Perhaps he did, but there is no hard evidence in the surviving original scores or parts to suggest it. There is so much that is not known. Bach's evolving creative focus can be seen in his production of self-sponsored keyboard publications that began with the first partita (BWV 825) in 1726 and continued with four other partitas (BWV 826–829), until 1731, when, instead of publishing the sixth partita (BWV 830) individually, he published all six partitas together as a complete collection, *Clavier Übung*, Opus 1 (BWV 825–830). Bach would have been preparing this when he wrote his final Misericordias Domini, Cantata 112, for Sunday, 8 April 1731.

For many centuries, David's Psalm "The Lord is my Shepherd" have been the go-to prayer, or mantra, for men and women of all faiths facing pain, distress, and anxiety. In Cantata 104 Bach brought into being music with voices and instruments that underscore the spiritual reassurance and comfort of these beloved words. In today's world of troubled news, daily reports of international unrest, and global uncertainties, the kindly music and encouraging text of this cantata could become a source of great consolation. It deserves to be better known, either in Bach's original version, or adapted appropriately (see Chapter 7) so as to inspire and spread its enheartening message of timeless goodness.

## Suggestions for Further Reading

For further details on the Shepherd cantatas see Hans-Joachim Schulze and James A. Brokaw II on https://doi.org/10.21900/wd.21, and Alfred Dürr (Oxford, 2005), 298–305. For more on Lutheranism see Michael Marissen (Oxford, 2016), 11–59, and Robin A. Leaver (2021), 217–247. For Bach's Calov Bible and its context see Albert Clement, ed. (2022). New insights into Anna Magdalena's life and career can be found in the blogspot by Eberhard Spree https://www.anna-magdalena-bach.com/en.

# 6

# Candlemas in Leipzig

'Ich habe genung'

The original score and parts for Cantata (BWV) 82, 'Ich habe genung' (I Have Enough) have survived in full, which is relatively rare for Bach's compositional materials. They are kept in the Berlin State Library (Staatsbibliothek zu Berlin), shelfmark D-B Mus.ms Bach P 114, and St 54 Fasz.1–4, and are freely accessible online (see Select Bibliography: Bach's Scores and Parts). The score is in Bach's handwriting and enclosed in a paper wrapper with a title written by his second son, Carl Philipp Emanuel (1714–1788). One can imagine the family collaboration: the detail-oriented young man helping organize his father's study, replacing scuffed and dog-eared covers while putting the scores and music in order. Neither father nor son wrote a date on the music to show when it was composed or first performed, but the watermark on the paper together with Bach's handwriting suggests that it was composed in early 1727.

Across the top of the first page of the full score Bach wrote *J. J. Festo Purificationis Mariae. Cantata* (Figure 6.1), meaning a cantata for the festival of the purification of Mary. Unusually he uses the term "Cantata" here, most probably because it is for a single solo voice, which makes it more song-like than the more usual cantata forces of several soloists and chorus. Purification is celebrated on 2 February. The festival is also frequently known as Candlemas, or as the Presentation of Christ. The invocation *J. J.* ("Jesus, help!") was particularly appropriate for this occasion because the prescribed introductory psalm, Psalm 12, begins "Hilff, Herr!" ("Help, Lord!"). At the foot of the first page of the score, Bach wrote: "NB. The vocal line must be transposed for Bass" (Figure 6.1). This is because he

**Figure 6.1** Bach's 1727 autograph of the opening of Cantata (BWV) 82, Mus.ms. Bach P 114. http://resolver.staatsbibliothek-berlin.de/SBB0001D6DB00000000. Staatsbibliothek zu Berlin, Preussischer Kulturbesitz.

had written out the first movement for alto soloist, and then for unknown reasons changed his mind and wrote the remaining movements for bass solo. Possible reasons for this are given below (see "Contexts of the First Performances"). The exchange of bass voice for alto was feasible without rewriting the score because the two voices have a similar range although an octave apart, and both sit particularly comfortably in the key of C minor. The score ends with the abbreviation *S.D.G.* (see Chapter 1).

In 1727 Candlemas happened to fall on a Sunday and so it is likely that the cantata would have been heard in Leipzig at the main early service at St. Nicholas Church and at the vesper service at St. Thomas Church.

Over the course of several years Bach adapted the cantata for different solo voices and different solo instruments, which also caused him to transpose the score to a different key. Evidence from the parts suggest the following performances:

- 2 February 1727 in C minor, possibly first conceived for alto, and then changed to bass soloist.
- 2 February 1730–1731 transposed up to E minor to suit a soprano soloist.
- 2 February 1736 in the original key of C minor suitable for a mezzo-soprano or high alto.
- 2 February 1746–1747 in the original version of C minor for bass solo.

The surviving instrumental and solo vocal parts are not all from the first performance. The C minor version has a solo oboe part for the first movement, and a solo oboe da caccia for the third movement, both in Bach's handwriting. The E minor version has a solo transverse flute part for movements 1, 3, and 5 in the handwriting of Christoph Friedrich Meißner (1716–?), a student at St. Thomas School. It seems plausible that the arrangements were chosen according to which vocal soloist was available.

The 2 February date given above for the performances, and standardly recognized in Bach research, assumes that the cantata was heard in the services for the festival of the Purification of the Blessed Virgin Mary, but as there are no dates on the scores it might also have been performed on other occasions. At some point after 1727 and before 1740 Anna Magdalena Bach transcribed the second and third movements into the later of her two surviving music notebooks, the 1725 *Clavierbüchlein*, (Figure 6.2) as a song for soprano solo in E minor with a figured bassline to be played on a home keyboard instrument. We know that before her marriage she had been a successful and accomplished professional soprano, and she might well have sung this at family gatherings, possibly at private parties or functions, or as part of the domestic devotions

**Figure 6.2** Page 111 from Anna Magdalena Bach's 1725 *Clavierbüchlein*, Mus.ms. Bach P 225. http://resolver.staatsbibliothek-berlin.de/SBB0001D81000270000. Staatsbibliothek zu Berlin, Preussischer Kulturbesitz.

of the Bach household. The chamber ensemble scoring with a solo voice and a solo, so-called *obbligato*, instrument make it supremely adaptable to different performing spaces, while the text itself is also appropriate for many different occasions.

## What Is Candlemas?

Forty days after Christmas it was the custom across Europe for candlelit processions to make their way through villages and towns toward churches, dispelling the frosty darkness of winter and creating a radiance at the center of each community. It was this display of light that caused the festival also to be known as Candlemas. After the reformation in the sixteenth century, the emphasis of this ancient festival of Mary was changed, transforming it into a more Lutheran festival of Christ, with the focus on Jesus, "the one light to lighten the Gentiles." In accordance with Levitical statutes, a woman would be pronounced ritually clean if she offered a lamb and a dove (or two doves) for sacrifice at the tent of meeting (Leviticus 12: 1–8) forty days after childbirth. In the Western church tradition, the fortieth day after Jesus' birth fell on 2 February, the day chosen to celebrate Mary and Joseph taking baby Jesus to the temple where they encountered the elderly Simeon. The incident is described in Luke 2:22–32, the Gospel reading prescribed for the feast day in the Leipzig lectionary. Verses 25–32 read:

> Now there was a man in Jerusalem called Simeon, who was righteous and devout. He was waiting for the consolation of Israel, and the Holy Spirit was on him. It had been revealed to him by the Holy Spirit that he would not die before he had seen the Lord's Messiah. Moved by the Spirit, he went into the temple courts. When the parents brought in the child Jesus to do for him what the custom of the Law required, Simeon took him in his arms and praised God, saying: "Sovereign Lord, as you have promised, you

may now dismiss your servant in peace. For my eyes have seen your salvation, which you have prepared in the sight of all nations: a light for revelation to the Gentiles, and the glory of your people Israel."

Simeon's song of praise is often known as the "Nunc dimittis" and is perhaps best known in the King James translation: "Lord, now lettest thou thy Servant depart in peace, according to thy Word." Inspired by the Holy Spirit, Simeon's prophetic identification of the baby Jesus as the Christ marks a paradigm shift from the old order of the Law, in which personal forgiveness required the death of animals, to the arrival of a new order, in which Jesus would offer himself as the perfect sacrifice, as the Easter, or Paschal, lamb. The gentle narrative of the blessed newborn baby and his grateful earthly parents, Mary and Joseph, changes radically when Simeon forewarns of the agonies that will befall Mary, in Luke 2:35: "And a sword will pierce your own soul too."

By January 1727 Bach had already composed two cantatas for Candlemas: Cantata (BWV) 83 'Erfreute Zeit im neuen Bunde' composed for 2 February 1724, and for 2 February 1725 Cantata (BWV) 125 'Mit Fried und Freud ich fahr dahin', a chorale cantata based on Martin Luther's hymn of the same name. By 1727 he had provided almost three years of weekly liturgical cantatas for his Leipzig churches; additionally, he had composed and performed a first and second version of his Passion according to St. John, and he was contemplating the first version of his Passion according to St. Matthew. There is no doubt that he was deeply versed in the theology of the passion story and all its characters, including the role of Mary, and the prophecy of Simeon.

The text of Cantata 82 was in all probability written for Bach by the theology student Christoph Birkmann (1703–1773), who was in Leipzig for three years (1724–1727) to study and observe the music performed in the churches. He also seems to have honed his creative poetic skills during this time (see "More on the Text and Its Structure" below). The libretto contains strong imagery of a physical relationship with Jesus: Verse 1 reads: "I have taken the Savior . . . into my eager arms"; "I have beheld him; my faith has pressed Jesus to my heart"; Verse 2 "Jesus would be my own and I am his. I hold him in faith"; Verse 4 "My God when will the beautiful 'now' come, when I will rest . . . there with you in the bosom." Belief in the physical resurrection of the body was a given for Lutherans of this period, and it required no justification or detailed explanation. The creaturely warmth of the relationship with the Savior is portrayed intimately. Far from the fatalistic, practical, or sentimental views of death common in the twenty-first century, this eighteenth-century poem faces death head on, allowing the sorrow of human mortality to coexist with unwavering confidence in everlasting life after the body has been shed. Birkmann's theology afforded him the conviction that knowing the Savior, knowing the cost He bore to buy salvation for the world, and the grace of eternal life, was enough. "It is enough."

## From Text to Music, Movement by Movement

Although in Leipzig the festival of the Purification of Mary was primarily a celebration of Christ, Bach very definitely chose to empathize with the feminine in this cantata. As the first-person singular voice is used throughout, a musical setting for solo voice was an obvious choice, in place of Bach's more usual four-part chorus and various soloists. The next decision was to select the instrumental forces. Bach opted for a small string ensemble and a solo instrument. The final decision was the form and structure of the cantata; this too needed to be fitting for the intimate message of the poetry. Its five stanzas suited a cantata in five movements, and Bach turned these into a satisfying formal symmetry: Aria–Recitative–Aria–Recitative–Aria, which he also emphasized by the symmetry of their time signatures: 3/8–C–C–C–3/8. See

Chapter 1 for more on the significance and theological meaning of symmetry.

The cantata opens with a lengthy solo melody, played in different versions on either an oboe or a flute, accompanied by a string ensemble. This instrumental section comes to an end with a pause on bar 33. To this point there have been no words, until the soloist enters in bar 34, when he/she sings that it is enough to take the Savior, the hope of the devout, into "my" arms. Throughout this aria the opening instrumental phrase is associated with the phrase "Ich habe genung" ("I have enough").

1. Aria

| | |
|---|---|
| Ich habe genung, | I have enough; |
| Ich habe den Heyland, das Hoffen der Frommen, | I have taken the Savior, the hope of the devout, |
| Auf meine begierigen Arme genommen; | Into my eager arms; |
| Ich habe genung. | I have enough! |
| Ich hab ihn erblickt, | I have seen him; |
| Mein Glaube hat Jesum ans Herze gedrückt; | My faith has pressed Jesus to my heart; |
| Nun wünsch ich noch heute mit Freuden | Now I wish, with joy, this very day |
| Von hinnen zu scheiden: | To depart from here: |
| Ich habe genung. | I have enough! |

The first line of the text recalls Jacob's words in Genesis 33:11, "Ich habe alles genung" and in Genesis 45:28 where he says, "Es ist genung." The biblical verses in Genesis and Luke's gospel are united by the thematic parallel of God's grace: both Jacob, in Genesis, and Simeon, in the gospel of Luke, are happy to die in response to the fulfilment of their longings. This theme is the topic of the opening phrase of the famous funeral hymn text "Es ist genung"

("It is enough") by Franz Joachim Burmeister (1633–1672). When Birkmann wrote his reflection he decided not to use the third-person singular, but to use the "I" form, as did Jacob in Genesis 33:11, "Ich habe alles genung." In Cantata 82, it is not clear if "I" is Simeon, or if the "I" of the soloist and solo instrument represents every believer. Perhaps it is both.

The opening, yearning instrumental phrase is remarkably similar in shape, structure, minor mode, compound three time, and mood to the opening of three other arias by Bach. The decorated ascent spanning a sixth is heard in the aria "Zerfließe, mein Herze" in the St. John Passion (BWV 245/35), in the aria "Erbarme dich" that was to be included in the St. Matthew Passion (BWV 244/39), performed for the first time on Good Friday, 11 April 1727, and it is also heard in the duet aria "Wann kommst du, mein Heil" in Cantata (BWV) 140 'Wachet auf, ruft uns die Stimme' composed in 1731. The opening phrases are not identical, but the similarity of figuration in their context suggests that the decorated ascending sixth was the starting point for an expression of deep longing. For example, the aria from the St. John Passion, "Zerfließe, mein Herze, in Fluten der Zähren" ("Dissolve, my heart, in floods of tears") for high soprano in F minor, follows the tenor's dramatic description of the aftershock of the death of Jesus: "While the whole world suffers as Jesus suffers, the sun is clothed in mourning, the temple curtain is torn, rocks split, the earth shakes, and graves open because they see their creator's body growing cold." The tenor asks: "My heart, what will you do?" and the answer is given by the soprano in the decorated ascending sixth phrase: "Dissolve, my heart, in floods of tears to honor the Almighty! Tell the world and heaven your distress: your Jesus is dead." Bach's attempt to encapsulate this cosmic event, the profundity of which no theologian has yet captured in words, was to choose a decorated ascending sixth in minor mode. Because composers carry ideas and fragments that gestate and reappear unbidden at appropriate moments, it is not surprising that Bach used this heart-rending figure in his expression of Simeon's prophetic song. The first time the exquisite melodic motive is heard in Cantata 82 one might sense a foreshadowing of the indescribable trauma that Mary was to experience thirty-three years later.

A similar melodic figure appears in "Erbarme dich, mein Gott, um meiner Zähren Willen" ("Have mercy, my God, for the sake of my tears") in the St. Matthew Passion, once more capturing a moment of heart-breaking distress. The alto soloist sings the words in B minor, in compound time, with a solo violin, using the same intervallic pattern of a broken rising sixth, giving voice to Peter's tears immediately after he has denied Christ three times, after he has heard the cock crowing, and then remembering how Jesus had foretold his devastating denial. Bach was most probably working on his St. Matthew Passion in January 1727 alongside writing 'Ich habe genung'. This could be one of the reasons why he automatically wrote the first movement of Cantata 82 for solo alto, before changing it to solo bass.

No exact timeline or proof is required to observe this kind of musical cross-fertilization, nor can a cold analytical description capture the musical expression of deep sorrow that these phrases contain. The common minor key, the yearning phrase with an upbeat to the tonic keynote, leading to the third note of the scale and descending again to the tonic, all in compound time, is an accurate technical description. But it is the living embodiment of the performers, the breath traveling through the oboist, flautist, and singer that brings the music to life, tapping into and expressing the broken fragility of the crushed eyewitness.

The opening four lines of the poem is in the symmetrical poetic "head form," discussed in Chapter 1. The words "Ich habe genung" occur three times in the libretto, whereas Bach asks his soloist to sing the phrase ten times. This opening phrase is then adapted in line 5, transforming sorrow into joy with "Ich hab ihn erblickt!" ("I have seen him!"). This causes us to hear the subsequent repetition of the opening instrumental introduction entirely differently, knowing that this final time "I" have actually seen him!

The layout of the first movement suggests that Bach might have planned a further layer of meaning in its structure. Although modern editions frequently mask Bach's intentions, the two surviving solo voice parts indicate thirty-three bars of rest at the beginning and thirty-three bars at the end of this first movement (Figure 6.3), a number that may have been an intentional reference to Jesus' age when he was crucified, an allusion also perhaps to Simeon's prophetic words to Mary.

> Bars 1–33 (33 bars) pause: Instrumental solo.
> Bars 34–75 (42 bars): I have taken the Savior, the hope of the devout, Into my eager arms; I have enough!
> Bars 76–106 (31 bars): Instrumental solo.
> Bars 107–176 (70 bars): I have seen him; My faith has pressed Jesus to my heart; Now I wish, with joy, this very day, to depart from here: I have enough!
> Bars 176/7–end (33 bars): Instrumental solo with an overlap of the soloist's final note.

However, it could only be an intentional emblematic allusion if Bach thought that Jesus died at the age of thirty-three. Investigating this potentially significant detail led me to discover the following. Jesus' age is referred to in Luke 3:23 when he began his public ministry: "And Jesus entered in his thirtieth year," but this does not give his age when he was crucified. Abraham Calov commented in parenthesis at this point in his amplified Bible: "(his age, which was the 4030th year of the World)." Many Lutherans in Bach's time still followed an ancient tradition of setting the date of creation at four thousand years before the birth of Jesus. However, the tradition that Jesus died at the age of thirty-three turns out to be more recent. (I am grateful to George van Kooten, Lady Margaret's Professor of Divinity at the University of Cambridge, for pursuing and solving the early history of this idea for me.) The

144　BACH'S *CHURCH CANTATAS*

**Figure 6.3**　Bass solo part for Cantata (BWV) 82, copied by J. S. Bach and by J. C. Altnickol, c. 1746–1748. Mus.ms. Bach St 54. http://resolver.staatsbibliothek-berlin.de/SBB0001E88400000000. Staatsbibliothek zu Berlin, Preussischer Kulturbesitz.

first written record is from the mid-fourth century, when Cyril of Jerusalem (312–386) wrote in his twelfth Catechetical lecture, 12:33: "The Savior passed the nine months period in the womb of the Virgin; but the Lord was a man for thirty-three years." Cyril wrote in Greek, and his works were still available and of interest in Bach's time. In fact, the Superintendent of Bach's Leipzig churches, Salomon Deyling (1677–1755), examined a sixty-page thesis on the life and writings of Cyril, published in Leipzig in 1726, and we know from the auction catalogue of Deyling's library after his death that he owned (page 65, item 1068) the *Opera Omnia* of Cyril's works, published by Milles of Oxford in 1703, interestingly earmarked by the auctioneers as "Exemplum Splendidum" and sold for the princely sum of 5 Thalers 4 Groschen. Deyling also owned (page 68, item 1139) a copy of the French translation of the Catechetical lectures published in Paris 1715. However, the tradition that Jesus died at the age of thirty-three was more widely transmitted in early Latin writings than in Greek, and by the 1500s was also firmly established in German-speaking Lutheran publications. The answer to my query was found finally in Heinrich Bünting's *Itinerarium Sacrae Scripturae* (originally published in 1582 but translated and reprinted in many languages up to the 1750s). Bach owned a copy of this volume, and he could have read that Jesus was thirty-three years old on Good Friday, when he was crucified (Figure 6.4).

Another potentially significant number in the first movement of Cantata 82 is 70, the numerical value of the name "Jesus" (see Chapter 1), and the number of bars that Bach chose for the final section of text "I have seen him; My faith has pressed Jesus to my heart; Now I wish with joy this very day to depart from here. I have enough." Bach had used the number 70 very obviously in 1725, in the central movement of Cantata (BWV) 42, a seven-movement cantata to celebrate the resurrected, but not yet ascended, Jesus. The disciples were afraid, gathered in a room behind a locked door, when Jesus appeared, and "stood in the middle of them" ("kam

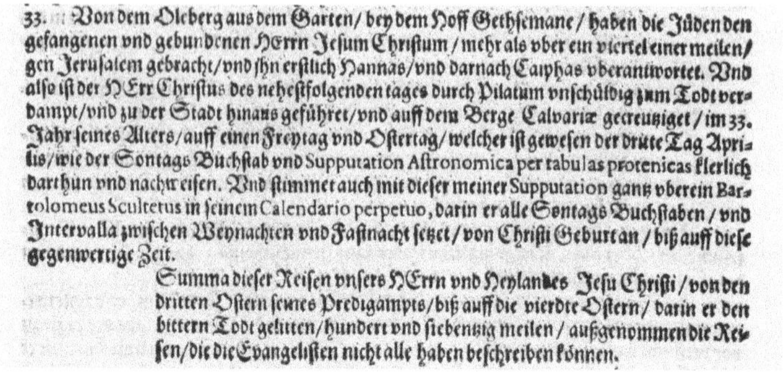

> 33. Von dem Oleberg aus dem Garten/ bey dem Hoff Gethsemane/ haben die Jüden den gefangenen vnd gebundenen Herrn Jesum Christum/ mehr als vber ein viertel einer meilen/ gen Jerusalem gebracht/vnd jhn erstlich Hannas/vnd darnach Caiphas vberantwortet. Vnd also ist der HErr Christus des nehestfolgenden tages durch Pilatum vnschüldig zum Todt verdampt/vnd zu der Stadt hinaus geführet/vnd auff dem Berge Calvariæ gecreutziget/im 33. Jahr seines Alters/auff einen Freytag vnd Ostertag/welcher ist gewesen der drute Tag Aprilis/wie der Sontags Buchstab vnd Supputation Astronomica per tabulas ptotenicas klerlich darthun vnd nachweisen. Vnd stimmet auch mit dieser meiner Supputation gantz vberein Bartolomeus Scultetus in seinem Calendario perpetuo, darin er alle Sontags Buchstaben/ vnd Intervalla zwischen Weynachten vnd Fastnacht setzet/von Christi Geburt an/biß auff diese gegenwertige Zeit.
>
> Summa dieser Reisen vnsers HErrn vnd Heylandes Jesu Christi/von den dritten Ostern seines Predigampts/biß auff die vierdte Ostern/darin er den bittern Todt gelitten/hundert vnd siebentzig meilen/auffgenommen die Reisen/die die Evangelisten nicht alle haben beschreiben können.

Figure 6.4 Heinrich Bünting, *Itinerarium Novi Testamentae* (1650), 28. https://opendata2.uni-halle.de//handle/1516514412012/33009. Halle (Saale) Universitäts- und Landesbibliothek Sachsen-Anhalt.

Jesus und trat mitten ein"). The symmetrical center of this cantata is the fourth movement with the text "Verzage nicht, o Häuflein klein": "Do not lose heart, oh little flock; although your enemies want to utterly destroy you and seek your downfall, which you are so distressed and fearful about, it will not last long," comforting and reassuring words of Jesus that Bach set to seventy bars. Jesus' physical presence is similarly described in this section of Cantata 82. The seventy-bar section can be clearly seen in the notation of the original vocal parts: a section of twenty-nine bars vocal solo, thirteen bars instrumental interlude, and twenty-eight bars vocal solo. Not that anyone other than a copyist checking bars would notice the number. But Bach knew, if this was an intentional compositional device, and his savior knew too, remembering that Jesus was the acknowledged source of help when he began composing the cantata (Figure 6.1 above). Although the entire cantata can be understood as a celebration of Christ, it is this seventy-bar section of text in the first movement that contains the most direct reference to the personal presence of Jesus: "I have seen him; My faith has pressed Jesus to my heart."

The simple texture of the subsequent recitative clears the soundscape and our emotions, to then establish the storyline. We now know that "I" is not Simeon, but that "I" is the believer who is responding "with Simeon" to the joy of the consolation of Jesus.

**2. Recitative**

| | |
|---|---|
| Ich habe genung! | I have enough. |
| Mein Trost ist nur allein, | My one and only consolation is |
| Dass Jesus mein und ich sein eigen möchte sein. | That Jesus would be my own and I his. |
| Im Glauben halt ich ihn, | I hold him in faith; |
| Da seh ich auch mit Simeon | Thus, with Simeon, I, too, already see |
| Die Freude jenes Lebens schon. | The joy of that life. |
| Lasst uns mit diesem Manne ziehn! | Let us go with this man! |
| Ach! möchte mich von meines Leibes Ketten | Ah, that from my body's chains |
| Der Herr erretten! | The Lord would rescue me! |
| Ach! wäre doch mein Abschied hier, | Ah, were indeed my leave-taking here, |
| Mit Freuden sagt ich, Welt, zu dir: | I would say with joy to you, world: |
| Ich habe genung! | I have enough! |

The expression in these fourteen short bars is achieved through varying speeds and textures. The phrase "Let us go with this man" is musically expressed by a walking movement in the **continuo** line; and the words "with joy" are emphasized because the soloist sings an exuberant sixteenth-note figure that reaches to the highest note in the movement before descending stepwise, a musical gesture that might express the joy of the believer departing this world.

## 3. Aria

| | |
|---|---|
| Schlummert ein, ihr matten Augen, | Fall into slumber, you weary eyes, |
| Fallet sanft und selig zu! | Droop gently and blissfully shut. |
| Welt, ich bleibe nicht mehr hier, | World, I will remain here no longer; |
| Hab ich doch kein Teil an dir, | I have indeed no share in you |
| Das der Seele könnte taugen. | That could be fit for my soul. |
| Hier muss ich das Elend bauen, | Here [on earth] I must build up misery, |
| Aber dort, dort werd ich schauen | But there [in heaven], there I will look upon |
| Süssen Frieden, stille Ruh. | Sweet peace, quiet rest. |

The recitative is followed immediately by yet another exquisite aria, frequently known as the "slumber aria" given its similarities to other cradle arias such as "Schlafe, mein Liebster" from the Christmas Oratorio, BWV 248. Most lullabies use the major key, because the major mode is thought to contribute to happy, secure, and peaceful sleep. The opening aria had been in wistful minor mode. The mood lifts as soon as this second aria begins in its major key, giving a positive emotional advantage and impetus even though the listener may not understand how or why. The largely stepwise melody of "Schlummert ein" opens with a rhythmic rocking on the first beat caused by a syncopated stepwise up-down figure. The major key combined with this lilting, lullaby-like phrase may be one reason why many modern listeners find the movement so restful and reassuring.

Bach's division of the eight-line text is quite unusual. He could have set the words just once, or emphasized the rhyme scheme. Instead, he chose to make the first two lines the focal point of the aria, repeating the words and its melody numerous times. The aria begins with the instruments playing the nine-bar melody, so that the tune is already familiar to the listener before the soloist gives it words. The soloist sings for eighteen bars, before the instruments repeat the opening nine bars. Bach then compresses the next three lines of text into a twelve-bar section of new music, followed then by a modified version of the familiar melody, again to the words "Schlummert ein." The final three lines of text are set to new music before the aria repeats the opening 9:18:9 bars. Pause indications interrupt the regular pulse of the aria five times, halting the onward momentum as if enacting the in-between state of almost, but not quite, having fallen asleep.

4. Recitative

| | |
|---|---|
| Mein Gott, wenn kömmt das schöne: Nun!, | My God, when will the beautiful "Now" come, |
| Da ich im Friede fahren werde | When I will go in peace, |
| Und in dem Sande kühler Erde | And rest in the sand of the cold earth |
| Und dort bei dir im Schosse ruhn? | And there with you in the bosom? |
| Der Abschied ist gemacht, | I have taken my leave, |
| Welt, gute Nacht! | World, good night. |

Bach set the fourth stanza as a short recitative. The words "When I will go in peace" recall the opening of Simeon's song: "Lord now let your servant depart in peace," although here they are combined with the more physical comfort of resting in God's bosom, like a child being comforted by its mother.

The text is heard clearly here because of the strikingly minimal continuo accompaniment, contrasting strongly with the full-bodied lyricism of the previous movement. Bach gives prominence to "nun" ("now") and "ruhn" ("rest") in this short movement. The high note of "nun" is emphasized by an unexpected upward leap of a sixth onto the first beat of the second bar, shocking the listener out of any lingering slumber.

5. Aria

| | |
|---|---|
| Ich freue mich auf meinen Tod, | I look forward to my death; |
| Ach! hätt er sich schon eingefunden. | Ah, if only it had taken place already. |
| Da entkomm ich aller Not, | There I will escape all the distress |
| Die mich noch auf der Welt gebunden. | That still bound me in the world. |

The final movement of the cantata has a text and musical setting that some find inappropriate and even distasteful. Although the words may be a source of distress to the modern listener, Bach emphasized their message by setting them in unmistakable dance style in 3/8 meter. Of this movement Alfred Dürr (1918–2011) wrote:

> It is one of those pieces close to dance—with clear, periodic phrase structure, enlivened by strong rhythmic impulses—that no doubt reveals Bach's great art, but in this case does not offer a balanced conclusion to what precedes it, with the result that the absence of a concluding chorale is doubly to be regretted.

Dürr was a twentieth-century scholar who arguably had the greatest experience and knowledge of Bach's church cantatas in his generation. I therefore take his opinions seriously, but I do wonder what he, and others since, have missed in Bach's intention for this verse. How did Bach understand the text, and why did he set it to such lively and joyful music? Bach had lost both parents before he was eleven years old, as well as siblings, and this must have left him with emotional scars and wounds. As an adult he had also lost several of his beloved children. His response to the text of this movement therefore could not possibly have been glib or coldly intellectual. The tension between the deep sorrow or loss, and the joy of future hope, must be heard somewhere in the music of this final movement.

Clues to what Bach might have been striving toward are suggested in several books that he owned and could have read. For example, in

Chapter 59, on page 1154 in a book of systematic theology, the author, August Pfeiffer, considered what it will be like after death: "On Heaven and Eternal Life"; Question 1: Will we eat and drink in heaven? Question 2: What will heavenly joy consist of? Pfeiffer's reassuring answers include that our bodies as well as spirits will be resurrected, and that our families and friends will also be there.

However illusory this might sound to modern ears, it was a widespread understanding and belief within Lutheranism of the period. It holds in tension the seeming contradiction between the sorrows of physical suffering and bodily death, and the future joy of eternal bliss. It is seen, for example, in the state-of-the-art Leipzig encyclopedia, when the author of the entry "Freuden-Tag des Hertzens Jesu" ("The Joyful Day of Jesus' Heart"), explains: "Yes, he [Jesus] rejoices in these days of suffering and death because he was gaining a beloved bride." Similar sentiments can be seen in poems, particularly those for funerals. On page 789 of his collection of poems, *Poetische Blumen-Garten* (1717), Johann Christoph Männling (1658–1723) takes the final words of Jesus from the cross given in John's Gospel (John 19:30) as his starting point, and chooses the head form (see Chapter 1), with each of the seven stanzas beginning "Es ist vollbracht" and ending "Welt gute Nacht!" Bach frequently set the phrase "Es ist vollbracht" in his church music, specifically in Cantatas (BWV) 159, 161, and most famously in his St. John Passion. Verse three of Männling's poem speaks of the joy of death.

| | |
|---|---|
| Es ist Vollbracht, | It is finished, |
| Die Siech-Last hat ihr Ende, | The burden of illness is over, |
| Die Seligkeit, | The blessedness, |
| So voller Freud, | So full of Joy, |
| Die faß ich in die Hände | Which I take in both hands, |
| So wohl hats Gott gemacht! | God has made it so good! |
| Welt gute Nacht! | World, good night! |

And this view of death is recommended to believers by Johann Olearius in a section devoted to lingering and protracted sickness.

> 270 Seel.Sterbekunst 2. B. von derer Erweisung.
> Und das ist der Gläubigen Triumph und Sieg/ sie singen frölich von der gnädigen Erlösung/loben und preisen Gott/ und dancken ihm/daß Er die seinen errettet/erhelt und beschützt.

**Figure 6.5** Johann Olearius, *Gymnasium Euthanasius Christliche Sterbeschule* (1669), 270. https://digital.slub-dresden.de/id367213427/286. Sächsische Landesbibliothek, Staats- und Universitätsbibliothek Dresden.

where he writes (Figure 6.5): "And this is the believer's triumph and victory—they sing joyfully of merciful redemption, praise and worship God, and thank him that he saves, enlightens, and protects his own." As a pastor, Olearius had of course witnessed firsthand the immense suffering and family sorrows caused by lingering mortal sickness, and yet he was still able to write this.

The same progression from suffering to eternal joy is seen in August Pfeiffer's twenty-four-verse chorale, "So gibst du nun, mein Jesus, gute Nacht!," a text that Bach set to music twice, as BWV 402 and as BWV 501, number 315 in the Schemelli hymnbook. Verse 24 reads:

| | |
|---|---|
| Dass ich mit Leib und Seel aus meiner Gruft | That with my whole body and soul |
| dem wunderschönen Aufgang aus der Höhe | I go with great leaps from my tomb, |
| entgegen werd gezücket in der Luft | drawn from on high into the air |
| und in sein Reich mit vollen Sprüngen gehe. | and into his kingdom to a wonderful resurrection. |

Living up to such a theological ideal, however logical, must have been extremely difficult. The conflicting emotions caused by this teaching can be seen in the heart-rending poems by Margarethe Susanna von Kuntsch (1651–1717) written for each of her deceased children, and particularly in her poetic dialogue between mother love and dutiful submission to God's will (page 90). It is these conflicting emotions that I sense Bach captured in the dance of the final movement of Cantata 82. The performers are asked to embody both the sorrow of deep loss, and the joyful hope of family reunions in eternal life. Just as Mary wept for her son hanging on the cross—a sword piercing through her heart—so have generations of parents looked at the empty shells of their lifeless offspring. Nothing can minimize their agony. The knowledge that even the mother of God went through it, that her son's death paved the way for the resurrection of our loved ones, must have helped Bach and his contemporaries to write with gratitude and confidence about the joys to come, even while in the depths of grief. It is a double-edged blessedness. Many modern performances of this movement ride roughshod over the context, creating a strange, almost offensive jollity. It feels important that this movement should not be characterized by muscular triumphalism.

## More on the Text and Its Structure

Bach was no stranger to the phrases "Ich habe genung" ("I have enough") and "Es ist genung" ("It is enough"). "Es ist genung" is the opening line of a hymn text by Franz Joachim Burmeister (1633–1672), who was born in Lüneburg and served as a pastor there until his death. Fourteen of Burmeister's texts were set to music by Mühlhausen-based composer Johann Rudolph Ahle (1625–1673), including the hymn "Es ist genung, so nimm Herr, meinen Geist," whose melody opens with four ascending steps of the whole-tone scale, creating the shocking and jarring effect of a tritone. Burmeister's text was transmitted in many hymnals and

Bach will have known it since childhood. In 1723 he used the fifth stanza of Burmeister's text to Ahle's melody in the final movement of Cantata (BWV) 60/5. The Burmeister text is also included as chorale 848 in the category of Sterbelieder (hymns for death) in Schemelli's hymnal, *Musicalisches Gesangbuch* (Leipzig, 1736), a collection of 954 old and new hymns, to which Bach contributed an unknown number of melodies and harmonizations.

Recently the libretto of Cantata 82 was discovered in a published cycle of cantata texts compiled and edited by Christoph Birkmann (1703–1771). Over seventy texts in the collection are of cantatas performed at the churches of St. Thomas and St. Nicholas while Birkmann studied in Leipzig. The authors of many of the texts are known, but there are some that have no attribution, and which are now thought to have been written by Birkmann himself. According to his autobiography, Birkmann took every opportunity while he was in Leipzig to interact with great scholars and immerse himself in cultural experiences, which included "diligently following the great master Bach and his choir, and in winter the *Collegia musica*." He was in the right place at the right time.

As discussed in Chapter 1, it was commonplace in Bach's time to adapt or parody preexisting poetic and musical materials. It would have been quite easy, even for an inexperienced poet, to take an eight-line stanza starting and ending with "Es ist genung," such as Burmeister's 1662 hymn, and create a new version with slightly adapted words "Ich habe genung." Many poets, including Birkmann and Männling, use this "Haupt-Ode" form to adapt Burmeister's famous hymn (see Chapter 1).

| F. J. Burmeister, 1662 | C. Birkmann, 1728 |
|---|---|
| 1. Es ist genung! | 1. Ich habe genung! |
| So nimm, Herr, meinen Geist zu Zions Geistern hin! | Ich habe den Heyland, das Hoffen der Frommen, |
| Lös' auf das Band, | Auf meine begierigen Arme genommen, |
| das allgemählich reißt; | Ich hab ihn erblickt, |

Befreie diesen Sinn
Der sich nach seinem Gott
　sehnet,
Der täglich klagt, der
　nächtlich thränet
Es ist genung, es ist genung!

Mein Glaube hat Jesum ans Herze
　gedrückt;
Nun wünsch ich noch heute mit
　Freuden,
Von hinnen zu scheiden!
Ich habe genung!

In 1702 Männling had done something similar, taking the opening phrase of Burmeister's "Es ist genung" and creating from it an entirely new seven-stanza poem (Figure 6.6).

F. J. Burmeister, 1662
5. Es ist genung, wenn es dir
　gefällt
So spanne mich doch aus!
　Mein Jesus kömmt; Nun
　gute Nacht, o Welt! Ich fahr
　ins Himmelshaus, Ich fahre
　sicher hin mit Frieden,
　Mein großer Jammer bleibt
　danieden. Es ist genung.

Männling, 1702, reprint 1717
1. Es ist genung! Ade o Welt!
Dein Glantz mich ferner nicht
　auffhält
Mein Jesus wincket mir.
Die Himmels-Pfort ist auffgethan
Ich schau den liebsten
　Heyland an.
O Süsses Lebens-Zier!
Hier ists genung / genung

Translated into English, the first and final stanzas of Männling's poem read:

It is enough! Farewell O world
Your beauties cannot detain me.
My Jesus is waving to me.
The Heavenly Gate is open,
I am looking at the dearest Savior.
O sweetest ornament of life!
Here it is enough, enough!

It is enough! Calm your spirit,
with God's wise counsel,
dear Friends, who shed tears.
We will after a little while
see one another soon there in
joyful eternity, in God's city.
Here it is enough! Enough.

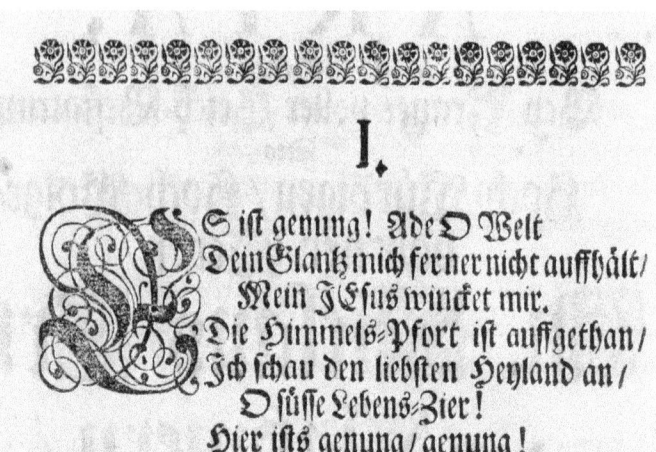

**Figure 6.6a and 6.6b** First and final stanzas of Johann Christoph Männling's *Aria* for the funeral of Nicolaus Ernst von Natzmer (1702), "Es ist genung!" n.p. https://resolver.staatsbibliothek-berlin. de/SBB0001EA1500000000. Staatsbibliothek zu Berlin, Preussischer Kulturbesitz.

Birkmann could easily have taken as his model for "Schlummert ein," a text published in 1725 by Gottfried Efraim Scheibel (1696–1758) and quickly made a parody text for Bach. As Robin A. Leaver has shown, the text for the festival of Purification in Scheibel's 1725 cycle of texts is "Schlummert ein, ihr Augenlieder, Fallet sanft in Frieden nieder."

## Contexts of the First Performances

By 1723 Bach had composed the Candlemas Cantata (BWV) 83 'Erfreute Zeit im neuen Bunde' for choir and soloists. Because the copyist Anon IIf made some new parts for Cantata 83, writing on paper bearing the same watermarks as those on the parts for Cantata 82, some scholars have suggested that Bach intended to perform Cantata 83 in 1727, in addition to performing the newly composed 'Ich habe genung', arguing that because Candlemas fell on a Sunday in 1727, two cantatas might have been required. Although the material evidence shows that Anon IIf was available to make copies for Bach in late January/early February 1727, this does not prove conclusively that Cantata 83 was performed on 2 February. Intriguingly, Bach composed cantatas for solo voice and small instrumental forces for two successive Sundays that year: Cantata 82 for 2 February, and for Cantata (BWV) 84 for Sunday 9 February 1727. The text for Cantata 84 was written in the first person "I," and was for solo soprano, solo oboe, and strings, with a chorus required only in the final chorale. This is the only known time in his career that Bach scheduled solo cantatas for two successive Sundays, which suggests several possible scenarios, the most persuasive being that the choristers at the school were unable to sing due to some kind of winter bug. Whether it was strep throat or hoarseness, or some other bacterial or viral infection, Bach decided that a solo cantata was the safest option for 2 February 1727 and that he should not risk scheduling a cantata that required full choir for the following Sunday either.

In addition to these uncertain circumstances, there is an entirely new scenario that may also explain the hasty handwriting in the score of Cantata 82, and the change from alto voice to bass.

I stumbled across the possibility when reading the published memorial essay and biography for the inventor and mathematician Jacob Leupold (1624–1727), known fondly as Leipzig's "Archimedes." Leupold died on 12 January 1727, three weeks before 'Es ist genung' was planned to be performed. The merchant Georg Heinrich Bose (1682–1731) was Leupold's friend and patron. Bose, the influential city councilor, was also closely connected to the Bach family, as their neighbor and family friend. The Bose family lived in the Bose house opposite St. Thomas Church, his daughter Christiana Sybilla (1711–1749) was Bach's wife's bosom friend ("Hertzens Freundin"), and his son Georg Mattias Bose (1710–1761) was to become a famous inventor and engineer like Jacob Leupold. Furthermore, in common with Bach, Jacob Leupold's father confessor was none other than Christian Weiß (1671–1737), pastor of St. Thomas Leipzig, and preacher at St. Nicholas while Bach was music director. Pastor Weiß, Jacob Leupold, and Pastor Tettelbach, author of Leupold's memorial pamphlet, were all members of the Society for Christian Love and Science (Societät Christlicher Liebe und Wissenschaften). Tettelbach writes in the pamphlet that Leupold's funeral was held in St Paul's Church, Leipzig, "with praiseworthy ceremonies befitting his station." According to the city's records his funeral was held on 15 January 1727 with "tota schola," that is, with the alumni of the St. Thomas School, and therefore likely to include special music. In addition to these social connections, I was struck by the final phrase of Tettelbach's essay: "Ich habe alles genug," referencing "Gen. XXIII,11" (*sic*!; see Figure 6.7). It is not an unusual phrase; nonetheless it caused me to ask if Cantata 82 might have been first performed at Leupold's funeral ceremony on 15 January, perhaps even as a favor to Bose in honor of his friendship with Leupold.

The phrase "Ich habe alles genug!" is spoken by Jacob Leupold's namesake, the patriarch Jacob, when he is attempting a

14      ❦ ( o ) ❦

Kirche angefügten Begräbniß mit löblichen und seinem Stande gemäßen Ceremonien *) zu Grabe ist bestattet worden.

Da er aber vorhero sich zu seinem Tode wohlbereitet, den aus GOttes Worte von seinem Beicht-Vater, tot. tit. Herrn D. Weißen empfangenen Trost gläubig angenommen, und sich denen treuen Vater-Händen GOttes im wahren Glauben an JEsum Christum mit vielen hertzlichen Seufftzern andächtig empfohlen hat; So ist kein Zweiffel, daß seine durch das Blut Christi gereinigte Seele alsobald, nach geschehener Auflösung, von denen heiligen Engeln ins ewige Leben werde seyn getragen worden, und nunmehro vor dem Throne des Höchsten stehen. Ἕυρηκα, ἕυρηκα, gefunden, gefunden, rief ehedem Archimedes voller Freuden aus, als er im Bade die Probe einer verfälschten göldenen Krone erfunden hatte. (Conf. Leupoldi Theatr. hydrostat. pag. 205. §. 10.) So wirds auch bey dem wohlseligen HerrnLeupold heissen, nachdem er im Himmel die Krone des Lebens gefunden. Wer will aber seine Glückseligkeit aussprechen? Denn er besitzet nunmehro der Seelen nach diejenigen Güther, derer Grösse kein Archimedes ausmessen, und kein Pythagoras mit seinen Zahlen ergründen kan. Ja er kan mit dem vergnügten Jacob (Gen. XXIII, 11.) sagen: Ich habe alles genug!

<small>*) Ejusmodi honoribus etiam Archimedes auctus fuit, licet in urbisSyracusarum direptione a milite occisus fuerit. Marcellus enim, interitum ejus permoleste ferens, honeste eum sepeliri jussit, cujus sepulchrum, obsoletum prorsus, & dumis atque vepribus obsitum, & ipsis adeo Syracusanis ignotum, Cicero, quæstor Siciliæ, cum illud ex descriptione quadam cognitum haberet, Senatui Syracusano demonstravit, centum triginta septem post annis. (Cic. l. 1. Tuscul. Quæst.) Imo Cæl. Rhodig. L. 17. c. 29. refert. Archimedi statuam honorificam fuisse positam, præcipuis ejus instrumentis ornatam, nempe Globo cœlesti & Cylindro.</small>

Figure 6.7 Final words of Gottfried Tettelbach's biography and memorial essay for Jacob Leupold, *Die letzte schuldige Freundschafft und Ehren-Bezeugung*. It should read "(Gen.XXXIII.11)." https://digital.slub-dresden.de/werkansicht/dlf/112935/14. Sächsische Landesbibliothek, Staats- und Universitätsbibliothek Dresden.

reconciliation with his brother Esau, recorded in Genesis 33:11 (not 23:11 as given in the pamphlet). I have not yet found a published funeral sermon or funerary materials relating to the ceremony on Wednesday 15 January, which might reveal what music, if any, was performed. Although one might expect the choir to sing the customary funeral motets, rather than a solo work, the final words of Leupold's essay, and the international status of Leupold, makes me wonder if Bach brought forward the first performance of 'Ich habe genung', and caused him to change the solo voice to bass to be appropriate to celebrate the life of Leipzig's internationally renowned engineer.

The Bach and Bose families became friends and neighbors despite the vast differences in social and financial status. Indeed, in the 1720s four Bose daughters became godparents to four Bach children. The Bachs had lived and worked alongside the aristocracy in Weimar, Weißenfels, and Cöthen where they would have learned how to behave and speak courteously, and perhaps it was this refinement that helped bridge the social divide. One can imagine that Georg Bose senior would have happily sponsored the Thomaskantor to perform the customary funeral aria or two in honor of his friend Jacob Leupold. There would also have been a memorial service for Leupold at either the main or the vespers service on Sunday 2 February, when Pastor Weiß might have preached, combining the memory of Jacob Leupold and celebrating the Purification of Mary. The printed booklets that would have included the cantata texts for Sundays 2 and 9 February 1727 have not yet been discovered, although they may not be accurate anyway, as they were most probably printed before any unforeseen outbreak of sickness or death, or last-minute changes. It is unlikely that we will ever discover the whole story; nonetheless, we do know that reappropriating excellent musical materials, accepting compositional and occasional performance commissions, and a dual-purpose Sunday service were all part of Bach's Leipzig experience.

## A Personal Connection?

The extended outpouring of emotion in Cantata 82 'Ich habe genung' expresses an intimacy with God that is lacking in Cantatas 83 and 125. The two items from Cantata 82 that Anna Magdalena Bach copied into her 1725 musical notebook were the recitative "Ich habe genung" and a truncated version of the aria "Schlummert ein" in soprano clef in E minor/G major. Although they appear as the thirty-fourth and thirty-eighth entry, it is difficult to ascertain when she added them. Their presence, though, suggests that they were intended for home music making, and possibly for family or private devotions. Tellingly, the first performance of Cantata 82 was just six months after the death of their firstborn child, three-year-old Christiana Sophia Henrietta (1723–29 June 1726). Perhaps the recitative phrase "Ich habe genung" and the lullaby "Schlummert ein" helped Anna Magdalena come to terms with the memories of seeing and feeling Christiana draw her last breath. It would not be the last time her motherly love would be tested—over the next five years she was to lose three-year-old Christian Gottlieb on 21 September 1728, fifteen-month-old Christiana Dorothea on 31 August 1732, and little Regina Johanna eight months later, who died on 25 April 1733 just before her fifth birthday. One can only imagine the mental, emotional, and spiritual resources required to live with such repeated losses. Remembering what would befall Mary, and her husband's intimate setting, must have been a source of comfort. But what of the final movement, that sits so uncomfortably today? Might its unmistakable dance too have given courage in anticipation of a joyful physical family reunion in eternity?

## Cantata 82 Today

Which features of the text and music transmit life-enhancing meaning to the listener today? The style of performance makes all the difference to the listener's response. Does the performance encourage me to empathize, to weep, to reflect on mortality, to appreciate the joy of life? Or does the performance distract me, diverting my attention away from the core meanings of the libretto?

Bach had lived with the reality and grief and loss through death since childhood. The tolling of the bells for funeral processions was a commonplace reality in Lutheran communities, and they had tolled for his nearest and dearest all too often. As a devout Lutheran, he believed that death was part of the divinely ordained cycle of birth, loss, and rebirth. One can glimpse in Cantata 82 the love of the mother, holding the broken, dying Christ in her arms, a universal model for vulnerable women after the extraordinary near-death experience of childbirth; the hormones kicking in to provide nourishment from deep within; the love of parents cut to the core by the fragility of a powerless, dependent newborn for whom they are suddenly responsible. This is the heart of love that breaks the deepest held prejudices, and the love that unifies as it offers to every generation the empathy and power to enrich humanity. Regardless of religion or philosophy, this love is our human connection with the divine. Perhaps this might also explain the indefinable affinity that many feel when they hear Cantata 82.

## Suggestions for Further Reading

For more on Cantata (BWV) 82 see Bettina Varwig, "Death and Life in J. S. Bach's Cantata *Ich habe genung* (BWV 82)" (2010) and Alfred Dürr, *The Cantatas of J. S. Bach* (2005), 654–666. Birkmann's background and role in Bach's performances is described by Christina Blanken in "A Cantata-Text Cycle of 1728 from Nuremberg" (2015), 9–30, and in German, *Bach-Jahrbuch*, 101 (2015), 13–74. For the possible origins of "Schlummert ein, ihr Augenlieder," see Robin A. Leaver (2021), 83–117.

# 7

# Glory from New Galleries

## Reimagining Bach's Church Cantatas

Just as the distance continues to increase between today and the Lutheran world in which Bach lived, so the gap will continue to widen between what Bach's music means to us and what it originally meant. What attracts each culture and generation to his music will also continue to evolve. The rate of changing taste has increased particularly swiftly since the international dissemination of recorded sound, and, more recently, with the global accessibility of music through the internet. Some pillars of today's knowledge about Bach's church cantatas are likely to remain unchanged, or only lightly revised, such as the musical notation and handwriting in his scores and parts, some of which are prized among the greatest examples of human and cultural endeavor. Some performance styles too, particularly those striving toward what might have been "authentic" in Bach's time, will, I suspect, also continue albeit with revised designs and sounds. Performances that serve a liturgical role within worship services in many Christian denominations are also likely to remain. But it must be remembered that Bach's church cantatas were jobbing compositions to be used once, and then put on a shelf until a suitable moment arose either for a second performance, or for the materials to be adapted or reused. This gives authentic license for the cantatas to be given entirely new forms, configurations, purposes, and interpretations. Opinions will differ.

In this chapter I will explore how the cantatas have been viewed since Bach's death, including some of the hidden, unattractive obstacles that have hindered or distorted their transmission. I will delve more deeply into their theology and underlying ideas and ask how these might help the cantatas to be seen afresh and performed in new ways.

## Disputes and Disagreements

The history of Bach scholarship is littered with public and private disputes caused by the desire to establish what Bach intended, and what was or is "correct." For example, there have been disagreements about Bach's theological persuasion, about the correct way of performing the vocal works, whether with one or more singer to a part, and whether Bach and his Passions were actively or subliminally anti-Semitic. The personal cost to individuals on both sides of such arguments and the divisions they cause between performers, listeners, and scholars are needless when ultimately everyone involved is trying to define and understand the best modern practice. A longstanding battle has been over the image of Bach. On page 35 of the *Introduction to Bach Studies*, Melamed and Marissen summarized it like this:

> The image of Bach as Great Pious Lutheran was first projected by C. H. Bitter, and put forward forcefully by Philipp Spitta. . . . Following upon the new chronological research of Alfred Dürr and Georg von Dadelsen in the 1950s, Friedrich Blume radically questioned this view, now seeing Bach as a begrudging, impious church musician and a sort of proto-Marxist. An avalanche of scholarly protests immediately followed.

There are many other areas of disagreement that color the understanding and performance of Bach's church cantatas.

Less-than-tolerant responses are often characterized by the dualistic premise that there is a right and wrong to all questions. Of course, differences of opinion have always been part of intellectual history and are necessary to sharpen and clarify understanding. However, there are kinder ways of evolving the intellectual process, and my hope is that intolerant, exclusive "right-wrong," and "acceptable-unacceptable" tendencies in the Bach community will be replaced by a more generous climate that encourages and welcomes new ideas and novel ways of discussing and performing the cantatas.

Disputes that affected Bach himself are well represented in the secondary literature. Less well represented, though, are the calls for tolerance and understanding that Bach could have read. There are many examples in the theological books that Bach owned, particularly in the writings of August Pfeiffer. Chapters 3 and 5 above include Pfeiffer's kindly view of the heathen, his comprehensive view of grace, and his understanding of the salvation story through the imagery of the Good Shepherd, and how these affect the understanding and performance of Cantatas 61 and 104. In the next section I will consider the racial in/tolerance within Bach's Lutheran society, and Bach's view of the non-Lutheran "other." This is important because numerous cantata libretti have ambiguous meanings that can be misread, and because of the unconscious bias that can be displayed in performance.

## Viewing the "Other"

The theology of Bach's Lutheran culture has frequently been presented as judgmental, anti-Semitic, anti-Catholic, and generally anti-Other. This can be seen in scholarly interpretations of cantata texts emphasizing "us" and "them," and which suggest that Bach presented Lutherans as "the goodies" and the Heathen, the Jews, the Turks, and the Catholics "the baddies." In German-speaking communities in Bach's time, however, views of humanity, of judgment and salvation for the believer, were more subtle.

Martin Luther's final tract "On the Jews and Their Lies" (*Von den Juden und ihren Lügen* (1543) did nothing to help the ugly and shameful history of anti-Semitism within Lutheran society. After 1539 Jews were allowed to do business in Leipzig at the three annual fairs, each lasting between two and three weeks, but the Jewish traders were not allowed to stay beyond this period, nor, until 1717, were they allowed to make their homes and raise families in Leipzig. This history suggests a uniformly hard-line intolerance of the Jewish people, but publications in Bach's library tell a more nuanced story. The widely distributed reference book about Judaism by the Hamburg preacher Johannes Müller (1626–1672), published in 1644, bears witness to the ongoing discussions about whether Jews should be allowed to live among Christians. A generation later, August Pfeiffer wrote in his systematic theology about the factual differences of belief between Jews and Lutherans. He cites the uncompromising verses in the Old and New Testament about the people of Israel and writes that believing Jews do not accept the Trinity (Chapter 3, §4), the divinity of the Messiah (Chapter 18, §1), or that Jesus is the Son of God (Chapter 18, §22). His overriding message, however, is one of God's grace toward the Jews. Bach's interest in the topic extended to owning a copy of Josephus' *History of the Jews* in German translation, which his wife, Anna Magdalena, was to inherit. In Leipzig the Bach family knew several scholars who studied oriental languages including Hebrew, Turkish, and Arabic, some teaching these in the universities and using them to communicate with the city's many foreign visitors. Bach's predecessor as Thomaskantor, Johann Kuhnau, was one who read and spoke several languages, including Hebrew.

Among the groups and individuals considered "other" by Lutherans were Christians espousing different doctrinal beliefs, including Calvinists, Catholics, Chiliasts, and mystics. Bach owned Pfeiffer's *Anti-Calvinismus* (1699). The title word "Anti" sounds aggressive to readers today, as if Pfeiffer was against everything the

Calvinists believed, but that is not the case. The book is a teaching volume, explaining how Calvinistic doctrines differ from Pfeiffer's understanding of Lutheran doctrines. For example, on the theme of God's merciful calling to all men, Pfeiffer asks (page 200 §5) "Whether God called every man from the beginning of the world onwards to his grace and mercy of eternal life. We answer Yes, but the reformers [the Calvinists] answer No," and (page 692 §7) "The logic [of the Calvinists] is as follows: God has chosen some, including me, or God has rejected the majority, but not me."

Pfeiffer published four other volumes with "Anti" in the title. In 1684 it was *Anti-Melancholicus* in which he gives encouraging biblical tips on how to combat melancholy; in 1691 *Anti-Chiliasmus* in which he systematically explains what a chiliast believes and gives the Lutheran view on the place of dreams and their interpretations. In 1692 he published *Anti-Enthusiasmus*, which is a careful examination of biblical prophecy, and an assessment of recent revelations by new mystics and self-styled prophets. And in 1702 it was *Anti-Papismus*, in which he uses Luther's shorter catechism to explain how Catholicism differed from Lutheranism in doctrine and lifestyle. The volume ends with the phrase "Gott Allein sei Ehr" ("To God alone be the Honor"), before which he cites as a prayer "Erleucht doch unser Sinn und Hertz", a verse from Jacob Ebert's chorale "Du Friedefürst, Herr Jesu Christ," ("You Prince of Peace, Lord Jesus Christ") on which Bach was to base his 1724 Cantata (BWV) 116.

| | |
|---|---|
| Enlighten our hearts and minds | Erleucht doch unser Sinn und Hertz |
| through the spirit of your mercy, | Durch den Geist deiner Gnad, |
| so that we may not act frivolously | Daß wir nicht treiben daraus ein Scherz, |
| to the harm of our souls | Der unsrer Seelen schad. |
| Lord Jesu Christ, | Herr Jesus Christ |
| you are the only one | Allein du bist, |
| who can accomplish this. | Der solchs wohl kan ausrichten |

Pfeiffer's aspiration in these "Anti-" volumes was to teach his readers. All the volumes include full indexes of topics to enable the reader to navigate the materials easily. Rather than presenting provocative anti-"other" views that would divide the community, Pfeiffer's purpose was to clarify the differences to build understanding. His writings illustrate the extent to which some theologians in Bach's time were chipping away at prejudices against the "other" and paving the way for a more tolerant and loving understanding of humanity. And he was not alone. In the classic history of Lutheran theology, *The Theology of Post-Reformation Lutheranism* (1970), Robert D. Preus demonstrates that such liberal views were a growing trend among theologians from late Lutheran Orthodoxy:

> There is nothing new about the doctrine of the truthfulness of Scripture as taught by the Lutherans during the late period of orthodoxy.... What is new is a rather marked preoccupation with the doctrine [of the truthfulness of Scripture] and a greater emphasis on it by Calov, Scherzer, Dannhauer, Quensted, and others at about the middle of the 17th century.... For the first time in the history of the church a freer attitude toward the inerrancy of Scripture is being taken by theologians ... who at the same time profess fidelity to the authority of Scripture.... It should not surprise us that many were thinking along more liberal lines. Empiricism and the scientific method were coming into their own in the 17th century and were gaining ascendancy over men's minds, especially the minds of men of letters, including theologians. (347–348).

Bach was living five or more generations after Martin Luther, toward the end of the period defined as "late orthodoxy." History shows that in Bach's time there was still a lot of regional anti-"other" attitudes living alongside religious tolerance and social development. In Hamburg, for example, there were riots in 1730, which are often cited in Bach scholarship to demonstrate how anti-Semitic the Lutheran clergy were. A closer look at the causes and the historical facts of these riots, however, shows that the situation was far more complex and open to numerous possible interpretations. In *Religious Toleration and Social Change in Hamburg 1529–1819* (1985), 94–95, Joachim Whaley describes the 1730 riots:

> Tension between Jews and Christians in the Neustadt obviously built up over a number of weeks. Witnesses later questioned by the judicial authorities told stories of impudent behavior by Jewish youths, one of whom apparently threw plum pips into the wig of a choir master, and of Christian aggression toward women on the streets. At the same time rumors were circulated by sailors that Jewish merchants were responsible for the recent loss of Hamburg sailors to pirates in Algiers. On the afternoon of 24 August, a group gathered on the Grossneumarkt, threatening the Jews with violence. It was easily dispersed by the militia, but it reassembled on the following day in the predominantly Jewish Elbstrasse nearby.... By 27 August, the violence was over and official inquiries into the disturbances began, although predictably little helpful evidence was found, and only six men, including one Jew, received minor punishments on 13 September. By any standard the riot was a relatively mild affair. It passed without bloodshed, without even destruction of property. The militia had never lost control of the situation and, at a crucial point on 26 August, the appearance of [Bürgermeiter Garlieb] Sillem on the streets probably saved the day. The Jews too behaved discreetly by keeping off the streets for a few days.

The growth of the Jewish communities in Hamburg had been relatively trouble-free since 1720 (page 94) but the actions and policies of the Hamburg Senate marginalized the orthodox Lutheran clergy who felt themselves forced into a "face-saving" exercise. To defend their position, they produced lengthy documents on the topic of Jews and salvation, including their preaching policy. The Senate, however, would have nothing of it, and continued their task of keeping the peace in the diverse and international city of Hamburg. Chief among the aggressively outspoken and intolerant orthodox clerics was Pastor Erdmann Neumeister, who wrote and published several cantata cycles (see Chapter 3). Nonetheless it is important to remember that Neumeister's views were not representative of all Lutheran theologians or citizens. August Pfeiffer put forward a refreshing and kindly alternative to the many judgmental and intolerant views of Christian salvation. Bach would have turned to his copy of Pfeiffer's widely published *Evangelische Christen-Schule* when he had theological questions about God's grace, God's love, and God's justice: a treasured volume that he bequeathed to his daughter Elisabeth Juliana Friderica (1726–1781), the future wife of Bach's student, Johann Christoph Altnickol (1720–1759).

Chapter 35 of this enormous tome is devoted to the Gospel and its primary message. The chapter is divided into questions and subdivided into answering paragraphs. Question four, on page 823, is: "What is the whole sum of the Gospel?," the answers to which are given over five paragraphs §7–§11. The following is a short selection:

> §7 The entire content of the Gospel is found in the golden power-saying of Christ, John 3:16 "For God loved the world so much that he gave his one and only Son so that whoever believes in him shall not perish, but have everlasting life," because it is these words, in their right and complete understanding, that put before our eyes the entire gospel sermon of grace:

> §9 It sounds strange enough at first when Christ says: "God loved the world." Do not understand this to mean the enormous expanse of heavens and of earth, but rather Adam and all the children of men in the world, who descended from him in the common course of nature. Not a single one is excluded, in a word, God loves the **human** world. ...

> If only we had stayed like our first parent, as he had created us in God's own image, we wouldn't be amazed by the phrase "God loves the world so much." What would be so peculiar if God loved his own image? But now because of the fall of man, it is a very strange phrase. . . . Goodness, what has God seen in this evil world to love? Beloved, is this not an absolute paradox, an amazing, miraculous, and unbelievable statement: "God loved the world"? §10 Although this is strange, nonetheless it is true. . . . It is understood that we see God's grace-filled affection, pity, and mercy in this love. . . . It is not because of our beauty, virtue, or splendid qualities that he loves us, but because of our wretchedness and need. §11 Why then did God not have mercy on the fallen angels in the same way that he has mercy on us fallen human beings? Because it was the guilt of the stranger, Adam, that caused and brought about our fall—it was not our hatred and defiance against God, as in the case of the fallen angels (Revelation 12). As Moses said: "O how the Lord loves the people" (Deuteronomy 33), and "See what love the Father has lavished on us" (1 John 3).

God's love was so fundamental to Pfeiffer's theology and to his life that he chose it as the sermon text for his funeral. A poem composed for his funeral was also entitled "Divine Love" ("Göttliche Liebe"). He saw God's love as an unconditional gift to every single human being.

In Chapter 31 he addressed life's questions head on, asking about the dispensation of grace toward the heathen: "There is nevertheless a remarkable inequality in the divine dispensation of his calling," which he follows by one of the hardest questions (pages 726–727):

> §13 If God wanted all people to know the truth, why did he not allow his Word to be clearly accepted by everyone? To which we

answer: It is enough ["Es ist genung," the theme of Chapter 6] that God gives every man sufficient instruction that he may come to the knowledge of the truth and be saved. God is free to pour out his spiritual gift of grace to a lesser or greater extent to one or another (Romans 11:35). God has power to do what He will with his own (Matthew 20:15).

Pfeiffer's sense of human justice forced him to probe the logic of this theology, on page 732–733:

> §15 Why then do many thousands of heathen children die before they even know left from right? What can they do who were not born into the Christian faith, or who died before they reached the age of understanding? The answer is: If you assume that such heathens, including Turks [Muslims] and Jews, would be damned, then God would not be doing unjustly, BUT God in his Word says that he does not want **any** to be damned (Matthew 23:37) and in these situations we have to trust to God's righteous mercy, because God can do more in these cases than we know or understand. [Gott kan in solchen Fällen mehr thun, als wir wissen och verstehen].

He explains that God wrote his natural law in the hearts of humans, to enable them to know the right way of honoring God. He gives examples of God's mercy toward different Old and New Testament peoples, writing on page 736:

> §17 When Jesus said he was sent only to the lost sheep of the house of Israel (Matthew 24:24) he was speaking of his personal preaching mission, and not of the merciful calling of God, which especially includes the Jews. His recommendation to his disciples in Matthew 10:5 not to walk along foreign streets was a temporary recommendation and does not contradict the ever-valid

command (*mandato perpetuo*) to teach all heathens and to preach the gospel to all creatures.

This statement, that the loving and kind God can be trusted to do more than we can ever know or understand, is light years away from the impression given of the condemnatory, judgmental God often communicated in the literature on the Lutheran theology in Bach's cantatas. Pfeiffer upholds a gentle theology, citing the imagery in Matthew 23:37 of the loving God longing to protect and gather all his loved ones, as a hen gathers her chicks under her wings. Based on the principle that God loves the whole world, Pfeiffer concludes that God does not wish any to be condemned, and that we must trust to God's fair and just mercy. It is no surprise that as an Orientalist with a passion for reading, teaching, and speaking numerous Middle Eastern languages, Pfeiffer had love in his heart for all those who spoke these languages, and for every single person who was "other" than a card-carrying German-speaking Lutheran. He believed there was grace for the heathen from all foreign lands and culture.

Pfeiffer also considered the question of women, and why St. Paul, in his letters, stated that they were not allowed to preach. Although not going as far as many today would wish, he points out that the wives of the apostles accompanied them when they were preaching (1 Cor. 9:5), and continues (Chapter 48, page 1159):

> §3 [Not being allowed to preach] is not a slur to the female sex (for is it not enough glory for them that the eternal Son of God wished to be born of a woman? Gal. 4:4). They are also joint heirs of the grace of life, 1 Peter 3:7, in Christ where there is neither male nor female, Gal. 3:28. God also wants to pour out his spirit on women as well as men, equipping them with his gifts and enlightening them, Joel 2:28–29. Women also have power over their children and servants, and over others who

need to be taught privately, and Paul wants all women to be good teachers, Titus 2:3.

## Bach and Tolerance

Against all this background, the obvious question is whether Bach himself was as kindly as Pfeiffer was toward the foreigner, the heathen, the Muslim, the Jew, and the Catholic, or if he subscribed to an exclusive theology where only "insiders" were accepted? When Bach wrote his various settings of "Nun komm der Heyden Heyland," including Cantata 61 (see Chapter 3), did he imagine the heathen as Pfeiffer did, with God's inclusive love embracing everyone from different cultures and foreign lands? Did he see the Savior of the heathen as loving and welcoming to all? The answer to these questions will affect the interpretative choices made by the performers of the cantatas and of his wordless organ preludes on "Nun komm der Heyden Heyland." When he sets texts that seem to emphasize the godly crusade against the heathen, did he subscribe to the message, or was he describing a story text as an opera composer might? For example, how do we square Pfeiffer's gentle theology with Bach's inclusion of Martin Luther's words in Cantata (BWV) 126: "Preserve us Lord with your Word and control the murderous rage of the Pope and Turks [Catholics and Muslim] who would want to cast down Jesus Christ, your son, from his throne"? Part of the answer may be contained in Bach's musical solutions: after a dramatic opening based on Luther's uncompromising words, Bach's music and the subsequent text become a lesson in unity and peace, more in line with Pfeiffer's understanding of God's grace and love to people from all nations and races.

Although Pfeiffer sees God's love (John 3:16) as the central motivation of the Gospel, the issues are nonetheless very complex. It is not possible to soft-pedal the significance for Lutherans of Jesus' death on the cross and his resurrection as the means of salvation, and this has logical implications for those who do not subscribe to the beliefs. Bach could have read the following section from John 12:37–40 in his copy of Abraham Calov's amplified commentary concerning the exclusion of the Jews and of all who do not believe in Jesus (Figure 7.1). Translated into English, with the biblical text in bold and Calov's comments in parentheses, the section cites prophecies from Isaiah 53:1, and Isaiah 6:10, and reads:

> **v. 37 Even after he had performed many signs** (so many beautiful sermons, and so many signs and miracles) **in their presence, still they would not believe him** (because of their blind, stubborn, and unrepentant minds and hearts). **v. 38 This was to fulfil the words** (which have truly been fulfilled) **of the prophet Isaiah** (even here he is speaking of the life, suffering and death of the Messiah, Isaiah 53:1, compare to Romans 10:16), **when he said: Lord, who has believed our message, and to whom has the arm of the Lord** (the power of God, of Christ, 1 Corinthians 1:24) **been revealed?**
>
> **v. 39 For this reason they** (the Jews) **could not believe, because, as Isaiah says elsewhere** (again specifically prophesied of them, namely of the Israelites in these last days).
>
> **v. 40 He** (the Lord God, Rom. 11:8) **has blinded their eyes** (the eyes of their hearts and understanding, Eph. 4:18), **and hardened their hearts** (through the justice of Holy Judgement, as was prophesied in Is. 6:10 which is applicable to the time and to all you who are now living, as is also written in Matth. 13:14–15 and in Acts 28:27) **so that they can neither see with their eyes** (because they have been blinded by the spirit of this world) **nor understand with their hearts** (because of the stubbornness of their hearts) **and turn to me that I** (the Savior of the world) **might help them** (even though I came first and foremost to help them, Matth. 15.24 and became their servant. Rom. 15.8).

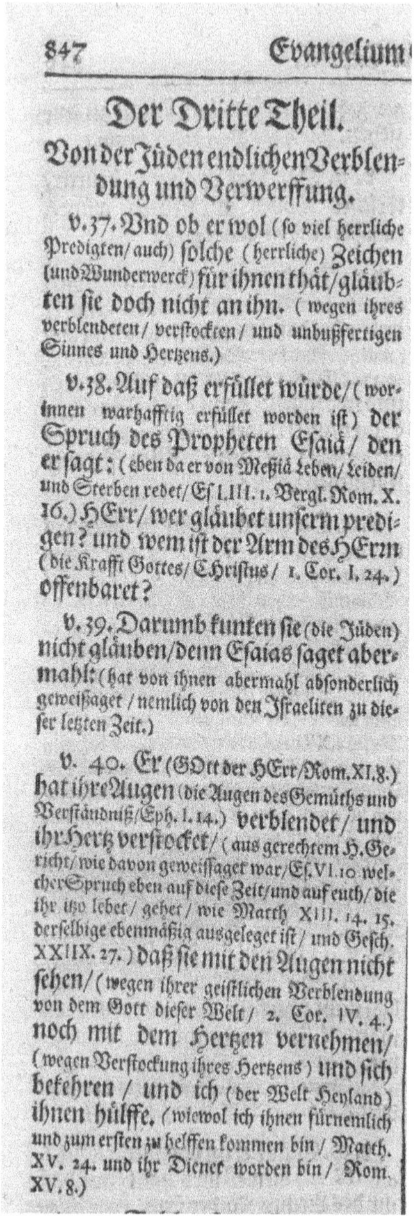

## Der Dritte Theil.
### Von der Jüden endlichen Verblendung und Verwerffung.

v. 37. Und ob er wol (so viel herrliche Predigten/ auch) solche (herrliche) Zeichen (und Wunderwerck) für ihnen thät/ gläubten sie doch nicht an ihn. (wegen ihres verblendeten/ verstockten/ und unbußfertigen Sinnes und Hertzens.)

v. 38. Auf daß erfüllet würde/ (worinnen warhafftig erfüllet worden ist) der Spruch des Propheten Esaiä/ den er sagt: (eben da er von Meßiä leben/ leiden/ und Sterben redet/ Es LIII. 1. Vergl. Rom. X. 16.) HErr/ wer gläubet unserm predigen? und wem ist der Arm des HErrn (die Krafft Gottes/ Christus/ 1. Cor. I, 24.) offenbaret?

v. 39. Darumb kunten sie (die Jüden) nicht gläuben/ denn Esaias saget abermahl: (hat von ihnen abermahl absonderlich geweissaget/ nemlich von den Israeliten zu dieser letzten Zeit.)

v. 40. Er (GOtt der HErr/ Rom. XI. 8.) hat ihre Augen (die Augen des Gemüths und Verständniß/ Eph. I. 14.) verblendet/ und ihr Hertz verstocket/ (aus gerechtem H. Gericht/ wie davon geweissaget war/ Es. VI. 10 welcher Spruch eben auf diese Zeit/ und auf euch/ die ihr itzo lebet/ gehet/ wie Matth XIII. 14. 15. derselbige ebenmäßig ausgeleget ist/ und Gesch. XXIIX. 27.) Daß sie mit den Augen nicht sehen/ (wegen ihrer geistlichen Verblendung von dem Gott dieser Welt/ 2. Cor. IV, 4.) noch mit dem Hertzen vernehmen/ (wegen Verstockung ihres Hertzens) und sich bekehren / und ich (der Welt Heyland) ihnen hülffe. (wiewol ich ihnen fürnemlich und zum ersten zu helffen kommen bin/ Matth. XV. 24. und ihr Diener worden bin/ Rom. XV. 8.)

**Figure 7.1** John 12:37–40 in *Die Heilige Bibel... ausgearbetetet und verfasset von Abraham Calov. Das Neue Testament* (1682), 847. http://resolver.staatsbibliothek-berlin.de/SBB0000351300010000. Staatsbibliothek zu Berlin, Preussischer Kulturbesitz.

Calov holds in tension the almost impossible-to-reconcile paradox of God's love and his judgment, leaving it up to the individual to decide how to live with the paradox.

Jesus is ever present in Bach's cantatas. In the five cantatas illustrated in this book, he is portrayed as loving and kind, welcomed into the soul of the believer, frequently with expressions of intimacy. In Cantata 106 the soprano sings, "Yes, come Lord Jesus, come." In Cantata 61 the tenor sings, "Come, Jesus, to your church" and the soprano "Open yourself, my whole heart, Jesus comes and enters in." In Cantata 147 the soprano sings, "Prepare the highway for you, Jesus, My Savior, choose my believing soul," and the tenor "Help, Jesus, help that I too may profess you," and the final chorale affirms that "Jesus remains my joy, the consolation and blood of my heart." Cantata 104 is entirely about Jesus the Good Shepherd; and in Cantata 82 the soloist sings about taking the Savior into "my" arms and "pressing him to my heart."

Leipzig was a cosmopolitan city with regular influx of foreign visitors from all nations. When trading stopped and the city gates closed during church services, there was little else to be done other than go to church, where, even if the German language or the sermon were incomprehensible, music would be heard. There is no record of how many non-Lutheran or visitors attended the Sunday services in St. Thomas or St. Nicholas. Might those unable to find a place of worship according to their customs have gone to the spiritual center of Leipzig and experienced this "strange" Lutheran Sunday morning? Imagine the liturgy interspersed with twenty minutes of a Bach cantata—however imperfectly performed—after weeks of traveling, uncomfortable lodgings, and little to be heard other than the babbling sounds of foreign languages. Music did not need words to be understood. Did Bach's music touch and move the hearts of visitors from different cultures? Does Pfeiffer's gentler brand of God's love explain why Bach's music can so readily be adapted to different languages, instruments, and tolerate different tempi and performance styles?

## Bach's Church Cantatas for the Future

Bach's fame and his reputation as one of the greatest composers in history dates to about fifty years after his death when he was hailed by Christian Friedrich Daniel Schubart (1739–1791) as the "Orpheus of the Germans" and as the musical equivalent of Isaac Newton (1643–1727). Bach had no idea he would be remembered in such an extravagant way. His music soon became known as universally accessible and as the epitome of masterful composition. In the early decades of the 1800s musicians eagerly bought or copied any composition by Bach as soon as it was available. In 1850 the Bach Gesellschaft was established to publish the first complete edition of Bach's works. As a result, libraries across the world became proud owners of the volumes. Even though not primarily intended to be used for performance, the Bach Gesellschaft edition nonetheless ensured global dissemination of Bach's music. The keyboard works were adopted as teaching materials, which guaranteed new generations of Bach lovers, while eminent performers and teachers created their own editions, adding expression marks and interpretative details to Bach's largely unadorned scores.

Some pieces were beloved by world-renowned classical performers, becoming even more popular through recorded sound. Jazz, pop, and rock artists also continue to draw on Bach's music, adapting it to their own genres and styles, but his two hundred church cantatas are mostly excluded from popular knowledge. This is probably because, in contrast to Bach's other compositions, the church cantatas have largely lost their original function. Naturally there is a tradition of the cantatas being performed in a worship context on the appointed liturgical dates in churches across Germany and internationally, including in the States where there has been a Bach Vespers series at Holy Trinity Lutheran Church, New York, since 1968. Nonetheless, the German-speaking Lutheran church serves a minority, and the liturgy itself has changed so much over the past three hundred years that Bach would hardly recognize it today.

Over the past century, recorded sound and the wireless have enabled some of Bach's cantatas to become known, and over the past fifty years Bach's complete cantata output has been the subject of concert series and recording projects spearheaded by eminent conductors, including Gustav Leonhardt, Nikolaus Harnoncourt, Helmuth Rilling, John Eliot Gardiner, Masaaki Suzuki, and Philippe Herreweghe. Coinciding with the development of the internet, and ventures such as Bach Digital, these cantata recordings spawned the need for Bach fans to discuss details of their favorite works, which led to the setting up of online forums. Numerous open-access video performances of the cantatas also began to appear online, including the J. S. Bach Stiftung performances, and the Netherlands Bach Society "All of Bach" series. Music festivals too continue to help promote knowledge of the cantatas. Among these is the enormously popular Bachfest Leipzig, which featured the Bach Cantata Ring (2018) and comprehensive coverage of the cantatas under the title "We Are Family" (2022–2024), and the venerable Bethlehem Bach festival in Pennsylvania. Despite these developments, the cantatas remain a niche for the dedicated Bach enthusiast.

What, then, can be done to facilitate the wonderful music in the cantatas to reach their full potential in the future? Bach's music was composed when belief in the unity of all created things was fundamental. This belief is common to very many different religious traditions worldwide and seems to be one of the elements that helps Bach's music speak to different faith traditions, and to cross national and political borders. Freed from its original purpose, the cantata music can now be heard not just from the church or choir gallery, or in the quasi-sacred space of the concert hall at specific times, but 24/7 in homes, schools, in the streets, in gardens, in shopping malls, in fact anywhere. However, as we have seen, the poetic texts that Bach set in his cantatas and passions contain concepts and ideas that are largely bound to his culture and time. There must be ways to release the music of the cantatas from the bondages of their libretti, so that new generations can experience

Bach's music. If not, the risk is that these church cantatas will become part of an increasingly rarefied museum culture. This raises questions about whether the spiritual intention of the original texts can in fact be separated from Bach's music, or if the spirituality is integral to the music, regardless of their texts. If so, wherein lies the spirituality? Is it in the specific instrumentation, or in Bach's vocal choices, in their forms and structures? How much can be changed so that it still sounds like Bach and retains the spiritual comfort, reassurance, and original joy? Where does the intention of Bach as composer begin and end?

For over two hundred years musicians have been trying to make Bach's St. John and St. Matthew Passions more approachable. Initially it was through translating the texts into the vernacular. Then it was the style of performance that changed, from the enormous mid-twentieth-century mass educational experience with adult and children's choirs, noses in their scores, to the intimacy of the early twenty-first-century one-to-a-part semi-staged, memorized performances, such as the St. Matthew Passion by Solomon's Knot, dramatized by John La Bouchardière. Equally radical has been the arrangement of the St. John Passion for tenor, percussion, and keyboard (tenor, Benedikt Kristjánsson; harpsichord/organ, Elina Albach; percussion, Philipp Lamprecht) live-streamed from St. Thomas Church in Leipzig, unforgettably at the height of the pandemic on Good Friday 2020 and, performed two years later in the Leipzig city square, miked up and amplified, with the stage projected on gigantic screens, and the "congregation" made up of complete strangers and friends singing the chorales together. There have also been numerous adaptations of single arias from the passions to make them more culturally accessible, "Erbarme dich, mein Gott" ("Have Mercy, My God") from Bach's St. Matthew Passion being among the most popular. Entirely different emotional effects are created by, for example, the raw and moving version in Arabic with its distinctive style of string playing by Sarband and Fadia el-Hage, and the astounding vocal strength in the flawless performance by Tim Mead and period instruments of the Netherlands Bach Society. The same aria can also be heard in an arrangement for cello replacing the solo voice performed by Hauser and Lana Trotovsek's with the Zagreb Philharmonic Orchestra. Such adaptations sound startlingly different when compared to Bach's original, and yet each performance can be equally "spiritual".

It has long been proven that Bach's music tolerates every type of instrument. A cut-and-pasted selection of different movements can still sound like Bach if done expertly. New music and ideas will result from reclothing the cantata arias, which, in fact, is what Bach and his contemporaries regularly did. They were experts in using parody techniques and equally adept at hiding their methods. Bach himself commandeered his own music and music composed by others and reworked the materials into something new. It seems entirely appropriate, then, for every generation to unapologetically continue this practice and adapt the wonderful music of his cantatas.

Michael Maul, the artistic director of the Leipzig Bachfest, reflected on these issues in the introduction to program of the 2023 festival *Bach for Future*:

> Original and originality are not necessarily contradictory. This is why we want to show what the music of Leipzig's Thomaskantor has represented for the past 300 years with some unusual formats: its substance is timeless and thus adaptable, and consequently effective in all kinds of different contexts.

In 2021 Maul created "Bach's Messiah" with music from Bach's cantatas, oratorios, and passions, to piece together the story of Jesus' life, from the annunciation of Christ's birth, the Christmas story, the numerous parables and miracles of Jesus, and, lastly, his Passion, to his resurrection and ascension. Numerous newly reworked cantatas have since been premiered at the Bachfest. There is no end to the possible ways of rethinking the music to make it appropriate for future generations.

Reclothing music and adapting performance styles can be troubling for those who care deeply about the authenticity of Bach's original compositions. In 1964 the composer Benjamin Britten (1913–1976) reflected with anxiety about the impact of recorded music and listening in private rather than public spaces, concluding that something important is lost when the music is not heard live. In his acceptance speech of the first Aspen Prize in Colorado, he said:

> Music is now free for all. If I say the loudspeaker is the principal enemy of music, I don't mean that I am not grateful to it as a means of education or study, or as an evoker of memories. But it is not part of true musical *experience*. Regarded as such it is simply a substitute, and dangerous because deluding. Music demands more from a listener than simply the possession of a tape-machine or a transistor radio. It demands some preparation, some effort, a journey to a special place, saving up for a ticket, some homework on the programme perhaps, some clarification of the ears and sharpening of the instincts. It demands as much effort on the listener's part as the other two corners of the triangle, this holy triangle of composer, performer, and listener.

Sixty years later we take for granted, and are no longer shocked, that we can listen to any of Bach's church cantatas in the kitchen while preparing meals or while taking a long walk in a forest. It is undoubtedly different from listening to a live performance, and there are gains and losses. Repeated listening facilitates committing the music to memory and aids focus while doing mechanical tasks. Britten would most probably have been disturbed and saddened by this use of music, just as today's music lovers might be disturbed and saddened by how Bach's music will be heard sixty years hence. Whether consciously or unconsciously, today's generation of performers and listeners are living with the consequences of the ideal of getting back to the original text and reconstructing historically informed views of the past, known as the Urtext mentality. The next generation will be responding to the legacies we leave. We owe it to them to hold lightly to our preferences and to adopt and embrace tolerance.

Bach's life was about service to his fellow citizens and, in common with many of his contemporaries, he aspired to live in honor and to the glory of God (*Soli Deo Gloria*), with the help of Jesus (*Jesu Juva*). He believed in the Harmony of the Universe, and that working with music was the closest he could get to the Creator, the source of life and love. His was a privileged life philosophy. Today existence is seen differently. While many today do not acknowledge the same life source as Bach did, nonetheless kindness, loving, giving, and goodness remain at the common core of humanity.

On 11 November 1705 Bach was asked by his Arnstadt employers to declare if he was willing to make music with the students, as his contract stipulated. The question implies that he had not yet worked with the schoolboys. And yet he had "invited an unfamiliar maiden to come into the choir gallery to make music there," where women were not generally welcome, the very space from which his "God-glorifying church music" was heard. This incident suggests that Bach had a clear view of his calling and was prepared to act on it even when it caused him to contravene the cultural norms of his day. For his church cantatas to continue to fulfill their potential, we too need to be prepared to release them from any restricting traditions or norms. Their music and spirituality deserve to reach across the centuries and across the globe to all communities. In short, these cultural treasures require new galleries from which to display their glories.

## Suggestions for Further Reading

Details of the one-to-a-part debate can be found in Joshua Rifkin (1982) and Andrew Parrott (2000). For anti-Semitism in Bach's music see Michael Marissen (2016). For the definitive studies on the integration of Jewish communities in Hamburg see Joachim Whaley (1985), and on post-Reformation Lutheran see Robert Preus (1970 and 1972). Numerous adaptations of Bach's cantatas can be found on YouTube.

# Glossary

**Cadence:** a simple harmonic formula that signals closure or resolution. Akin to a period in grammar, it affirms the central key of a discrete section or an entire piece.

**Canon:** a procedure in which a melody is repeated against itself (note for note) at staggered intervals of time. A canon may also incorporate complementary voices that do not imitate the canonic melody.

**Circle of fifths:** a tool for describing and executing chord progressions by ascending or descending fifth. The resulting series of functionally related harmonies allows for tonic and dominant functions for each of the twelve chromatic pitches and is often depicted by a circle summarizing those relationships.

**Continuo** (*basso continuo*): the Baroque practice of realizing a bass line and numerical figures (whether indicated or implied) that specify intervals or chords above that bass.

**Counterpoint:** two or more interdependent musical lines in a shared texture. Unlike melody-dominated music, counterpoint mandates certain manners of voice leading between the parts, whose totality produces harmony.

**Fair copy:** a clean hand copy of a work, which may incorporate revisions to earlier versions of the same piece. In Bach's day a fair copy commonly served for either performance or as a reference for additional copies or a published edition.

**Fugue:** a procedure premised on a melody or "subject" that is developed imitatively, with staggered entries initially in all the parts and reappearances of that melody in various guises as the fugue runs its course.

**Imitation:** the repetition in multiple voices of a short motive or melody at varying intervals of time.

**Inversion (melodic):** turning a melody upside down to make all its intervals move in the opposite direction, creating a mirror image of the original.

*Ricercar*: literally, a piece that "searches out" or "seeks" (der. from the Italian verb *ricercare*).

*Ritornello*: Italian for "little return," a short recurring instrumental section in a movement, often beginning and ending a chorus or aria.

**Sequence**: a series of repeating motives or harmonic patterns at multiple pitch levels.

# Select Bibliography

The bibliography begins with primary sources from which I drew a wealth of new information for this book. Most are open access and can be found, read, and downloaded, by searching author or title on the following sites: https://vd17.k10plus.de/ for seventeenth-century sources and https://vd18.k10plus.de/ for those from the eighteenth century. Bach's scores and parts, together with information about their copyists and dates, can be found through searching https://www.bachdigital.de/content/index.xed.

The bibliography ends with a selection of valuable secondary sources.

A note on translation: The English translations of the cantata texts are based on Marissen and Melamed https://bachcantatatexts.org/ Unless otherwise stated, all English translations are mine, in a style that tends toward dynamic equivalence.

## Primary Sources

*Printed Books and Pamphlets*

Bach's Own Bible. *Die Heilige Bibel . . . ausgearbetetet und verfasset von Abraham Calov.* Facsimile of Bach's copy signed 1733. Franker, Amersfoort, Netherlands: Van Wijnen, 2017.

Becker, Cornelius. *Der Psalter Davids Gesangweis, Auff die in Lutherischen Kirchen gewöhnliche Melodyen zugerichtet.* Leipzig: Cum Privilegio, 1602.

Birkmann, Christoph. *GOtt-geheiligte Sabbaths-Zehnden/bestehend aus Geistlichen Cantaten auf alle Hohe Fest- Sonn- und Feyer-Täge der Herspruckischen Kirch-Gemeinde zu Gottseeliger Erbauun.* Nürnberg: Lorenz Bieling, n.d. [Preface 26 October 1728].

Bünting, Heinrich. *Itinerarium Sacrae Scripturae.* Braunschweig, Magdeburg: Kirchner, 1650.

Calov, Abraham. *Die Heilige Bibel . . . ausgearbetetet und verfasset von Abraham Calov. Das Neue Testament.* Wittenberg: Christian Schrödter, 1682.

Creide, Hartmann. *Nuptialia Oder Fünfftzig Christliche Hochzeit-Sermonen.* Beyer: Franckfurt am Mayn, 1661–1670.

De Marees, Pieter. *Siebende Schiffahrt In das Goldreiche Königreich Guineam in Africa gelegen.* Translated by Levinus Hulsius into German from the original Dutch. Wolfgang Richter: Frankfurt Am Mayn, 1603.

Deyling, Salomon. *Catalogus Bibliothecae Deylingiae Auctionis Lege . . . Die XXI Juni.* Leipzig: August Samuel Cruciger, 1756.

Deyling, Salomon. *S. Cyrillum Hierosolymitanum*. Leipzig: Andreas Martin Schede, 1726.
Franck, Salomon. *Evangelische Sonn- und Fest-Tages-Andachten*. Weimar & Jena: Johann Felix Bielcke, 1717.
Franck, Salomon. *Geistliche- und Weltliche Poesien*. Jena: Johann Felix Bielcke, 1711.
Frohne, Johann Adolph. "Christliche Leich-Predigt." In *Reminiscere Amoris et Honoris*. Mühlhausen: Tobias David Brückner, 1709.
Fux, Johann Joseph. *Gradus ad Parnassum*. Translated by Lorenz Christoph Mizler. Leipzig: Mizler, 1742.
Geier, Martin. *Zeit und Ewigkeit nach gelegenheit der ordentlichen Sontags Evangelien in des Herrn Furcht hiebevor der Christlichen Gemeine in Leibzig Anno 1664 fürgestellet*. Leipzig: Lanckisch, 1670.
Henrici, Christian Friedrich. *Picanders Ernst- Schertzhaffte und Satyrische Gedichte*. Leipzig: Boëtius, 1727–1751. Vol. 1 (1727), Vol. 2 (1729), Vol. 3 (1732), Vol. 4 (1737), Vol. 5 (1751).
Hiltebrandt, Gustav Adolph. *Neu-Eröffneter Anmüthiger Bilder Schatz . . . Zur Lustigen Beschawung und Gemüths-Ergötzung*. Mayntz, Franckfurt: Ludvvig Bourgeat, 1674.
Hunold, Christian Friedrich. *Menantes Academischer Neben-Stunden Allerhand neuen Gedichte*. Halle, Leipzig: Johann Friedrich Zeitler, 1713.
Josephus, Flavius. *Deß hochberühmten Jüdischen Geschicht-Schreibers Historien und Bücher*. Numerous German language editions published from 1532–1782.
Kuntsch, Margaretha Susanna von. *Sämmtliche Geist = und weltliche Gedichte. Nebst einer Vorrede von Menantes*. Halle, Magdeburg: Neuen Buchhandlung, 1720.
Männling, Johann Christoph. *Aria Welche Bey Trauer-Voller Leich-Bestattung Des . . . Hn Nicolaus Ernst von Natzmer*. Stargard: Johann Nicolaus Ernst, 1702.
Männling, Johann Christoph. *Der Europäische Parnassus, Oder Kurze und deutliche Anweisung zu der Deutschen Dichtkunst*. Wittenberg: Brüning, 1685.
Männling, Johann Christoph. *Poetische Blumen-Garten*. Breslau: Bleßing, 1717.
Mattheson, Johann. *Behauptung der himmlischen Musik*. Hamburg: Christian Hérold, 1747.
Mattheson, Johann. *Neu Eröffnete Orchestre*. Hamburg: Schiller, 1713,
Mattheson, Johann. *Der Vollkommene Capellmeister*. Hamburg: Christian Hérold, 1739.
*Meckbachs-Zinckisches Ehren-Denckmahl*. Mühlhausen: Tobias David Brückner, 1709, 1712.
Mizler, Lorenz Christoph. *Musicalische Bibliothek*. 4 vols. Leipzig: Mizler, Braun, 1739–1754.

Neumeister, Erdmann. *Geistliche Poesien . . . auf alle Sonn = und Fest = Tage durch gantzes Jahr.* Eisenach: Johann Adolph Boëtius, 1717.
Neumeister, Erdmann. *Geistliches Singen und Spielen.* Gotha: Christoph Reyhern, 1711.
Neuss, Heinrich Georg. *Kurtzer Entwurf von der Music.* Leipzig: Heinsius, 1754.
Olearius, Johann. *Biblische Erklärung.* 5 vols. Leipzig, Halle: Johann Christoph Tarnow, David Salfeld, 1678–1681.
Olearius, Johann. *Christliche Bet-Schule.* Leipzig: Frommann, 1664.
Olearius, Johann. *Gymnasium Euthanasius Christliche Sterbeschule.* Leipzig: Georg Heinrich Frommann, 1669.
Pfeiffer, August. *Apostolische Christen-Schule. Darinnen die ordentlichen Sonntags- und vornehmste Fest-Episteln Durchs gantze Jahr richtig disponiret . . . und deutlich erkläret.* Lübeck: Krüger, 1704.
Pfeiffer, August. *Evangelische Christen-Schule, Darinnen Das Gantze* SYSTEMA THEOLOGIAE, *Oder die Articul der Christlichen Religion In ihrer richtigen Ordnung, aus denen Evangelischen Sonn- und Fest-Tags-Texten deutlich gewiesen.* Leipzig, 1688, 1710, 1724.
Pfeiffer, August. *Gazophylacion Evangelicum: Evangelische Schatzkammer.* Nürnberg: Hofmann Froberg, 1686.
Pfeiffer, August. *Nuptialia, Das is: Zehen auserlesene Hochzeit-Predigten.* Frankfurt und Leipzig: Pfeiffer, 1705.
Praetorius, Michael. *Syntagma Musicum.* 3 vols. Wittenberg: Richter, 1615–1620.
Riederer, Johann Friedrich. *Die Bedenckliche Und Geheimnisreiche Zahl Drey.* Frankfurt, Leipzig, 1732.
Rist, Johan. *Himlische Lieder.* Lüneburg: Heinrich Stern, 1641–1642.
Rittmeyer, Johann. *Himmlisches Freuden-Mahl Der Kinder Gottes auf Erden. Oder Geistreiche Gebehte So vor- bey- und nach der Beicht und H. Abendmahl kräfftig zu gebrauchen.* Helmstädt: Wolfgang Hamm, 1683.
Schmolck, Benjamin. *Das Saiten-Spiel des Hertzens.* Breslau, Liegnitz: Michael Rohrlachs, 1721.
Schweinitz, David von. *Hundert Todes-Gedancken: Das ist Vorbereitung Eines Christlichen Lebens Zum Seeligen Sterben.* Breßlau: Fellgiebel, 1664.
Tettelbach, Gottfried. *Die letzte schuldige Freundschafft und Ehren-Bezeugung.* Dresden: Harpeterischen Schrifften, 1727.
Vockerodt (Vokkerod), Johann Arnold. *Glükwunschende Abend-Musik . . . welche . . . Kunraht Mekbachen . . . den 8 Januari 1679 zum Bürgermiester daselbsten erwehlet wurde zu ehren . . .* Mühlhausen: Hüter, 1679.
Walther, Johann Gottfried. *Praecepta der musikalischen Composition.* Edited by Peter Benary. Leipzig: Breitkopf & Härtel, 1955 (orig. 1708).
Werckmeister, Andreas. *Musicalische Paradoxal-Discourse.* Quedlinburg: Theodor Philipp Calvisius, 1707.
Winkworth, Catherine. *The Chorale Book for England.* Edited by William Sterndale Bennett and Otto Goldsmith. London: Longman & Green, 1863–1865.

## Bach's Scores and Parts

Cantata (BWV) 106. The earliest surviving score is by an anonymous scribe, 1768. It is held in Staatsbibliothek zu Berlin, D-B Mus.ms. Bach P 1018. https://digital.staatsbibliothek-berlin.de/werkansicht/?PPN=PPN1046854291.

Cantata (BWV) 61. The full score is held in Staatsbibliothek zu Berlin, D-B Mus.ms. Bach P 45, Faszikel 6. https://digital.staatsbibliothek-berlin.de/werkansicht?PPN=PPN845728342&PHYSID=PHYS_0097&DMDID=DMDLOG_0044.

Cantata (BWV) 147. The full score is held in Staatsbibliothek zu Berlin, D-B Mus.ms. Bach P 102. https://digital.staatsbibliothek-berlin.de/werkansicht/?PPN=PPN84777578X. The parts are held in Staatsbibliothek zu Berlin, D-B Mus.ms. Bach St 46. https://digital.staatsbibliothek-berlin.de/werkansicht/?PPN=PPN871678500.

Cantata (BWV) 104. The parts are held in Staatsbibliothek zu Berlin, D-B Mus.ms. Bach St 17. https://digital.staatsbibliothek-berlin.de/werkansicht/?PPN=PPN869937294.

Cantata (BWV) 82. The original score can be seen here: https://digital.staatsbibliothek-berlin.de/werkansicht/?PPN=PPN861911474. The original parts can be seen here: https://digital.staatsbibliothek-berlin.de/werkansicht/?PPN=PPN872352986.

## Secondary Sources

"Analytical Perspectives on the Bach Cantatas." *Discussing Bach* 8 (January 2025) https://bachnetwork.org/discussing-bach/db8/

"Bach and Jesus." *Discussing Bach* 2 (July 2021). https://bachnetwork.org/discussing-bach/db2/

"Bach Cantata Texts, Poetic Techniques, and Meanings." *Discussing Bach* 5 (November 2022). https://bachnetwork.org/discussing-bach/db5/.

Bartel, Dietrich. *Andreas Werckmeister's* Musicalische Paradoxal-Discourse. A Well-Tempered Universe. Translated with commentary by Dietrich Bartel. Lanham, MD: Lexington Books, 2017.

Blanken, Christina. "A Cantata-Text Cycle of 1728 from Nuremberg: A Preliminary Report on a Discovery Relating to J. S. Bach's So-Called 'Third Annual Cycle.'" *Understanding Bach* 10 (2015): 9–30. https://bachnetwork.org/ub10/ub10-blanken.pdf.

Britten, Benjamin. *On Receiving the First Aspen Award.* London: Faber and Faber, 1965.

Chafe, Eric T. *Tonal Allegory in the Vocal Music of J. S. Bach.* Oakland: University of California Press, 1991.

Chafe, Eric T. *Tears into Wine: J. S. Bach's Cantata 21 in Its Musical and Theological Contexts.* Oxford: Oxford University Press, 2015.

Crist, Stephen A., and Daniel R. Melamed, eds. *The Cambridge Companion to Bach Cantatas*. Cambridge: Cambridge University Press, 2025.

David, Hans T., and Arthur Mendel, eds. *The New Bach Reader: A Life of Johann Sebastian Bach in Letters and Documents*. Revised by Christoph Wolff. New York: W. W. Norton, 1998.

Dürr, Alfred. *The Cantatas of J. S. Bach*. Revised and translated by Richard D. P. Jones. Oxford: Oxford University Press, 2005.

Harris, Ernst Charles. *Johann Mattheson's* Der Vollkommene Capellmeister: *A Revised Translation with Critical Commentary*. Ann Arbor, MI: UMI Research Press, 1981.

Heber, Noelle M. *J. S. Bach's Material and Spiritual Treasures: A Theological Perspective*. Martlesham, Suffolk: Boydell Press, 2021.

Irwin, Joyce. *Foretastes of Heaven in Lutheran Church Music Tradition: Johann Mattheson and Christoph Raupach on Music in Time and Eternity*. Lanham, MD: Lexington Books, 2015. English translation of Christoph Raupach's *Deutliche Beweis-Gründe* (1717) and Johann Mattheson's *Behauptung der himmlischen Musik* (1747).

*Johann Sebastian Bach's Personal Copy of Abraham Calov's Bible Commentary: History, Significance, Perspectives*. Edited by Albert Clement. Utrecht: Uitgeverij Van Wijnen, 2022.

Kevorkian, Tanya. *Baroque Piety: Religion Society, and Music in Leipzig 1650–1750*. New York: Routledge, 2007.

Kevorkian, Tanya. *Music and Urban Life in Baroque Germany*. Charlottesville: University of Virginia Press, 2022.

Koch, Ernst. *Musik der Menschen und Musik der Engel*. Leipzig: Evangelische Verlagsanstalt, 2021.

Leaver, Robin A. *Bach Studies: Liturgy, Hymnology, and Theology*. London, New York: Routledge, 2021.

Leaver, Robin A. *Bach's Theological Library*. Neuhausen: Hänssler-Verlag, 1983.

Leaver, Robin. A. *J. S. Bach and Scripture: Glosses from the Calov Bible Commentary*. St. Louis: Concordia, 1985.

Leaver, Robin A. "Emblematic Jesus." *Discussing Bach 2* (July 2021). https://bachnetwork.org/discussing-bach/db2/.

Marissen, Michael. *Bach & God*. Oxford: Oxford University Press, 2016.

Marissen, Michael. "The Character and Sources of the Anti-Judaism in Bach's Cantata 46." *Harvard Theological Review* 96, no. 1 (January 2003): 63–99.

Marissen, Michael, and Melamed, Daniel R. *Texts and Historically Informed Translations for the Music of Johann Sebastian Bach*. https://bachcantatatexts.org/.

Maul, Michael. *Bach's Famous Choir: The Saint Thomas School in Leipzig, 1212–1804*. Translated by Richard Howe. Martlesham, Suffolk: Boydell Press, 2012.

Melamed, Daniel R., and Marissen, Michael, *An Introduction to Bach Studies*. Oxford: Oxford University Press, 1998/2006.

Merkel, Kerstin, and Heide Wunder, eds. *Ungewöhnliche Frauen: Deutsche Dichterinnen, Malerinnen, Mäzeninnen aus vier Jahrhunderten*. München, Zürich: Piper Verlag, 2007.

Parrott, Andrew. *The Essential Bach Choir*. Martlesham, Suffolk: Boydell Press, 2000.

Peters, Mark A. *A Woman's Voice in Baroque Music: Mariane von Ziegler and J. S. Bach*. Aldershot and Burlington, VT: Ashgate, 2008.

Peters, Mark A., and Reginald L. Sanders, eds. *Compositional Choices and Meaning in the Vocal Music of J. S. Bach*. Lanham, MD: Lexington Books, 2018.

Petzoldt, Martin. *Bach Kommentar*. Band I: *Die geistlichen Kantaten des 1. bis 27 Trinitatis-Sonntages*. Bachakademie Stuttgart. Kassel: Bärenreiter, 2004.

Petzoldt, Martin. *Bach Kommentar*. Band II: *Die geistlichen Kantaten vom 1. Advent bis zum Trinitatisfest*. Bachakademie Stuttgart. Kassel: Bärenreiter, 2007.

Petzoldt, Martin. *Bach Kommentar*. Band III: *Fest- und Kausalkantaten, Passionen*. Bachakademie Stuttgart. Kassel: Bärenreiter, 2018.

Petzoldt, Martin. "Liturgy and Music in Leipzig's Main Churches: The Church Book and the Agenda." Translated by Thomas Braatz from the original German. https://www.bach-cantatas.com/Articles/Leipzig-Churches-Petzold.pdf.

Preus, Robert. *The Theology of Post-Reformation Lutheranism*. Vol. 1: *A Study of Theological Prologemana*. Vol. 2: *God and His Creation*. St. Louis: Concordia, 1970, 1972.

Rathey, Markus. *Bach in the World: Music Society, and Representation in Bach's Cantatas*. Oxford: Oxford University Press, 2023.

Rathey, Markus. "Ästhetik eines 'Fragments'—Anmerkungen zur Traditions des Schlußsatzes der Kantate 'Nun komm der Heiden Heiland' BWV 61." *Bach-Jahrbuch* 88 (2002): 105–117.

Rathey, Markus. "'Gottes Zeit ist die allerbeste Zeit'—Anmerkungen zu einer unbeachteten Quelle für den Eingangschor des Actus Tragicus." *Bach-Jahrbuch* 110 (2024): 185–193.

Rifkin, Joshua. "Bach's Chorus: A Preliminary Report." *Musical Time* 123, no. 1677 (November 1982): 747–751, 753–754.

Rose, Stephen. *The Musician in Literature in the Age of Bach*. Cambridge: Cambridge University Press, 2011.

Schulze, Hans-Joachim, and James A. Brokaw II. *Commentaries on the Cantatas of Johann Sebastian Bach: An Interactive Companion*. https://doi.org/10.21900/wd.21.

Schulze, Hans-Joachim. "Die Bach-Kantate 'Nach dir, Herr, verlanget mich' und ihr Meckbach-Akrostichon." *Bach Jahrbuch* 97 (2011): 255–257. https://journals.qucosa.de/bjb/article/view/2294/2220.

Schulze, Hans-Joachim. "The Parody Process in Bach's Music: An Old Problem Reconsidered." *Bach* 20, no. 1 (Spring 1989): 7–21. https://www.jstor.org/stable/41640315.

Schmalfuß, Hermann, "Johann Sebastian Bachs 'Actus Tragicus' (BWV 106): Ein Beitrag zur Entstehungsgeschichte." *Bach Jahrbuch* 56 (1970): 36–43. https://journals.qucosa.de/bjb/article/view/1572.

Shabalina, Tatiana. "Activities around the Composer's Desk: The Roles of Bach and His Copyists in Parody Production." *Understanding Bach* 11 (2016): 9–38. https://bachnetwork.org/ub11/ub11-shabalina.pdf.

Snyder, Kerala. "From Abendmusic to *Christmas Oratorio*." *J. S. Bach and the Oratorio Tradition, Bach Perspectives* 8 (2011): 69–95. Edited by Daniel R. Melamed.

Spree, Eberhard. *Blog: Anna Magdalena Bach*. https://www.anna-magdalena-bach.com/en.

Steiger, Renate. "Actus tragicus und ars moriendi: Bachs Textvorlage für die Kantate 'Gottes Zeit ist die allerbeste Zeit' (BWV 106)." *Musik & Kirche* 59 (1989): 11–23.

Talle, Andrew. *Beyond Bach: Music and Everyday Life in the Eighteenth Century.* Urbana: University of Illinois Press, 2017.

Tatlow, Ruth. *Bach's Numbers: Compositional Proportion and Significance.* Cambridge: Cambridge University Press, 2015.

Tatlow, Ruth. *Bach and the Riddle of the Number Alphabet.* Cambridge: Cambridge University Press, 1991.

Tatlow, Ruth. "Handling Unruly Sources." *Discussing Bach* 6 (December 2023) https://bachnetwork.org/discussing-bach/db6/

Tatlow, Ruth. "The Theology of Bach's church Cantatas", *Discussing Bach* 8 (January 2025). https://bachnetwork.org/discussing-bach/db8/

Varwig, Bettina. "Beware the Lamb: Staging Bach's Passions." *Twentieth Century Music* 11, no. 2 (September 2014): 245–274. https://doi.org/10.1017/S1478572214000097.

Varwig, Bettina. *Music in the Flesh: An Early Modern Musical Physiology.* Chicago: University of Chicago Press, 2023.

Varwig, Bettina. "Death and Life in J. S. Bach's Cantata *Ich habe genung* (BWV 82)." *Journal of Royal Musical Association* 135, no. 2 (2010): 315–316.

Whaley, Joachim. *Religious Toleration and Social Change in Hamburg 1529–1819.* Cambridge: Cambridge University Press, 1985.

Wolff, Christoph. *Johann Sebastian Bach: The Learned Musician.* New York: W. W. Norton, 2000.

Wolff, Christoph. *Bach's Musical Universe.* New York: W. W. Norton, 2020.

Wolff, Christoph, ed. *The World of the Bach Cantatas: Early Selected Cantatas.* New York: W. W. Norton, 1995.

Wunder, Heide. *He Is the Sun, She Is the Moon: Women in Early Modern Germany.* Translated by Thomas Dunlop. Cambridge, MA, London: Harvard University Press, 1998.

Yearsley, David. *Bach and the Meanings of Counterpoint.* Cambridge: Cambridge University Press, 2002.

# Index

*For the benefit of digital users, indexed terms that span two pages (e.g., 52–53) may, on occasion, appear on only one of those pages.*

Figures are indicated by an italic *f* following the page number.

acrostic, 23–25, 27, 57–58, 61–62
*Actus Tragicus*, 34–65
Ahle, Johann Georg (1651–1706), 60, 64
Ahle, Johann Rudolph (1625–1673), 153–54
alphabet, number, 23, 24*f*, 42, 75, 101
Altnickol, Elisabeth Juliana Friderica (1726–1781), 130–31, 169–70
Altnickol, Johann Christoph (1720–1759), 144*f*, 169–70
anagram, 23
architecture, 11, 12–14
Arnstadt, 4, 34–35, 60–61, 64, 183

Bach, Anna Magdalena (1701–1760), née Wilcke (Wülcke), 28–29, 94, 104, 105–6, 127–28, 129, 166
  *Clavierbüchlein* (1725), 136–37, 136*f*, 161
Bach, Carl Philipp Emanuel (1714–1788), 66–67, 110–11, 128
Bach, Catharina Dorothea (1708–1774), 28–29, 45–47, 66, 128
Bach, Christian Gottlieb (1725–1728), 129–30, 161
Bach, Christiana Sophia Henrietta Bach (1723–1726), 94, 127–28, 161
Bach, Christiana Dorothea (1731–1732), 161
Bach, Elisabeth Juliana Friderica (1726–1781). *See* Altnickol
Bach family, 23–25, 28–29, 47–49, 66, 90, 93–94, 110–11, 127–28, 133–35, 136–37, 157–58, 160, 166
Bach, Friedelena Margaretha (1675–1729), 28–29
Bach, Gottfried Heinrich (1724–1763), 127–28, 129
Bach, Johann Christoph Friedrich (1732–1795), 110–11
Bach, Johann Gottfried Bernhard (1715–1739), 128
Bach, Johann Jacob (1682–1722), 45–46
Bach, Johann Lorenz (1695–1773), 70
Bach, Johann Ludwig (1677–1731), 130–31
Bach, Johann Sebastian (1685–1750)
  Works
    'Alles mit Gott und nichts ohn' Ihm', BWV 1127, 13, 23–25
    B Minor Mass, BWV 232, 21–22
    Cantata (BWV) 4, 19–20
    Cantata (BWV) 7, 19–20
    Cantata (BWV) 29, 21–22
    Cantata (BWV) 30.2, 21–22
    Cantata (BWV) 36.1, 21–22

Bach, Johann Sebastian
(1685–1750) (*cont.*)
Cantata (BWV) 36.5, 21–22
Cantata (BWV) 42, 145–46
Cantata (BWV) 46, 21–22
Cantata (BWV) 60, 153–54
Cantata (BWV) 61, 5–6, 66–86, 174, 177
Cantata (BWV) 70.1, 89, 111
Cantata (BWV) 71, 47, 59
Cantata (BWV) 75, 6
Cantata (BWV) 82, 31, 133–62, 177
Cantata (BWV) 83, 53, 138, 157, 161
Cantata (BWV) 84, 157
Cantata (BWV) 85, 129–30, 131–32
Cantata (BWV) 95, 53
Cantata (BWV) 104, 13, 113–32, 177
Cantata (BWV) 106, 13, 22, 34–65, 177
Cantata (BWV) 112, 131–32
Cantata (BWV) 116, 167
Cantata (BWV) 125, 53, 138, 161
Cantata (BWV) 126, 174
Cantata (BWV) 131, 47, 60
Cantata (BWV) 140, 5–6, 141–42
Cantata (BWV) 147, 5–6, 19, 22, 29, 87–112, 177
Cantata (BWV) 150, 23–25, 61
Cantata (BWV) 159, 151
Cantata (BWV) 161, 151
Cantata (BWV) 182, 66–67
Cantata (BWV) 186.1, 89, 111
Cantata (BWV) 198, 56
Cantata (BWV) 199, 25
Cantata (BWV) 213, 21–22
Cantata (BWV) 214, 21–22
*Clavier Übung*, Part 1, BWV 825–30, 29, 131–32
*Clavier Übung*, Part 3, BWV 675–77, 129–30
Christmas Oratorio, BWV 248\, 21–22, 148
'Dein Wort laß mich bekennen', BWV 348, 108
Magnificat, BWV 243, 92
Musical Offering, BWV 1079, 23–25
St John Passion, BWV 245, 56, 128–29, 141–42, 151, 180–81
St Matthew Passion, BWV 244, 56, 141–42, 180–81
"Erbarme dich, mein Gott," 180–81
"Es ist Vollbracht," 56, 151
'So gibst du nun, mein Jesus, gute Nacht', (BWV 402, & BWV 501), 152
Bach, Maria Barbara (1684–1720), 28–29, 66
Bach, Maria Elisabeth (1644–1694), 28–29, 34–35, 45–46, 61–62
Bach, Regina Johanna Bach (1728–1733), 161
*Bach Compendium*, 29
Bach Digital, 29–31, 111, 179
Bach Gesellschaft, 29–31, 178
Bach-Werke-Verzeichnis, 29–31
Bach, Wilhelm Friedemann (1710–1784), 61–62, 66, 110–11, 128
baptism, 45–46, 66–68
Basso continuo, 35, 44–45, 185
Becker, Cornelius (1561–1604), 114, 125–27, 129–30, 131
*Der Psalter Davids Gesangweis* (1602), 126f, 129–30
Bible verses
Genesis 18:27, 82
Genesis 33:11, 140–41, 157–60, 159f
Genesis 45:28, 140–41

## INDEX

Leviticus 12:1–8, 137
Deuteronomy 33, 171
2 Samuel 12:3, 117–18
2 Chronicles 5:13, 93–94, 95*f*, 104–5
Psalm 12, 133–35
Psalm 23, 114, 117–18, 120, 125–27
Psalm 49, 117–18
Psalm 51:10–12, 81–82
Psalm 80:1–2, 114, 120
Psalm 89, 113
Psalm 90:12, 38, 50–51
Psalm 102, 68
Psalm 119, 117–18
Song of Solomon 6:5, 117–18
Wisdom 11:20, 12–13
Sirach 14:18, 39–40
Isaiah 6:10, 174–75, 176*f*
Isaiah 11:1–5, 91
Isaiah 38:1, 52, 52*f*
Isaiah 40:31, 61–62
Isaiah 53:1, 174–75, 176*f*
Isaiah 53:6–7, 117–18
Jeremiah 3:12, 117–18
Ezekiel 34:11, 117–18
Joel 2:28–29, 173–74
Zechariah 13:7, 117–18
Matthew 6:6, 62–63
Matthew 9:36, 117–18
Matthew 10:5, 172–73
Matthew 10:30, 54–55
Matthew 10:32, 101–3
Matthew 11:28, 117–18
Matthew 13:14–15, 175, 176*f*
Matthew 15:24, 175, 176*f*
Matthew 20:15, 171–72
Matthew 21:1–9, 68
Matthew 23:37, 172, 173
Matthew 24:24, 172–73
Luke 1:5–25, 106
Luke 1:39–56, 91
Luke 3:23, 143–45
Luke 10:42, 52
Luke 21:17–18, 54–55
Luke 2:22–40, 53, 137–38
Luke 2:35, 138
Luke 23:43, 42
Luke 10:42, 52
John 3:16, 76, 170, 174–75
John 10:11–16, 114, 120
John 12:37–40, 174–75
Acts 17:28, 50–51
Acts 28:27, 175, 176*f*
Romans 5:12, 117–18
Romans 8:31, 57–58
Romans 10:16, 175, 176*f*
Romans 11:8, 175, 176*f*
Romans 11:35, 171–72
Romans 12:9–16, 91
Romans 13:11–14, 68
Romans 15:8, 175, 176*f*
1 Corinthians 1:24, 175, 176*f*
1 Corinthians 9:5, 173
Galatians 3:28, 173–74
Galatians 4:4, 173–74
Ephesians 4:18, 175, 176*f*
1 Timothy 4:7, 49–50
Titus 2:3, 173–74
1 Peter 1:18, 117–18
1 Peter 3:7, 173–74
1 John 3, 171
Revelation 3:20, 78–79
Revelation 7:12, 43–44
Revelation 12, 171
Revelation 22:17–20, 39–40, 82–83
Birkmann, Christoph (1703–1773), 8–9, 21, 138–39, 140–41, 154, 156–57
Bose, Christiana Sybilla (1711–1749), 157–58
Bose family, 13, 160
Bose, Georg Heinrich (1682–1731), 13, 157–58, 160
Bose, Georg Mattias (1710–1761), 157–58
*breve,* 9, 16–17

Britten, Benjamin (1913-1976), 182-83
  *On Receiving the First Aspen Award* (1964), 182
Bünting, Heinrich (1545-1606)
  *Itinerarium Sacrae Scripturae*, 143-45, 146f
Burmeister, Franz Joachim (1633-1672), 21-22, 153-54
  'Es ist genung', 140-41, 153-54, 155
Buxtehude, Dieterich (1637-1707), 82-83

cadence, 78-79, 185
Calov, Abraham (1612-1686), 168
  Calov Bible, 94, 95f, 114-15, 143-45, 174-77, 176f
Calvinist, 4-5, 72, 89-90, 166-67
canon, 13, 185
cantata cycles, 6, 20-21, 169-70
Chafe, Eric, 74-75
*Cchiasmus*, 19-20
chromatic steps, 31-32, 37, 185
chronogram, 23
circle of fifths, 127, 185
Cöthen, 4-5, 28-29, 90, 129, 160
counterpoint, 13, 185
Cyril of Jerusalem (312-86), 143-45

Decius, Nikolaus (1485-1541), 131
*devise*, 45, 57-58
Deyling, Salomon (1677-1755), 128-29, 143-45
Drese, Johann Samuel (1644-1716), 66-67, 89
Drese, Johann Wilhelm (1677-1745), 66-67, 89
Dürr, Alfred (1918-2011), 32, 150, 164

Eberhardine, Electress Christiane (1671-1727), 56
Eilmar, Georg Christian (1665-1715), 46-47, 57-58, 61-64

Eisenach, 67-68, 69
emblem, 13-14, 16, 23-25, 42, 57-58, 61-62, 76, 101, 115-16, 115f, 143-45
Erdmann, Georg (1682-1736), 130-31

fair copy, 70, 87-89, 185
Franck, Salomo (1659-1725), 20-21, 87-112
  *Evangelische Sonn- und Fest-Tags-Andachten* (1717), 87, 88f, 92-93
  *Evangelische Schatzkammer* (1686), 115-16
  *Geist- und Weltliche Poesien* (1711), 101-3, 102f
Frohne, Johann Adolf (1652-1713), 48-49, 62-63, 63f
fugue, 13, 38-40, 185
funeral, 2, 41, 45-46, 47-49, 51-52, 53, 54-56, 62-64, 140-41, 151, 156f, 162, 171
Fux, Johann Joseph (1660-1741), 12-13

gamba, viola da, 35, 38, 41-42, 43, 55, 56, 57f
Geier, Martin (1614-1680), 48-49
  *Zeit und Ewigkeit* (1670), 114-15
Gotha, 89-90
grace, 56, 73, 85-86, 93-94, 99-100, 116-17, 118-19, 138-39, 140-41, 165, 166, 169-70, 171, 173, 174
Graupner, Christoph (1683-1760), 108-9
  Dein Wort laß mich bekennen (GWV) 1163/16, 108-9, 109f

Hamburg riots (1730), 168-70
Handel, George Frideric (1685-1759), 18-19, 66
  *Messiah*, 18-19, 181-82

harmony, musical, 1, 13, 21, 32
Harmony, Universal. *See* Universal Harmony
heart, 1, 13, 25, 26f, 26f, 41, 71, 73–74, 79, 80f, 82
Henrici, Christian Friedrich (1700–1764). *See* Picander
Hess, Dame Myra (1890–1965), 110–11
Hiltebrandt, Gustav Adolph (1632–1695)
　*Ner-Eröffnete Anmüthiger Bilder Schatz,* 13–16, 15f
hope, 62–63, 74–75, 119, 125, 140, 150, 153
Hulsius, Levinus (1550–1606), 72
Hunold, Christian Friedrich (1680–1721) aka Menantes, 56, 57f
　*Menantes Academischer Neben-Stunden* (1713), 56, 57f

imitation, 93–94, 185
inversion, 36, 124f, 124, 185

Jahn, Martin (c. 1620–1682), 100
Jesu, meiner Seelen Wonne, 91, 92–93, 100, 105, 106, 109–10
Jesu, Joy of Man's Desiring, 100, 105, 108–10
*Jesu Juva* J.J., 3–4, 133–35, 183
Josephus, Flavius (c. 37–c.100), 166
joy, 2, 13–14, 36–37, 42, 55, 56, 92–93, 100, 117–18, 153, 177, 179–80

kindness, 97, 119, 121, 127–28, 183
*Kirchen-Agenda,* 7–8
*Kirchen-Ordnung,* 7–8
Kohlroß, Johann (1487–1560), 108
Kuntsch, Margarethe Susanna von (1651–1717), 153
Kurtàg, György and Márta, 64–65

Lämmerhirt, Tobias (1639–1707), 45–46, 48–49, 59, 61
Leaver, Robin A., 156–57
Leibniz, Gottfried Wilhelm (1646–1716), 18, 77
Leipzig, Bachfest, 179, 180–81
Leipzig, St Nicholas, 5–6, 110–11, 157–58, 177
Leipzig, St Thomas, 5–6, 84f, 90, 110–11, 177
Leipzig, St Thomas School, 127, 157–58
Leipzig Thomaskantor, 83, 90, 128, 181
Leopold, Prince of Anhalt-Cöthen (1694–1728), 4–5, 28–29, 89–90
Leupold, Jacob (1624–1727), 157–60
*libretti,* 20
light, 72–73, 76–77, 137–38
liturgy, Leipzig, 5–6, 7–8, 83–85, 84f, 91, 177
liturgy, Lutheran, 2, 9, 43–44, 92, 178
love, 2, 16, 129–30, 153, 161–62, 173
love, God's, 72, 73, 85–86, 101, 169–70, 171, 174–75, 177, 183
Luther, Martin, 82
　Mit Fried und Freud ich fahr dahin, 2, 53, 138
　Nun komm der Heyden Heyland, 69, 74
　*Von den Juden und ihren Lügen* (1543), 166

Magnificat (Mary's song), 91–92, 96–97, 98
Männling, Johann Christoph (1658–1723), 21, 23, 155, 156f
　*Europäische Parnassus* (1685), 21–22
　*Poetische Blume-Garten* (171)
Marees, Pieter de (fl. 1602), 72

Mattheson, Johann (1681–1764)
　*Behauptung der Himmlischen*
　　*Musik* (1747), 2
　*Das Neu-Eröffnete Orchestre*
　　(1713), 17
　*Der Vollkommene Capellmeister*
　　(1739), 8, 11
Maul, Michael, 181–82
Meckbach, Conrad Meckbach
　(1637–1712), 23–25, 56,
　60, 61
　*Christum Meum Desidero*, 57–58,
　　61
Meckbach, Maria Elisabeth
　(1645–1709), 61–62, 64
　*Meines Erlösers Mahlzeichen*
　　*Geben Zierde*, 57–58
Meckbach, Paul Friedemann
　(1674–1731), 61–62
Meißner, Christoph Friedrich, 135
Menantes, see Hunold
mercy, 91–92, 117–19, 142, 166–67,
　171, 172, 173, 180–81
Meuslin, Wolfgang (1497–1563), 131
mirror image, 1, 13, 124, 124f
Mizler, Lorenz Christoph (1711–
　1788), 9, 12–13, 16–17
　Corresponding Society of the
　　Musical Sciences, 9–10
　*Musicalische Bibliothek*, 10, 40
Morhof, Daniel Georg (1639–1691),
　22
motet, 34–35, 84f, 85, 158–60
motto, 13–14, 23–25, 27, 45–46,
　57–58, 113, 115–16
Mühlhausen, 4, 47–48, 59,
　61–62, 64
Müller, Heinrich (1631–1675), 114–15,
　166

Neumeister, Erdmann (1671–1756),
　6, 21, 169–70
　*Geistliche Poesien...*(1717), 67–68,
　　69–71, 78–79, 82–83

Neuss, Heinrich Georg (1654–1716)
　*Kurtzer Entwurf von der Music*
　　(1754), 13
Newton, Isaac (1643–1727), 178
Nicolai, Philipp (1556–1608)
　Wie schön leuchtet der
　　Morgenstern, 74, 82–83
number alphabet, 23, 101
　Heyland=65, 101
　Jesus=70, 23, 145–46
　Jesu=52, 23, 75, 76
*numerus musicus*, 12–13, 16–17
*numerus poeticus*, 22

oboe d'amore, 124, 131
Olearius, Johann ((1611–1684), 43–44,
　49–50
　*Biblische Erklärung* (1681), 114–15
　*Christliche Bet-Schule* (1664), 49, 50f
　*Christliche Sterbeschule* (1669),
　　151–52, 152f

Pachelbel
　*Hexachordum Apollinis* (1699), 23
paragram, 23, 24f
parallel, 23–25
parody, 21–22, 154, 181
peace, 2, 42, 117–18, 137–38, 148–
　49, 174
Penzel, Christian Friedrich
　(1737–1801), 44–45
Pfeiffer, August (1640–1698), 71, 73,
　114–16, 165, 171
　*Anti-Calvinismus* (1699), 167
　*Anti-Chiliasmusu* (1691), 166–67
　*Anti-Enthusiasmus* (1692), 167
　*Anti-Melancholicus* (1684), 167
　*Anti-Papismus* (1702), 167
　*Apostolische Christen-Schule*
　　(1704), 52f, 52
　*Evangelische Christen-Schule...*
　　*SYSTEMA THEOLOGIAE*
　　(1688), 71–73, 116–19,
　　150–51, 169–74

*Evangelische Schatzkammer*
     (1686), 13–14, 115–16,
     129–30
"So gibst du nun, mein Jesus, gute
     Nacht!", 152
Picander, 8–9, 20–21, 23
   *Ernst- Schertzhaffte und Satyrische
     Gedichte* (1727–1751), 22, 24*f*
   *See also* Henrici, Christian
     Friedrich
picture rhyme, 25
Praetorius, Michael (1571–1621), 9,
     16–17
Preuss, Robert D
   *The Theology of Post-Reformation
     Lutheranism*, 168
proportion, 13–14, 40
Purification of Mary, 53, 64–65

rastrum, 27
Rathey, Markus, 58, 82–83
recitative, 5–6
Reiche, Gottfried (1667–1734), 94
rhyme, 21–23, 25, 81–82
rhyme scheme, 92–93, 122–23,
     148–49
*ricercar*, 23–25, 186
Riederer, Johann Friedrich
     (1678–1734), 23
   *Die bedenckliche und geheimnisreiche
     Zahl Drey,* 23–25
*ritornello,* 19, 93, 122–23, 186
Rittmeyer, Johannes (1636–1698)
   *Himmlisches Freuden-Mahl*
     (1683), 79–82, 80*f*

sacred, 2, 3, 179–80
sacred-secular division, 3
Scheibel, Gottfried Efraim
     (1696–1758), 156–57
Schemelli's *Gesangbuch* (1736), 109–10,
     135, 153–54
Schmolk, Benjamin (1672–1737), 23

Schubart, Christian Friedrich Daniel
     (1739–1791), 178
Schulze, Hans-Joachim, 29
Schweinitz, David von (1600–1667),
     50–51, 58, 64
   *Hundert Evangelische Todes-
     Gedancken*, 58*f*
*senarius*, 16–17
sequence, 19–20, 43, 127, 186
Simeon, Song of, 2, 42, 53, 137–38
sketch, 11
Snyder, Kerala, 82–83
Society for Christian Love and
     Science, 157–58
*Soli Deo Gloria* S.D.G., 3–4, 133–35,
     167, 183
spirituality, 179–80, 183
Steffani, Agostino (1654–1728), 8, 74
Steiger, Renate (1934–2006), 49–50
story, 5–6, 31, 53, 71, 89, 91, 105–8,
     147, 160, 174, 181–82
Strecker, Adolph (1624–1708), 48–49,
     61
   Romans 8:17–18, 48–49
symmetry, 12–14, 19–20, 23–27, 77,
     124*f*, 124, 139–40, 142,
     145–46

Telemann, Georg Philipp (1681–1767),
     66–68, 75–76
*tempus clausum,* 90–91
Tettelbach, Gottfried (d. 1748),
     157–58
   *Die letzte schuldige Freundschafft,*
     159*f*
Thomaskantor. *See* Leipzig
     Thomaskantor
Tilesius, Dorothea Susanna
     (1674–1708), 46–48, 61
Tilesius, Johann Adolph
     (1668–1728), 46–47, 61
triad, 19, 36, 93, 124, 124*f*
tritone, 37, 39–40, 153–54

unity, 12–13, 35, 106–7, 174, 179–80
Universal Harmony, 12–13, 179–80, 183

vibrations, 18–19
Vopelius, Gottfried (1645–1715), 125–27
　*Neu Leipziger Gesangbuch* (1682), 125–27
*Vox Christi,* 42, 78–79, 129–30

Walther, Johann Gottfried (1684–1748), 1
Weimar, 4–5, 28–29, 59, 87
Weiß, Christian (1671–1737), 128, 157–58

Weißenfels, 94, 160
Wilhelm Ernst, Duke of Saxe-Weimar (1662–1728), 23–25, 27, 28–29, 87, 89
Wolff, Christoph, 29
Wülcke, Anna Magdalena (1701–1760). *See* Bach
Wülcke, Johann Caspar (1660–1733), 94

Zachow, Friedrich Wilhelm (1663–1712), 66
Zarlino, Gioseffo (1517–1590), 16
Zerbst, 94
Ziegler, Christiane Mariane von (1695–1760), 8–9, 20–21

www.ingramcontent.com/pod-product-compliance
Ingram Content Group UK Ltd.
Pitfield, Milton Keynes, MK11 3LW, UK
UKHW041018010326
468442UK00019B/124